DETERM
TO BELI

CW00497487

"*Lennox is no fool. Nor does he rush in, though he bravely explores ground where angels may fear to tread. And the overall debate about freedom is an 'argument for the sake of heaven' that no Christian should duck – because it bears on our view of the character of God, of human dignity, of moral responsibility, and therefore on our mission and public witness. Gracious, patient, tenacious, persistently biblical, and eschewing argument by labels, Lennox is a model of how to handle issues that are divisive but important. It is up to each of us to read, study, think, pray, and decide for ourselves. The heart, face, and voice of our faith are all at stake in the answers we give.*"

Os Guinness, author of *Impossible People*

"*Professor Lennox raises serious biblical, theological, and philosophical questions about theological determinism – the belief that God has foreordained and rendered certain all that happens including who will be saved and who will not be saved. Anyone curious about this belief must read* Determined to Believe?"

Roger E. Olson, Foy Valentine Professor of Christian Theology and Ethics, George W. Truett Theological Seminary, Baylor University

"*With grace, humility, wisdom, and boldness, John Lennox offers a readable, biblically-informed guide that tackles important questions about freedom and fatalism, salvation and sovereignty, faith and foreordination, regeneration and reprobation. This book will be a help for those perplexed by – and even pressured into accepting – a theological system that strikes them as undermining genuine moral responsibility and calling into question the assurance of salvation.*"

Paul Copan, Professor and Pledger Family Chair of Philosophy and Ethics, Palm Beach Atlantic University and author of *An Introduction to Biblical Ethics* and *A Little Book for New Philosophers*

"John Lennox is widely recognized as one of the top Christian intellectuals of our time. Yet he is also rightly admired for his uncanny ability to get right down to the basic issues in a discussion and to write about them with a simple clarity that still exemplifies depth and range of treatment. And, as one would expect, Determined to Believe? is a model of these virtues. This is no ordinary rehash of old debates about Calvinism vs. Arminianism, God's sovereignty vs. free will and moral responsibility, and so on. In fact, the real brilliance of the book lies in Lennox's insistence that we set aside old labels and try a fresh approach with new eyes to the topics related to the acceptance or non-acceptance of theological determinism. As a result, this is a treasure trove of clear, easy to understand biblical exegesis, helpful definitions of key terms like "foreknowledge" and "predestine", and coverage of theological determinism as it relates to the human condition, the nation of Israel and the hardening of Pharaoh's heart, and the assurance a believer may rightly claim regarding one's salvation. I highly recommend this refreshing and helpful book."

– J. P. MORELAND, Distinguished Professor of Philosophy, Talbot School of Theology, Biola University, La Mirada, California, USA

"John Lennox, one of today's finest evangelical minds, treats the reader to a well-argued position on this controversial contemporary debate among evangelicals. Scriptural in content, philosophical in argument, comprehensive in scope, and irenic in tone, it rescues the debate from much of partisan rhetoric so often found in books on the same subject. Finally, a book that avoids a proof-texting approach placing the discussion in the context of the entire Judeo–Christian narrative crafted with exegetical integrity and intellectual rigor. Reading it is like having a stimulating conversation with a good friend."

– BRUCE LITTLE, Senior Professor of Philosophy, Southeastern Baptist Theology Seminary

"In this wide-ranging book that is sure to garner much interest, the polymath and apologist John Lennox turns his attention to issues of long-standing debate within Christian theology: freedom and necessity, sin and grace, predestination and perseverance. In his characteristically insightful and winsome way, Lennox offers probing but charitable criticisms of popular views and suggests a way forward. This book will be helpful in many ways – even (and perhaps especially) for those inclined to disagree with its conclusions."

– **THOMAS H. MCCALL,** Professor of Biblical and Systematic Theology, Director, Carl F. H. Henry Center for Theological Understanding, Trinity Evangelical Divinity School

"Determinism, whether biological, emotional or even spiritual, may have shattering effects at all levels, including faith. I have been eyewitness of the shipwreck caused by its influence on some people's lives. In an age prone to extremisms, even in Christian circles, Determined to Believe? *is a wise and profoundly biblical demonstration that God's truth cannot be a source of despair or frustration, but a spring of abundant life in Christ. John Lennox's work comes as a necessary and excellent vaccination against the dangers of determinism on the life of faith."*

– **PABLO MARTÍNEZ,** psychiatrist, author and Bible teacher

DETERMINED TO BELIEVE?

THE SOVEREIGNTY OF GOD, FREEDOM, FAITH, AND HUMAN RESPONSIBILITY

John C. Lennox

MONARCH
BOOKS

Published by Monarch Books
an imprint of
Lion Hudson IP Ltd
Wilkinson House, Jordan Hill Road,
Oxford OX2 8DR, England
Email: monarch@lionhudson.com
www.lionhudson.com/monarch

ISBN 978 0 85721 872 8
e-ISBN 978 0 85721 873 5

First edition 2017

Acknowledgments
Unless otherwise indicated Scripture quotations are from the Holy Bible, New International Version, copyright © 1973, 1978, 1984 by the International Bible Society. Used by permission of Hodder & Stoughton, a member of the Hodder Headline Group. All rights reserved.

Scripture quotations marked ESV are from The Holy Bible, English Standard Version, Anglicized Edition, published by HarperCollins Publishers, © 2001 by Crossway Bibles, a division of Good News Publishers. Used by permission. All rights reserved.

pp. 28–29 Extract from "The Humanitarian Theory of Punishment" in *The Twentieth Century: an Australian Quarterly Review* © 1970 C. S. Lewis, reprinted by permission of The C. S. Lewis Company Ltd.

pp. 95–96 Extract from *Why I Am a Christian* © 2003 J. R. W. Stott, reprinted by permission of IVP.

pp. 195–96 Extract from "On Original Sin" in *International Journal of Systematic Theology* © 2015 Oliver D. Crisp, reprinted by permission of John Wiley and Sons Limited.

A catalogue record for this book is available from the British Library

Printed and bound in the UK, September 2017, LH29

This book is for Ben and Rachel
and all others who ask the hard questions

Acknowledgments

I am deeply indebted to many friends for comments on the contents of this book, most of which were gratefully taken on board. In particular, I would like to thank Chris Clarke, Tim Costello, David Cranston, Paul Ewart, David Glass, Max Baker Hytch, Tom McCall, Pablo Martinez Vila, and my ever helpful research assistant Simon Wenham. I am also grateful to my publishers, Lion Hudson, for their constant support and for their provision (once more) of a truly excellent editorial consultant in Richard Herkes.

Contents

Prologue

The nineteenth-century mathematician and historian of philosophy Augustus De Morgan once issued a warning for the scientist who tried to venture into metaphysics: "When he tries to look down his own throat with a candle in his hand," he said, he needs to "take care that he does not set his head on fire."

Philosopher Thomas Nagel in *The View from Nowhere* wrote: "I change my mind about the problem of free will every time I write about it…"

The apostle Paul said:

> *And he made from one man every nation of mankind to live*
> *on all the face of the earth, having determined allotted periods*
> *and the boundaries of their dwelling place, that they should*
> *seek God, in the hope that they might feel their way towards*
> *him and find him.*
>
> (Acts 17:26–27 ESV.)

One of the most famous encounters between Christianity and philosophy occurred in ancient Athens when the apostle Paul was invited to address the philosophers at the Areopagus Court. The historian Luke tells us that Paul had been discussing the Christian faith with the crowds in the market place when he was approached by representatives of the two leading philosophical schools, Stoics and Epicureans. These philosophers were initially confused about Paul's teaching and wished to know more, so they gave Paul the opportunity to address them in the formal setting of the Areopagus.

Greek philosophers were interested in the nature of ultimate reality and the relationship of human beings to whatever that ultimate reality might turn out to be. The Stoics, whose philosophy was popular among the intellectual élite, had come to the view that there was a rational principle, a universal reason or *logos* that ruled the universe by an inexorable fate, and that man's best wisdom was to co-operate with that fate. The Epicureans, on the other hand, were materialists who believed that the gods (who were made of atoms like everything else) were distant and took no interest in the world. Man's best wisdom was to seek *ataraxia* – tranquillity. Human thought was in their view, like everything else, a chance process, in the last analysis nothing but the random swerving of atoms in the void of empty space.

We at once recognise the contours of two major ideas that have occupied the human mind for centuries and have lost none of their fascination – necessity and chance, the law-like and the random, the determined and the free. The Creator God, if there is one, sovereign; his human creatures, free and responsible.

The battle – and it is a battle – to understand these issues is currently raging on two fronts. The first front is the atheist attempt to eliminate human free will and inevitably, with it, any concepts of absolute morality. This atheistic onslaught enlists the powerful authority of the natural sciences – especially neuroscience. And then, on the Christian front, the spread of theological determinism raises many questions for Christians. Clearly, even if I were competent to do so, one small book would be entirely inadequate to deal with both fronts. For that reason I have decided to concentrate on the issues raised for me and my fellow Christians by theological determinism.

However, I have thought it sensible first of all to look at free will and determinism from the point of view of our human experience and from a philosophical perspective, in order to set the discussion in a broader space than that of Christian theology. I am aware that a Christian reader may well raise a principled objection to such a procedure, by saying there is a danger that we shall end up framing God in our own image, based on our convictions about the nature of human freedom. I accept the point, but awareness of the risk diminishes it; and I hope that what I have done will prove useful, in that it at least broadens understanding of what these issues mean to those who do not necessarily share the Christian worldview.

What This Book is About

This book is written mainly for Christians who are interested in or even troubled by questions about God's sovereignty and human freedom and responsibility. One of my main reasons for writing is that I have been persuaded to do so by those who (perhaps over-generously) profess to have found my comments in lectures and conversations on these topics helpful in getting to grips with Scripture for themselves. It is in that spirit that I write. I do not for a moment suppose that I have provided definitive solutions to these difficult questions. Indeed, I am inclined to think that our very finiteness imposes a limitation that will mean that, in the end, even with our best attempts to understand Scripture, there will remain deep mysteries and unsolved problems. We should therefore approach these matters with humility and reverence. What I find encouraging in this daunting task is the fact that Scripture speaks on these topics, and it is therefore incumbent upon us – indeed is part of our worship – to try to understand what God has revealed, as we depend on the Spirit of truth.

The book divides into five parts, as follows.

Part 1: The Problem Defined

1. THE NATURE AND LIMITATIONS OF FREEDOM

We first of all consider the concept of freedom, what it generally means to us, and to what extent we think we have it. We distinguish the liberty of spontaneity and the liberty of indifference. We then explore the connection between freedom and morality and that between free will and love. We think about the oft-repeated atheist claim that religion destroys human freedom and argue that, as far as Christianity is concerned, true freedom is part of its core message.

2. DIFFERENT KINDS OF DETERMINISM

We give examples of various takes on determinism and give examples of some well-known atheist thinkers who espouse physical determinism – the idea that everything is predetermined essentially by physics and chemistry – as well as a few that do not espouse that view. We also bring in the views of some leading neuroscientists.

We then move on to theistic or theological determinism – the idea that everything is predetermined by God. Our starting point is, not surprisingly, the biblical teaching on origins and in particular the way in which human beings are defined as moral beings gifted by God (we might say, sovereignly gifted by God) with a certain amount of freedom – to eat or not to eat of a specified tree. We cite Alvin Plantinga on the difference between God's creation of free creatures and their actions being caused by him. We next give examples of theological determinism, claiming that the issue for Christians is not whether it teaches the sovereignty of God – it does as one of its essential doctrines – but what the sovereignty of God actually means as revealed in Scripture.

3. REACTIONS TO DETERMINISM – THE MORAL PROBLEM

Here we continue our analysis of the moral problem that besets determinism, as seen by a variety of authors. Then we give some of the historical background to the tension between followers of Calvin and those of Arminius, leading to the Synod of Dort and the famous acronym TULIP which encapsulates some of the main issues involved.

4. WEAPONS OF MASS DISTRACTION

From this point on the book concentrates on biblical teaching, and the reader who wishes to skip the preliminaries may wish to dive in here – although, in my view, many of them are of importance as general background.

This chapter discusses the *biblical* attitude to a question of methodology – the all too prevalent danger of dealing with deep theological questions by the simple expedient of affixing labels on the representatives of the various positions taken and then conducting a seemingly endless discussion of what those labels might mean. Experience shows that this tends to bypass the important job of getting down to what Scripture actually says about the fundamental issues in question. We study what Paul has to say in 1 Corinthians about this tendency to label, and we find that he tells us in no uncertain terms that this is not a helpful way to proceed – not even if the labels contain the names of the very apostles themselves!

This leads me to say something more about my motivation in writing this book.

Part 2: The Theology of Determinism

5. GOD'S SOVEREIGNTY AND HUMAN RESPONSIBILITY

Here we introduce some of the biblical teaching on this topic and comment on the spectrum of theological opinion on it.

6. THE BIBLICAL VOCABULARY

We give a brief survey of the main biblical concepts employed in connection with our topic: foreknowledge, predestination, and election, demonstrating that they cover a wider range of meaning than is sometimes assumed.

Part 3: The Gospel and Determinism

7. HUMAN CAPACITY AND ITS LIMITS

One of the glories of the gospel is that its message of salvation is a message of the grace of God. What humans neither deserve nor can merit, God offers as a free gift to those who put their faith in Christ as Saviour and Lord. This raises many questions: what is the status of such faith? Is it a response to God of which human beings are capable, or does their sin render them completely incapable? Those who take the latter view raise three arguments that are central to the debate.

Argument 1. If human beings were capable of trusting God, they would be contributing to their salvation and therefore meriting it. Salvation would no longer be by grace and God's glory would thereby be diminished. It is claimed that the only way out of this is to hold that faith itself must be a gift of God, distributed according to his sovereign will, completely independent of any attitude, desire, or behaviour of those he elects to save. This view is called "unconditional election".

Argument 2. Human beings are incapable of believing because they are *dead in... trespasses and sins* (Ephesians 2:1) as a result of the sin that Adam introduced into the world. This view is often called the "total depravity" of man, although this phrase does not occur in Scripture. Just as dead creatures cannot respond to any stimulus, so men and women are constitutionally unable to respond to God. In order to be able to respond they must receive new life (i.e. they must be *born again*, John 3:3). Only then can they respond with the faith that God gives them. Without any action on their part (they are dead and therefore cannot act) God regenerates those he elects, by his Spirit; they are then, and only then, able to believe in Christ.

Argument 3. Although human beings are incapable of believing in God, for the reason given under Argument 2, it is nevertheless their fault that they do not believe. Therefore God may justly condemn them. This has to do with their connection to Adam who brought sin into the world: when he sinned, they sinned.

In this chapter we begin to think about these arguments in light of the biblical teaching on faith and regeneration.

8. THE HUMAN CONDITION – DIAGNOSIS AND REMEDY

We focus here on the biblical doctrine of justification by faith which lies at the heart of the gospel. This leads to an analysis of what it means to be dead in trespasses and sins, based on the biblical teaching about the entry of sin into the world.

9. DRAWN BY THE FATHER AND COMING TO CHRIST

The Gospel of John has a great deal to say about God's initiative in salvation. For instance, Jesus says that *all that the Father gives me will come to me... no-one can come to me unless the Father who sent me draws him* (John 6:37, 44). In this chapter we give a detailed exposition of these statements in their contexts, asking whether or not they are to be read as evidence of theistic determinism.

10. THE IRREVERSIBILITY OF REGENERATION

Here we turn first to Argument 2 and the biblical teaching on regeneration and its relationship to faith in Christ. We discuss the pros and cons of the widespread view that, in light of human incapacity, regeneration must precede salvation. We then investigate Argument 3 regarding the nature of Adam's sin and its consequences.

11. THE GOSPEL AND HUMAN MORAL RESPONSIBILITY

In this chapter we look at a major section of the Gospel of John, chapters 7–10, which are devoted to giving us different aspects of the way in which Jesus communicated his message to the world. We shall observe that he treated his hearers as morally responsible for what they did with what they heard, and we shall consider his statement *but you do not believe because you are not my sheep* (John 10:26), and what, if any, deterministic significance it might have.

Part 4: Israel and Determinism

We next devote five chapters to thinking through that major section of the letter to the Romans, chapters 9 to 11, where Paul considers the status of the nation of Israel before God. The reason for doing this is that the description of God's dealings with Pharaoh in Romans 9 is often regarded as the main pillar supporting theological determinism, and we wish to study it in its wider context in Romans. The chapters run as follows:

12. Israel and the Gentiles
13. Why Doesn't Israel Believe?
14. The Hardening of Pharaoh's Heart
15. Is Israel Responsible?
16. Has Israel a Future?

Part 5: Assurance and Determinism

The next four chapters address the question of Christian assurance, looking at two sets of issues: first, those raised by theological determinism, where the elect are secure but where it seems problematic to know whether or not one is actually elect; and secondly, those raised by the teaching that it is possible for a genuine believer to lose their salvation and eventually perish.

17. Christian Assurance
18. Will Faith in God Endure?
19. Warning in Hebrews
20. Assurance in Hebrews

PART 1

THE PROBLEM DEFINED

CHAPTER 1

The Nature and Limitations of Freedom

Most humans rank freedom among the highest of ideals. Freedom, we feel, is every human being's birthright: none has the right to deprive us of it against our will (except, of course, in cases of proven criminality). Even to attempt to remove someone's freedom is regarded as a crime against the essential dignity of what it means to be human.

Yet one of the key questions for any of us is: how free am I, if at all? There are people who think that human freedom is severely limited or even illusory. Some of them are atheists, and they ask: how can I be free, since the universe is completely responsible for my existence? Others are believers in God, and they may ask the very same question with a radically different starting point: how free am I, if at all, when God is completely responsible for my existence and behaviour?

Historically, the longing to be free has played a major role in the human drama. Robert Green Ingersoll wrote: "What light is to the eyes – what air is to the lungs – what love is to the heart – liberty is to the soul of man." In his State of the Union Address in 1941 US President Franklin D. Roosevelt enunciated the famous Four Freedoms:

Freedom of speech
Freedom of worship
Freedom from want
Freedom from fear.

Such freedoms are almost universally regarded as central to what it means to be human. In the preamble to the UN Charter of Human Rights the four freedoms are described as the "highest aspiration of the common people". Many who possess them to a certain degree tend to take them for granted. For many more these freedoms seem a distant, impossible dream – unrealisable yet tantalising.

If we are asked what we mean by "freedom" many of us will respond by saying that it means that we should be able to choose what we do; that we should be able to exercise our will, make our own decisions, and be able to implement them, provided we do not infringe other people's space and curtail their freedom.

Now we all realise that our freedom, whatever it involves, has certain inbuilt limitations. We are not free to run at fifty kilometres per hour, we are not free to live without food or air, and so on. However, we sense that we are free, provided there is availability and we have the resources, to choose between peas and beans, a green shirt or a blue one. We are free to support one football team rather than another, to tell the truth or to lie, to be kind or to be awkward. In fact, trying to decide between the endless different offerings on the supermarket shelves sometimes makes us wish we did not have so much freedom of choice.

We are also well aware that on occasions we voluntarily limit some of our freedoms – sometimes even for pleasure. For instance, if I am a member of a football team I cannot simply play as I like, inventing the rules as I go along. The whole point of the game is that I limit myself to playing within the rules, subject to the leadership of the captain. That is what makes football a game.

There are also more important contexts in which we submit to limitations, for the sake of our own safety and security: different nations choose which side of the road their citizens should drive on. This is an arbitrary choice, but once made it would be foolish and dangerous to ignore it and simply drive as we choose. More generally, as citizens of a civilised state, we voluntarily submit to the laws of the land (in theory, at least), foregoing part of our freedom as individuals. We do this for the sake of the higher good of enjoying the benefits of living together in a peaceful and civilised society.

When it comes to the right of human beings to essential freedom, all of us – whatever worldview we hold – would agree that this right should be regarded as inviolable. Sadly, in some parts of the world there is still a sorry failure to achieve anything approaching the Four Freedoms. It therefore rightly rouses our indignation to see any human being enslaved – treated as nothing more than a cog in a machine, a mere means to the end of another person's pleasure or profit. Every human being, man or woman, boy or girl, of whatever race, colour, or creed, from whatever part of the world, has a right to be treated as an end in himself or herself, never as a mere statistic, or simply as a means of production, but as a person with a name and a unique identity, born to be free.

But what is freedom? To what extent do we have it?

Two kinds of freedom

From the time of philosophers John Locke and David Hume distinctions have been made between two kinds of freedom – the liberty of spontaneity and the liberty of indifference.

The "liberty of spontaneity" is the freedom to follow our own motives, to do whatever we want to do, without anybody or anything else – say, the government – forcing us to do something we don't want to do, or stopping us from doing what we want to do. Granted that we have the health, ability, money, and necessary circumstances, and are not subject to any external constraint or restraint, most people agree that we have this liberty of spontaneity.

The "liberty of indifference" (libertarian freedom[1]) is the freedom to have done otherwise than in actual fact we chose to do on any occasion in the past. Faced with a choice between two courses of action in the future, liberty of indifference would imply that the choice is completely open. I can choose either course of action indifferently; and having chosen the one course of action, I can, on looking back, know that I could equally well have freely chosen the other course. I can choose, or could have chosen, to do X or not-X.

---

1   The adjective "libertarian" is somewhat unfortunate since it has other connotations, particularly in the moral sphere, that should not be imported here. The use of the term "indifference" is not a great deal better; but these terms have stuck and there is not much we can do about them.

In this book when I use the term "free will" I shall understand it in this sense.

Suppose, for instance, Jim has reached the point where he must choose to marry either Rose or Rachel. He has the liberty of spontaneity: no one is going to force him to marry the one rather than the other. He thinks, however, that he also has the liberty of indifference. He feels that he could just as easily marry either one of them "indifferently".

Augustine (theologian and philosopher from the fourth and fifth centuries), in common with Hume and many others, would deny that Jim has this kind of liberty. They hold that various complex subconscious physical and psychological processes constrain and determine his choice. Jim is free to marry the girl he chooses; however, the choice he will eventually make is already determined by these deep-seated processes inside him. He is not free to choose and act other than he does choose and act. The upshot of this is that some philosophers think that freedom of spontaneity is compatible with determinism – a view called compatibilism. Of course, libertarian freedom is the direct opposite of determinism. *The Oxford Handbook of Free Will* says:

> ... debates about free will in the modern era since the
> seventeenth century have been dominated by two questions,
> not one – the "Determinist Question": "Is determinism true?"
> and the "Compatibility Question": "Is free will compatible
> or incompatible with determinism?" Answers to these
> questions have given rise to two of the major divisions in
> contemporary free will debates, between **determinists** *and*
> **indeterminists**, *on the one hand, and between* **compatibilists**
> *and* **incompatibilists**, *on the other.*[2]

Freedom and morality

It is beyond dispute that our taste in food or art or music, or our choice of spouse, or indeed any of our decisions and choices, are

---

2   *The Oxford Handbook of Free Will*, Oxford, OUP, 2011, p. 5.

heavily *influenced* by elements in our physical or psychological make-up. However, whatever inner psychological traumas, desires, or urges may dispose us to break the moral or even the civil law – and we all have these – most of us believe that, as normal human beings, we are still free to choose to control our urges and keep both the moral and the civil law. We are, therefore, morally responsible to do so. This is the only basis on which civilised society can function. Thus there is a close connection between (libertarian) freedom and responsibility.

Indeed, the very existence of civil and criminal law demonstrates that members of civilised societies have a deep-seated conviction that they possess not only the liberty of spontaneity but the liberty of indifference. An essential part of what it means to be mature human beings (so discounting here both infants and the severely mentally ill) is the freedom to choose between A and not-A, such that we are morally responsible and hence accountable for our actions. The Supreme Court of the United States of America says that a belief in determinism "is inconsistent with the underlying precepts of our criminal justice system" (United States vs. Grayson, 1978).

To be a moral creature, one first of all needs moral awareness. Human beings, as far as we know, are the only creatures on earth that have such awareness. You can train a dog by rigorous, painful discipline not to steal a joint of beef from the table, but you will never succeed in teaching a dog why it is morally wrong to steal. It has no concept of morality and never will have.

Secondly, if one is going to behave morally, one must not only be aware of the difference between moral good and moral evil; one must have sufficient freedom of will in order freely to choose to do good or to do evil. In this respect there is a whole category difference between even the most advanced computer and a human being. A computer might give you the answers to moral questions which it is programmed to give you; but it would not itself understand, or be aware of, morality. It cannot, therefore, be held morally responsible for its choices and behaviour. If a computer is involved in the design of land-mines which ultimately cause the maiming or death of thousands of children, it makes no sense to accuse it of morally reprehensible behaviour. It had no free will or choice. It did what it was programmed to do. It is not a moral being and so is not responsible for its actions.

Human beings, by contrast, are not in that sense programmed (not unless they have been subjected to deep psychological conditioning). They have the ability to choose and, therefore, to make moral decisions. What is more, they generally pride themselves on it. No one would prefer to be a humanoid, computerised robot. When a man has chosen, for instance, to face danger for the sake of standing by his moral principles rather than take the cowardly way out and deny them, he likes to be regarded as having been responsible for his moral choice – and sometimes even to be praised for it. It is usually when we have done something very wrong that we are tempted to deny moral responsibility and to say, "I couldn't help it."

Cambridge neuroscientist Harvey McMahon writes:

> *Free-will also underpins ethics, where choices are made in the light of moral principles. In fact free-will underpins all choices. Furthermore, free-will underpins the role of intentionality and guilt in the judicial system... The very idea of rules or laws implies that we have a choice or ability to obey. How can the law command us to do certain things if we do not have the ability to do them? Thus, even the concept of obedience implies we have a choice.*[3]

Indeed, most civilised people regard as reprehensible and dehumanising the tendency in totalitarian states to treat those who take a moral stand against the state as "deviant" or "ill" rather than possessing the moral capacity to choose.

C.S. Lewis addressed this danger of regarding wrongdoing as essentially pathological in a brilliant essay entitled "The Humanitarian Theory of Punishment":

---

3   H. McMahon, "How free is our free-will?", *Cambridge Papers*, vol. 25, no. 2, June 2016.

> *The Humanitarian theory removes from Punishment the concept of Desert. But the concept of Desert is the only connecting link between punishment and justice. It is only as deserved or undeserved that a sentence can be just or unjust... Thus when we cease to consider what the criminal deserves and consider only what will cure him or deter others, we have tacitly removed him from the sphere of justice altogether; instead of a person, a subject of rights, we now have a mere object, a patient, a "case"...*
>
> *To be "cured" against one's will and cured of states which we may not regard as disease is to be put on a level with those who have not yet reached the age of reason or those who never will; to be classed with infants, imbeciles, and domestic animals. But to be punished, however severely, because we have deserved it, because we "ought to have known better", is to be treated as a human person made in God's image.*

Lewis proceeds to outline some of the chilling implications of the so-called humanitarian view. They are even more relevant today[4] than they were when he wrote them since, as we shall see, determinism has made great inroads in the areas of psychology and cognitive science. The idea of religion being a neurosis, or a delusion, as in the title of Richard Dawkins' bestseller *The God Delusion* has gained considerable traction.

Lewis continues:

> *We know that one school of psychology already regards religion as a neurosis. When this particular neurosis becomes inconvenient to government, what is to hinder government from proceeding to "cure" it?... And thus when the command is given, every prominent Christian in the land may vanish overnight into Institutions for the Treatment of the Ideologically Unsound, and it will rest with the expert gaolers*

---

4   It is a sobering thought that Lewis had to publish his essay in Australia as he could find no interest in the UK.

to say when (if ever) they are to re-emerge. But it will not be persecution. Even if the treatment is painful, even if it is life-long, even if it is fatal, that will be only a regrettable accident; the intention was purely therapeutic. In ordinary medicine there were painful operations and fatal operations; so in this. But because they are "treatment", not punishment, they can be criticized only by fellow-experts and on technical grounds, never by men as men and on grounds of justice.

This is why I think it essential to oppose the Humanitarian theory of punishment, root and branch, wherever we encounter it. It carries on its front a semblance of mercy which is wholly false. That is how it can deceive men of good will.[5]

For those interested in pursuing this matter further see the article by Stuart Barton Babbage entitled "C.S. Lewis and the Humanitarian Theory of Punishment".[6]

Free will and love

Another capacity that would be impossible without free will is the capacity to love. The existentialist writer Jean-Paul Sartre captured this idea well:

The man who wants to be loved does not desire the enslavement of the beloved. He is not bent on becoming the object of passion which flows forth mechanically. He does not want to possess an automaton, and if we want to humiliate him, we need try to only persuade him that the beloved's passion is the result of a psychological determinism. The lover will then feel that both his love and his being are cheapened…

5   C.S. Lewis, "The Humanitarian Theory of Punishment", *The Twentieth Century: An Australian Quarterly Review*, vol. III, no. 3, quoted in C.S. Lewis, *God in the Dock*, Grand Rapids, Eerdmans, 1970, pp. 287–94.

6   www.churchsociety.org/docs/churchman/087/Cman_087_1_Babbage.pdf

If the beloved is transformed into an automaton, the lover finds himself alone.[7]

The endowment of men and women with free will inevitably implies the possibility that they might use that free will to choose evil, and to reject love, even the love of God. Hence we must consider some necessary implications of human free will for the structure of nature. If the free will and free choice that God gave to human beings were intended to be genuine, that very fact necessitated that nature should possess a certain degree of autonomy.

C.S. Lewis puts it this way:

People often talk as if nothing were easier than for two naked minds to "meet" or to become aware of each other. But I see no possibility of their doing so except in a common medium which forms their "external world" or environment... What we need for human society is exactly what we have – a neutral something, neither you nor I, which we can both manipulate so as to make signs to each other. I can talk to you because we can both set up sound waves in the common air between us.[8]

Lewis then points out that this and other neutral fields – matter, in other words – must have a certain fixed nature, a certain autonomy as Lewis calls it. Suppose the contrary were the case. Imagine, for example, that the world was structured in such a way that a beam of wood remained hard and strong when used in the construction of a house, but it became as soft as grass when I hit my neighbour with it. Or if the air refused to carry lies and insults. Indeed, says Lewis:

If the principle were carried to its logical conclusion evil thoughts would be impossible, for the cerebral matter which we use in our thinking would refuse its task when we attempted to frame them. All matter in the neighbourhood

---

7   J-P. Sartre, *Being and Nothingness*, New York, Pocket Books, 1984, p. 478.

8   C.S. Lewis, *The Problem of Pain*, London, HarperCollins, 2002, p. 18.

of a wicked man would be liable to undergo unpredictable alterations.[9]

The result would be, of course, that real freedom of human will and choice would be negated.

Nature, then, must have a certain autonomy, in order that there can be a society of beings with free will, able to make real moral decisions for good or evil, and to carry them out in practice. The potential of evil thought and act to produce evil effects cannot be annulled without simultaneously removing the necessary condition for free will to function. This is a moral universe.

So far, so good, but what lies behind all of this? How does this universe come to be a moral universe; and if we are to be free within it, what are the basic conditions for achieving that freedom?

Worldview considerations

A key question is the following: are human beings the highest and sole rational authority in the world – or, indeed, in the universe, so far as we know and so far as it affects us? And in that case, are we completely free to decide how we shall behave, what is wrong and what is right, what our ultimate values are, what, if any, is the purpose of our existence, and what our ultimate goal should be? Are we ultimately responsible to none but ourselves? Or is there a God who, having created the universe and us within it, has the right to lay down, and in fact has laid down, not only the physical laws of nature, the boundary conditions of human existence, but also the moral and spiritual laws that are meant to control human behaviour? Are humans held responsible by this God for the way they behave, and will they be called upon at last to render account to him?

These answers reflect two different worldviews – atheism and theism. They are so utterly distinct that many atheists think that theism is the great enemy of human freedom, and follow the late Christopher Hitchens in regarding the God in whom they do not

---

9   C.S. Lewis, *The Problem of Pain*, London, HarperCollins, 2002, p. 21.

believe as a great North-Korean-style dictator in the sky who is constantly spying on us and restricting our freedom by his threats. They regard religion as a source of oppression, slavery, and war that stands in direct contradiction to human dignity and freedom. By the same token many theists point to atheistic ideology as a root cause of an incalculable amount of human oppression, and a denial of the basic human right to freedom, particularly in the twentieth century – think of Stalin, Mao, and Pol Pot.

This point needs careful attention, for there is oppression, violence, and war in many countries today that is directly connected with both atheism and religion. However, not all such systems are violent, and attempts to tar them with the same brush are unfair and, indeed, ludicrous.

If we consider the religions in the world today, for example: the peaceful Amish have nothing in common with violent Islamist terrorists. (I write as a Christian, a follower of Christ who explicitly repudiated violence and taught his disciples to love their enemies.[10])

A common response is that, even if some religions do not espouse violence, the God-postulate itself demeans human beings by compromising their autonomy. Karl Marx expressed this view as follows:

> *A man does not regard himself as independent unless he is his own master, and he is only his own master when he owes his existence to himself. A man who lives by the favour of another considers himself a dependent being. But I live completely by another person's favour when I owe to him not only the continuance of my life but also its creation, when he is its source ... Man is the highest being for man.*[11]

This is the heart of contemporary humanist philosophy:

---

10 For fuller discussion of this and related issues, see the author's *Gunning for God*, Oxford, Lion Hudson, 2011, pp. 59–82 and 117–44.
11 "The Difference between the Natural Philosophy of Democritus and the Natural Philosophy of Epicurus", translated in K. Marx and F. Engels, *On Religion*, Moscow, Foreign Languages Publishing House, 1955, pp. 517, 519.

A humanist has cast off the ancient yoke of supernaturalism, with its burden of fear and servitude, and he moves on the earth a free man, a child of nature and not of any man-made gods.[12]

It is a sad irony that it is Marx's atheist philosophy itself that might well be the greatest ideological weapon of mass destruction against human freedom that the world has ever seen. Yet Marx's observation merits more nuanced comment. For the idea is very common that making space for God in our worldview effectively reduces our freedom and so demeans us as humans.

Atheists are not the only people who value the instinctive desire of the human heart for freedom. According to theists, that desire is God-given and is both fundamental and central to their experience of God. Religious Jews, for example, will point to the experience that was the original, formative element in their existence and identity as a nation: their nation's deliverance by God from the Egyptian slave-labour camps in the second millennium. The clarion call of God's prophet Moses to the then Egyptian pharaoh, *Let my people go, so that they may worship me*, has resounded in Jewish hearts down the centuries. Jews have celebrated it ever since in the annual Feast of Passover (*Pesach*). The faith it has fostered in God as sustainer and liberator has maintained their hope during the many oppressions they have since suffered at the hands of totalitarian, anti-Semitic governments.

Christians will add that freedom is a core constituent of the gospel of Christ. They will cite Christ's statement of his mission:

The Spirit of the Lord is on me, because he has anointed me to proclaim good news to the poor. He has sent me to proclaim freedom for the prisoners and recovery of sight to the blind, to release the oppressed, to proclaim the year of the Lord's favour.

(Luke 4:18–19.)

---

12   *The Humanist*, no. 5, 1954, p. 226.

Underlying the atheists' desire to throw off any concept of a Creator God is their criticism of religion – sadly often borne out of personal experience – as an oppressive enslavement of the human spirit, and a cause of man's alienation from his true self.

Other religious viewpoints must rightly speak to this issue for themselves, but writing as a Christian I can well understand this objection. For mere religion as distinct from a living personal faith in God easily degenerates into a form of slavery. This is a danger of which the Bible itself is well aware. Paul exhorts his fellow Christians:

> It is for freedom that Christ has set us free. Stand firm, then, and do not let yourselves be burdened again by a yoke of slavery.
>
> (Galatians 5:1.)

The yoke of slavery that he refers to here is a form of legalistic religion. He earlier describes it as:

> Formerly, when you did not know God, you were slaves to those who by nature are not gods. But now that you know God – or rather are known by God – how is it that you are turning back to those weak and miserable principles? Do you wish to be enslaved by them all over again? You are observing special days and months and seasons and years! I fear for you, that somehow I have wasted my efforts on you.
>
> (Galatians 4:8–11.)

As the Christian sees it, the atheist's mistake here is that, in seeking to escape from oppressive, legalistic, superstitious and opiate religion, he rejects God, who himself denounces such religion. Far from increasing human freedom, it is the rejection of God that actually diminishes it and leads to a pseudo-religious anthropocentric ideology, whereby each individual man and woman becomes a prisoner of non-rational forces that will eventually destroy them in complete disregard of their humanity.

However, it is not our purpose to pursue these issues here, or further discuss the tension between theism and atheism over freedom in general. We shall focus instead on the increasing emphasis on determinisms of various kinds, both among atheists and theists (mainly Christians). Some atheists believe that nature's laws ultimately do the determining, while some theists believe that God does it.

CHAPTER 2

Different Kinds of Determinism

The Oxford Handbook of Free Will cheerfully tells us that there are ninety different kinds of determinism. We shall have to be content with very few. For instance, causal determinism is the view that every event is caused by prior events according to the fixed laws of nature. Some causal determinists are physical determinists – they admit only physical causes. Others are open to mental causation.

On the other hand, theistic determinism (theological determinism, divine determinism) is the view that everything is determined by God. In its general form theistic determinism does not lay down *how* God does the causing, only *that* he does so.

Physical determinism

The most famous living theoretical physicist, Stephen Hawking, is a physical determinist.

> *It is hard to imagine how free will can operate if our behaviour is determined by physical law, so it seems we are no more than biological machines and that free will is just an illusion.*[13]

He concedes, however, that human behaviour is so complex that predicting it would be impossible, so that in practice we use "the effective theory that people have free will".[14]

---

13 S. Hawking and L. Mlodinow, *The Grand Design*, London, Bantam Press, 2010, p. 45.
14 S. Hawking and L. Mlodinow, *The Grand Design*, London, Bantam Press, 2010, p. 47.

Richard Dawkins writes of a morally indifferent universe that controls human behaviour:

> In a universe of blind physical forces and genetic replication, some people are going to get hurt, other people are going to get lucky and you won't find any rhyme or reason in it, nor any justice. The universe we observe has precisely the properties we should expect if there is, at the bottom, no design, no purpose, no evil and no good. Nothing but blind, pitiless indifference. DNA neither knows nor cares. DNA just is. And we dance to its music.[15]

Neuroscientist Sam Harris writes:

> You seem to be an agent acting of your own free will. As we shall see, however, this point of view cannot be reconciled with what we know about the human brain… All of our behavior can be traced to biological events about which we have no conscious knowledge: this has always suggested that free will is an illusion.[16]

Paul Bloom, professor of psychology and cognitive science at Yale University agrees:

> Our actions are in fact literally predestined, determined by the laws of physics, the state of the universe, long before we were born, and, perhaps, by random events at the quantum level. We chose none of this, and so free will does not exist… Determinism has been part of Philosophy 101 for quite a while now, and arguments against free will were around centuries before we knew anything about genes or neurons. It's long been a concern in theology; Moses Maimonides, in the 1100s, phrased the problem in terms of divine omniscience: If God

---

15 R . Dawkins, *Out of Eden*, New York, Basic Books, 1992, p. 133.
16 S. Harris, *The Moral Landscape*, New York, Free Press, 2010, pp. 102–12.

already knows what you will do, how could you be free to choose?[17]

Leading German neuroscientist Wolf Singer, co-author of the so-called "Manifesto of Brain Researchers", thinks that, since the mind will eventually be completely explained naturalistically in terms of physical states and processes in the brain, we should give up all talk of freedom of the will.[18] Similarly, experimental psychologist Wolfgang Prinz says that "the idea of a human free will cannot even in principle be reconciled with scientific considerations".[19]

It is evident from the above quotations that there is a close connection, particularly on the atheist side, between determinism and reductionism – the view that entities are no more than the sum of their parts and can therefore be completely explained when *reduced* to those parts in analysis. We are used to the behaviour of physical things being determined by physical law and, if human beings are merely physical entities, it follows that their behaviour is as determined as the fall of a stone under gravitational attraction. It is therefore important to point out that such physicalist reductionism is coming under increasing pressure, not only from Christian theists as one might expect, but also from among the atheist ranks – notably by leading philosopher Thomas Nagel in his book *Mind and Cosmos*.[20]

However, not all atheists are determinists. For instance, Peter Tse, a leading contemporary neuroscientist from Dartmouth College, explores "the ways in which free will might be realized in a particular kind of neuronal and associated information-processing architecture".[21]

However, it is true that many prominent neuroscientists reject free will. In a much cited paper that appeared in *Nature*, John-Dylan

17 *The Chronicle Review*, March 2012.
18 W. Singer and G. Roth in *Gehirn und Geist*, 2004.
19 W. Prinz, "Der Mensch ist nicht Gespräch", in C. Geyer (ed.), *Hirnforschung und Willensfreiheit*, Frankfurt, Suhrkamp, 2004.
20 T. Nagel, *Mind and Cosmos*, Oxford, OUP, 2012.
21 P. Tse, *The Neural Basis of Free Will: Criterial Causation*, Cambridge, MIT Press, 2013.

Haynes and colleagues argued that our "subjective experience of freedom is no more than an illusion".[22] Another neuroscientist of repute, Michael Gazzaniga, writes:

> *Neuroscience reveals that the concept of free will is without meaning, just as John Locke suggested in the 17th century... It's time to get over the concept of free will and move on.*"[23]

This is a strange conclusion to be drawn in the name of science when one of its greatest luminaries, Albert Einstein, held that scientific theories were free creations of the human mind. It is also odd in light of the fact that human freedom is connected in most people's minds with morality and human dignity. Do we really wish to leave morality behind, to say nothing of the concept of love? Yet, despite the obvious moral pitfalls of believing in determinism, Sam Harris insists that anyone examining their own life will "see that free will is nowhere to be found".[24]

Ironically, many of the so-called New Atheists continue to fulminate against religion as being an evil delusion that should be eliminated. Their use of the word "evil' shows that their rage is a moral rage and at once raises the question: how can they have any moral concepts at all if, as the Dawkins quote above says, they believe that "there is no good and no evil" and human behaviour is reduced to a dance of the music of our DNA; how could anyone be blamed for their actions?

On Dawkins' deterministic view the problem of evil doesn't exist, for the simple reason that according to his worldview there is no such thing as evil. And if this is the case, what is the sense of his

---

22 C. S. Soon et al., "Unconscious Determinants of Free Decisions in the Human Brain", *Nature Neuroscience*, 11, 2008, pp. 543–45.

23 M. Gazzaniga, "Free will is an illusion, but you are still responsible for your actions", *Chronicle of Higher Education*, 18 March 2012.

24 S. Harris, *Free Will*, New York, Simon and Schuster, 2012, p. 64. "Our sense of our own freedom results from not paying attention to what it is actually like to be what we are. The moment we do pay attention, we begin to see that free will is nowhere to be found, and our subjectivity is perfectly compatible with truth."

reaction to religion (or anything else) as being evil? Of course, not all atheists agree with Dawkins. Indeed, Dawkins' moral outbursts against Christianity (or anything else) show that Dawkins doesn't seem to agree with Dawkins all the time!

Dissolving the problem of evil into meaninglessness cuts no ice with the vast majority of people. Causal determinism, whether genetic or otherwise, overreaches itself. It not only destroys morality, it destroys all meaning. The supreme irony of all of this is that many of the atheists quoted are precisely the people who think that Christianity oppresses people, demeans them, and removes their freedom. Now they tell us that we have no freedom at all – such logic is wonderful to behold!

One of the main reasons advanced for rejecting free will is the causal nexus argument, exemplified by the above quote from Richard Dawkins. If what we call our decisions are simply part of a long chain of physical cause and effect going back to the basic physics and chemistry of the universe, then there can be no sense in which we are in control of our decisions – whatever the "we" in that statement means.

Philosopher of science Tim Lewens of Cambridge argues that this argument is not weakened by quantum indeterminacy:

> What we want from free will, it seems, is to secure the claim that we are in control of things. This is not what indeterminacy gives us. Instead, it suggests that, just as an excited atomic nucleus may or may not decay in a five-minute interval, so a resolved car buyer may or may not purchase a Ford in a five-minute interval. But indeterminism does not tell us that the atom is in charge of when it decays, and it does not tell us that a person is in charge of whether she buys a Ford... It is chance, not control, that dictates which of these futures will materialize.[25]

In any case, David Hodgson writes: "I think the general consensus of physicists favours indeterminism, and recently the possibility of a

25   T. Lewens, *The Meaning of Science*, London, Pelican, 2015, p. 231.

deterministic version of QM [quantum mechanics] has been strongly challenged by mathematicians John Conway (inventor of the famous "Game of Life") and Simon Kochen...".[26]

Lewens goes on to discuss experiments in neuroscience, like those of Benjamin Libet, understood by some to show that subconscious brain activity preceded conscious decision. As a result conscious decision comes too late for it to be a cause of certain types of activity. However, Lewens' conclusion is, "Neuroscience has not yet shown freedom to be an illusion."[27] Cambridge neuroscientist Harvey McMahon agrees:

> *There is no pure experimental paradigm to test free-will as meaningful choice. So although the Libet-type experiment is often invoked to claim we have no free-will, and it may well help explain how the brain can make choices that do not invoke active cognition or prepare for choices, it does not address how and when cognitive decisions are made.*[28]

One of the most useful books on the whole topic is *Mythos Determinismus (The Determinism Myth)*, subtitled "How much does brain research explain?" by Brigitte Falkenburg.[29] She finds that, in the debate surrounding brain and mind, fundamental questions have been culpably neglected. With refreshing honesty she shows that there are massive gaps in the explanations offered by brain research, and she concludes that, in spite of claims to the contrary, no one today knows whether the mind is only an illusionary expression that accompanies neuronal automata, a product of neuronal calculation. She says that: "In the end, brain research cannot show that neuronal behaviour determines the contents of our consciousness."

26 *The Oxford Handbook of Free Will*, p.70.

27 T. Lewens, *The Meaning of Science*, London, Pelican, 2015, p. 250.

28 H. McMahon, "How free is our free-will?", *Cambridge Papers*, vol. 25, no. 2, June 2016.

29 B. Falkenburg, *Mythos Determinismus: Wieviel Erklärt uns die Hirnforschung?*, Berlin, Springer-Verlag, 2012.

Theistic determinism

The underlying assumption behind many denials of free will is naturalism, or even materialism. The presupposition here is that only the natural or material world exists. There is no supernature, no top-down causation, no break in the causal chain linking every phenomenon to the basic stuff of the universe. The logic of all of this is impressive, if the premise is true. However, as a theist, indeed a Christian theist, I deny the premise. I also deny it because of and not in spite of the fact that I am a scientist. I hold that science itself – indeed the very fact that we can do science – points to the fact that this universe is not all that exists. I believe that science witnesses to the existence of an eternal Creator God, who caused the universe to come to be in the first place, and who subsequently holds it in being. There is something beyond nature – supernature.

Now this does not mean that there is no causal chain, but it does mean there is something more. God is not part of the natural world, yet he created it with its regularities that we describe as laws. He is no prisoner of those laws – they simply describe what normally happens. God is free to feed new events, phenomena, and so on into nature from "outside". In fact, the central Christian claim is that God has himself come into the world: what the Gospel of John calls *the Word* has become human in Jesus Christ.[30] Science can recognise how nature normally works, but it cannot prevent God from doing something new or different.

That brings us to the question of theistic determinism. If there is a Creator God who is the first cause and upholder of the universe, it is clear that certain things are predetermined. God has created a physical universe that exhibits the kind of law-like behaviour that facilitates prediction. Some at least of the systems within the universe are deterministic – at least at the macro level.

Yet God is not constrained by the causal nexus, and he has created human beings in his image who are not completely constrained by it either. That is to say, they possess real freedom.

---

30   John 1:14.

C.S. Lewis has argued that human rationality itself, which is intimately involved in what we determine to do or not to do, is part of supernature:

> If all that exists in Nature, the great mindless interlocking event, if our own deepest convictions are merely the by-products of an irrational process, then clearly there is not the slightest ground for supposing that our sense of fitness and our consequent faith in uniformity tell us anything about a reality external to ourselves. Our convictions are simply a fact about us – like the colour of our hair. If Naturalism is true we have no reason to trust our conviction that Nature is uniform. It can be trusted only if quite a different metaphysic is true. If the deepest thing in reality, the Fact which is the source of all other facthood, is a thing in some degree like ourselves – if it is a Rational Spirit and we derive our rational spirituality from It – then indeed our conviction can be trusted. Our repugnance to disorder is derived from Nature's Creator and ours.[31]

It is encouraging to see some leading atheist thinkers beginning to give weight to this argument. Philosopher Thomas Nagel, an atheist, thinks that the naturalism assumed by most of the atheist writers mentioned above – which, I remind you, seems largely responsible for their determinism – is in serious trouble.

> Consciousness is the most conspicuous obstacle to a comprehensive naturalism that relies only on the resources of physical science... if we take this problem seriously, and follow out its implications, it threatens to unravel the entire naturalistic world picture.[32]

---

31 C.S. Lewis, *Miracles*, New York, Simon and Schuster, 1996, p. 139.
32 T. Nagel, *Mind and Cosmos*, Oxford, OUP, 2012, p. 35.

If, on the other hand, naturalism is false and theism is true,[33] then, I repeat, it is surely conceivable that human beings made in the image of God might well have a certain degree of real freedom to decide into the causal nexus, and alter it.

One might therefore expect Christian theists to defend human freedom of will, and indeed very many do. Our main concern in this book, however, is with those Christians who don't, or at least appear not to – whose "theistic determinism" disturbs many people because of the image of God it carries with it.

Back to the beginning

Up to this point I have mainly been considering the question of free will and determinism from our human experience and philosophical perspective. Mindful of the danger mentioned in the prologue, that we end up framing God in our own image, I shall now redress the balance by moving to consider what the Bible has to say about the topic.

But where should one begin? I find it interesting that, when it comes to the subject matter of this book, many writers and speakers begin with New Testament passages like Ephesians 1 or Romans 9 (which address the topic of predestination) and then proceed to read everything else in light of their interpretation of those passages. Now these passages are extremely important and we shall consider them in due course; but they are far from being the beginning of the biblical story.

Surely the appropriate place to begin is at the very beginning, with the biblical account of creation which tells us that *in the beginning God created the heavens and the earth* (Genesis 1:1). Therefore God is the "First Cause" in that he has caused the universe to be. God is later said to be *sustaining all things by his powerful word* (Hebrews 1:3). That is, the God of the Bible is not some remote deistic god that inaugurates the universe and then retires, leaving it to run without

---

33 These are of course not the only alternatives, but they are the ones at issue in this book.

his involvement. God as revealed in the Bible is intimately involved in holding the universe in being. Thus he is the sovereign Lord of creation. Indeed, God's sovereignty is one of the central themes of the Bible, and this is where the issue of determinism raises its head; not now for atheists but for theists.

The key question is: just what does God's sovereignty involve?

God clearly determines the existence of the universe and humans in it. Hence the next thing to consider is what Genesis says about the status of human beings. We are informed that men and women were created in God's image. There is, therefore, something very special about them since, although the universe declares God's glory to us, it was not made in his image. Humans were.

Of particular relevance to our theme is the fact that the first humans were placed in a magnificent garden and told they could eat the fruit of everything except the tree of the knowledge of good and evil. Far from diminishing the status of humanity, that prohibition was essential to establish the unique dignity of humans as moral beings. For the biblical story here defines the irreducible ingredients that constitute humans as moral beings and enable them to function as such. In order for morality to be real, the humans must have a certain degree of freedom, and there must be a moral boundary. So God gifted them with the freedom to eat or not to eat from all of the trees that were in the garden. But God said they were not to eat of one particular tree. He told them that if they ate from the tree of the knowledge of good and evil they would be sure to die (see Genesis 2:17).

This passage is crucial for understanding what Scripture itself means by God's sovereignty. It is clearly to be understood not in terms of absolute control over human behaviour but as a much more glorious thing: the devolving of real power to creatures made in God's image, so that they are not mere programmed automata but moral beings with genuine freedom – creatures with the capacity to say yes or no to God, to love him or to reject him.

Of course, the word "sovereignty" (which does not, incidentally, appear in the Genesis narrative) could be understood to mean absolute control in every detail of life and, as we shall see, is taken to mean that by some theists. But this smacks of despotism and totalitarian dictatorship, rather than speaking of a God who makes a universe in which love can not only exist but is supremely characteristic of God himself.

Thus human freedom in this sense is fundamental to the biblical narrative. It chimes in with both logic and experience, but it is prior to both. It is the way God has created us, and it is to be celebrated as one of his greatest glories. It says that we humans mean something – we are morally responsible beings, our choices and decisions are significant.

A.W. Tozer captured these ideas very well when he wrote:

> Here is my view: God sovereignly decreed that man should be free to exercise moral choice, and man from the beginning has fulfilled that decree by making his choice between good and evil. When he chooses to do evil, he does not thereby countervail the sovereign will of God but fulfills it, inasmuch as the eternal decree decided not which choice the man should make but that he should be free to make it. If in His absolute freedom God has willed to give man limited freedom, who is there to stay His hand or say, "What doest thou?" Man's will is free because God is sovereign. A God less than sovereign could not bestow moral freedom upon His creatures. He would be afraid to do so.[34]

One of the best articulations of this position that has gained broad acceptance is given by Alvin Plantinga in his important book *God, Freedom and Evil*. He begins by defining what he understands by a person being free with respect to an action:

> a person is free to perform that action and free to refrain from performing it; no antecedent conditions and/or causal laws determine that he will perform the action, or that he won't. It is within his power, at the time in question, to take or perform the action and within his power to refrain from it.

---

34   A. W. Tozer, *The Knowledge of the Holy*, New York, Harper, 1961, chapter 22.

This, of course, is libertarian freedom. Plantinga's statement of the Free Will Defence then runs as follows:

> A world containing creatures who are significantly free (and freely perform more good than evil actions) is more valuable, all else being equal, than a world containing no free creatures at all. Now God can create free creatures but he can't cause or determine them to do only what is right. For if he does so, then they are not significantly free after all; they do not do what is right freely. To create creatures capable of moral good, therefore, he must create creatures capable of moral evil, and he can't give these creatures the freedom to perform evil and at the same time prevent them from doing so. As it turned out, sadly enough, some of the free creatures God created went wrong in the exercise of their freedom; this is the source of moral evil. The fact that free creatures sometimes go wrong, however, counts neither against God's omnipotence nor against his goodness, for he could have forestalled the occurrence of moral evil only by removing the possibility of moral good.[35]

Yet, as we shall see in detail, this understanding of the biblical position has been challenged in all kinds of ways – perhaps most famously by Martin Luther at the time of the Reformation. In his book *The Bondage of the Will*, written in response to Erasmus' essay *On Free Will*, Luther said:

> [The] omnipotence and foreknowledge of God, I repeat, utterly destroy the doctrine of "free-will"… Doubtless it gives the greatest possible offence to common sense or natural reason, that God, Who is proclaimed as being full of mercy and goodness, and so on, should of His own mere will abandon, harden and damn men, as though He delighted in the sins

---

35   A. Plantinga, *God and Other Minds*, Grand Rapids, Eerdmans, 1977, p. 132.

*and great eternal torments of such poor wretches. It seems an
iniquitous, cruel, intolerable thought to think of God; and it
is this that has been such a stumbling block to so many great
men down through the ages. And who would not stumble
at it? I have stumbled at it myself more than once, down to
the deepest pit of despair, so that I wished I had never been
made a man. (That was before I knew how health-giving that
despair was, and how close to grace.)*[36]

In this passage Luther seems to be aware that there is a deep moral
problem with aspects of his view – an issue that we shall explore in
detail.

Another famous and influential statement on the matter of
predestination was made by the French theologian John Calvin. He
wrote,

*By predestination we mean the eternal decree of God by which
he determined with himself whatever he wished to happen
with regard to every man. All are not created on equal terms,
but some are preordained to eternal life, others to eternal
damnation; and accordingly, as each has been created for one
or other of these ends, we say that he has been predestined to
life or to death.*[37]

We notice that the general statement "whatever he wished to
happen... to every man" is rapidly narrowed to focus upon the
eternal destiny of every man. The word "predestination" involves the
idea of destiny, and it is the fixing of human destiny that is one of the
major issues in the whole debate.

I need to pause at this point, since the mention of Luther and
Calvin is likely to produce a reaction among some Christians that
I can understand but would like to avoid. Some of my readers may
think, "Here comes yet another misguided attempt to question the

36   M. Luther, *The Bondage of the Will*, Grand Rapids, Baker, 1990, p. 217.
37   J. Calvin, *Institutes of Christian Religion*, III, xxi, 5.

cumulative wisdom of centuries of Reformed Theology based on the magisterial work of two of the greatest and most influential Christian scholars who ever lived. There is no point in reading any further."

I would be very sad if that were the reaction. The very fact that I am writing this book may well, from the perspective of history, be at least in part traceable to the phenomenal energy, ability, and courage of Luther, Calvin, and other Reformers – figures who inspired and achieved the monumentally important task of bringing Scripture back into the centre of Christianity and its witness to the world. Their emphasis on the glory and sovereignty of God, and their insistence on constantly going back to the biblical text – taking great pains to explain it clearly and only accepting what was consistent with it – form a model to which many of us lesser mortals rightly aspire.

Following that lead has been a great inspiration to many Christians today, myself included, who long for more solidity, more intellectual depth, more maturity in the expression of their Christian faith, more sense of God's holiness and more concern for God's reputation than is to be found in some of the frothy, insubstantial attempts to make the Christian faith more attractive to the outside world.

It is that sense of indebtedness, together with the awareness of my own inadequacies, that has made me hesitate for a very long time before deciding to write this book.

There is another reason for my hesitation: the all-important fact that at the heart of the Reformation was the Christian doctrine of salvation: justification by faith alone in Christ alone. The Reformers rightly held that the contrary idea was false – that human beings could earn their salvation by their own effort in terms of works, rituals, religious performances, and even payments. Salvation was from God, a free gift of his grace in Christ. What was at stake is absolutely fundamental to Christianity and urgently needs to be made clear to each succeeding generation.

It is easy to see that the central tension was, crudely put, between God's divine work and our human works, or between God's sovereignty and human responsibility and free will. The Reformers were rightly concerned to exalt and glorify God by attributing salvation to him alone and not conceding anything to human merit. In particular, it is worth reflecting on Luther's early vain struggles to find peace with God by becoming an Augustinian monk and subjecting himself to fasting, scourging, and endless varieties of punitive self-discipline. No matter how he bent his will and fired up his determination, he realised that he never could do enough to merit peace with God.

It was when he was delivering his first series of lectures as Professor of Theology in Wittenberg that there dawned upon him the truth of justification by faith in Christ without works. At long last he experienced peace with God, and it became inevitable that he would challenge the then Roman Catholic culture of extreme "works-righteousness" where God's favour could even be bought in terms of expensive indulgences, pilgrimages, and penances. Luther's Ninety-five Theses nailed to the door of the Castle Church in Wittenberg were a devastating indictment of such religious corruption. His courageous determination to go against the flow was a turning point in history.

In light of this I can begin to understand that Luther had difficulties with the question of human free will. After all, he had exerted his willpower to its limits in order to merit salvation and found he could not. That could be interpreted as indicating that the human will was not free in the sense that it was not "free enough" to enable a person to earn favour with God. In the theological introduction to their translation of Luther's *The Bondage of the Will*, J. I. Packer and O. R. Johnston make the following statement:

> *Luther and Erasmus were not arguing about, and did not disagree about, the reality or the psychology of human choice; though Erasmus did not altogether see this, and sometimes speaks as if Luther's determinism involved a doctrine of psychological compulsion. But Luther's denial of free will has nothing to do with the psychology of action. That human choices are spontaneous and not forced he knows and affirms; it is, indeed, fundamental to his position to do so. It was man's*

total inability to save himself, and the sovereignty of Divine grace in his salvation, that Luther was affirming when he denied free will, and it was the contrary that Erasmus was affirming when he maintained free will.

The translators go on to say that, in Luther's view, salvation

must be wholly of Divine grace, for he himself can contribute nothing to it; and any formulation of the gospel which amounts to saying that God shows grace, not in saving man, but in making it possible for man to save himself, is to be rejected as a lie. The whole work of God's salvation, first to last, is God's; and all the glory for it must be God's also. That was just what Erasmus would not say... Erasmus affirms that God's mercy is won by works. Luther that it is recognised and received by faith.[38]

Now if this interpretation is correct, thus far it would take much of the heat and misunderstanding out of the whole topic, although it might then well be said that, in retrospect, a denial of free will (with its immediate implications for human choice) might not have been the wisest way of expressing such an interpretation.

At this point I should stress that (for me and many others) the issue is not whether or not the Bible teaches the sovereignty of God – it does, and I believe in its teaching wholeheartedly. God's kingdom was, is now, and ever shall be. God is the initiator and source of a salvation that no human can merit. On the personal level, the sense of God's gracious care and guidance that my wife, family, and I have enjoyed for many years, and our conviction that God is ultimately in control of his universe as expressed in the beautiful Hebrew poetry of Psalm 139, have been of inestimable comfort and value:

For you created my inmost being;
    you knit me together in my mother's womb.

---

38   M. Luther, *The Bondage of the Will*, Grand Rapids, Baker, 1990, p. 53.

I praise you because I am fearfully and wonderfully made;
　　your works are wonderful,
　　I know that full well.
My frame was not hidden from you
　　when I was made in the secret place.
When I was woven together in the depths of the earth,
　　your eyes saw my unformed body.
All the days ordained for me
　　were written in your book
　　before one of them came to be.

(Psalm 139:13–16.)

How many times have the words of the magnificent hymn "Be Still My Soul" been a steadying influence:

Be still my soul: the Lord is on thy side!
Bear patiently the cross of grief or pain;
Leave to thy God to order and provide;
In every change He faithful will remain.

However, God's guidance is never purely and simply the kind of micro-management that leaves the individual no choice. The biblical narrative demonstrates this again and again. Abraham is an interesting case in point. God appeared to him at intervals and explicitly told him what he should do – leave Ur, for example. Yet in between such intervals there was often no specific guidance given him. He had to decide what to do – and he sometimes made the wrong decision. If God had instructed him at every turn what he should do, then his humanity would have been compromised, since he could not have learned what it means to be a responsible, morally competent human being and his relationship with God would not have been genuine. It is essentially the same with God's gracious and sovereign guidance in our own lives.

Nor is it the issue that the Bible teaches some things that are uncomfortable and particularly hard for the modern mind to grasp, so that if we are going to reach the current generation we must soften or omit them to avoid being open to ridicule. It is not only the sovereignty of God that the contemporary mind finds difficult. The incarnation, miracles, resurrection, and ascension of Jesus are all in that category, and I know all too well what it means to be intellectually ridiculed publicly at the highest level for believing them.

The issue, I emphasise, is not whether the Bible teaches the sovereignty of God – it does. The issue is what it means by that teaching. For there are different ways of understanding the concept of sovereignty. One is in terms of divine determinism. Another is that God is a loving Creator who has made human beings in his image with a significant capacity to choose, with all its marvellous potential of love, trust, and moral responsibility. God is not the irresistible cause of human behaviour, whether good or bad – otherwise our actions and characters would be deprived of moral significance and it would make no sense to talk of us doing or being "good" or "bad".

It is one of God's greatest glories that he invests us with moral significance. That fact is most clearly shown in God's offer of salvation. That salvation is all of God, we cannot merit it; but in the preaching of the gospel we are challenged to use our God-given capacity to trust Christ to receive it. That trust is called "faith", and it is, according to Paul, the opposite of works, as we shall see.

Divine determinism, however, holds that it is even more glorifying to God to believe that human beings do not have these capacities and that their behaviour is completely determined by God. However, many, including myself, regard this view as going so far beyond the biblical teaching on God's sovereignty that it ends up detracting from the glory of God, to such an extent that it turns people away from the message of the gospel. To put it bluntly, it raises the question as to whether the God of theistic determinism is the God of the Bible.

It is therefore important to test the validity of our thinking in the light of Scripture. It is, of course, Scripture that is inspired and not our interpretation of it, and it would therefore be sad if what was giving offence was not the word of God but our misreading of it. The motivation behind this book, therefore, is my desire to understand Scripture better, and it is up to the reader to see whether I have been in any way successful.

More examples of theistic determinism

Let us first give some more recent examples of theistic views that are at the deterministic end of the spectrum.

B. B. Warfield:

> *All things without exception, indeed, are disposed by Him, and His will is the ultimate account of all that occurs... It is He that... creates the very thoughts and intents of the soul.*[39]

Paul Helm:

> *Not only is every atom and molecule, every thought and desire kept in being by God, but every twist and turn of each of these is under the direct control of God.*[40]

In spite of this apparently extreme deterministic position Helm nevertheless denies that God directly causes sin.

Edwin H. Palmer goes further:

> *Nothing in this world happens by chance. God is in back of everything. He decides and causes all things to happen that do happen. He is not sitting on the sidelines wondering and perhaps fearing what is going to happen next. No, he has foreordained everything "after the counsel of his will" (Ephesians 1:11): the moving of a finger, the beating of a heart, the laughter of a girl, the mistake of a typist – even sin.*[41]

---

39 B. B. Warfield, "Biblical Doctrines" art., "Predestination", p. 9, quoted in L. Boettner, *The Reformed Doctrine of Predestination*, Phillipsburg, P & R Publishing, 1971, pp. 31–32.
40 P. Helm, *The Providence of God*, Leicester, IVP, 1993, p. 22.
41 E. H. Palmer, *The Five Points of Calvinism*, Grand Rapids, Baker, 2009, p. 30. We should note, however, that the Westminster Confession explicitly states that "God is not the author of sin"; Art. 3, Para. 1.

R. C. Sproul echoes Paul Helm:

> *The movement of every molecule, the actions of every plant,*
> *the falling of every star, the choices of every volitional creature,*
> *all of these are subject to his sovereign will. No maverick*
> *molecules run loose in the universe beyond the control of the*
> *Creator. If one such molecule existed, it could be the critical fly*
> *in the eternal ointment.*[42]

We should notice that none of these quotations restricts itself to human destiny but attributes everything in the universe, including the behaviour of individual molecules, to the direct control of God. This, of course, raises the question of what we mean by "control". Very deep issues are involved here. We have little idea what human consciousness and mind are, to say nothing of God who is not material but Spirit. We have no real notion what it means for God who is Spirit to have created matter, let alone to have created minds other than his own. The human mind bears the image of God. Like the mind of God it also can control molecules. I can decide to move my arm, and its constituent molecules obey me. By uttering the word "fire" in a crowded room I can "control" the constituent molecules of many people's bodies so that they run out into the street.

What Helm and Sproul seem not to appreciate is that, if God takes over and "directly controls" the molecules in my arm – for instance, as it swings to hit you – then my responsibility has gone and I cease to be fully human. Surely the remarkable thing about the creation of human minds in the image of God is that he has chosen to cede to them, to some extent at least, a real capacity to act independently of his direct control. In other words, human freedom is real.[43]

---

42   R. C. Sproul, *What Is Reformed Theology?*, Grand Rapids, Baker, 2016,
      p. 172. Sproul elsewhere says that the person who does not believe
      this should be an atheist. Ironically, with God replaced by Nature, it is
      exactly what atheistic determinism does believe!
43   The reader interested in more on my views on mind and matter is
      directed to my chapter in R. A. Varghese (ed.), *Missing Link*, Lanham,
      University Press of America, 2013.

I am aware that my list of examples is very short and does not do justice to the immense amount of *historical* research available in the literature. My mention of Luther and Calvin may lead those people aware of that historical material to protest that I have failed to give due weight to the wide range of teaching of the great Reformers on these topics. That is perfectly true. There is, for example, much to be said on what exactly Calvin meant by predestination and how it is to be understood in light of the fact that he did believe in a certain degree of free will. Indeed, Richard Muller persuasively argues in his recent book, there is great variety among seventeenth-century theologians in the reformed tradition, many of whom even opposed determinism. He lists as important the book *Reformed Thought on Freedom*[44] and cites a review of it by Keith Stangin: "This historical investigation issues a tacit challenge to modern Calvinists, especially those that subscribe to a metaphysical determinism that brings with it intolerable theological conclusions"– such as, Muller adds, "the identification of God as the author of sin and the removal of human moral responsibility".[45]

Muller also points out that:

> *The debate became significantly more complex as some Reformed thinkers of the eighteenth century adopted the premise of the new rationalist and mechanical philosophies and argued overtly in favour of a deterministic reading of Reformed doctrine. The thought of Jonathan Edwards is paradigmatic of this new determinism and to the extent that Edwards has been identified as a "Calvinist", his work accounts for much of the more recent identification of Reformed theology as deterministic".*[46]

Furthermore, Muller gives a fascinating analysis of the influence of patristic and medieval scholarship on early Protestant thought

---

44 Willem J. van Asselt (ed.), Grand Rapids, Baker Academic, 2010.
45 R. Muller, *Divine Will and Human Choice*, Grand Rapids, Baker Academic, 2017, pp. 30–31.
46 *Ibid.*, p. 19.

demonstrating that even earlier opposition to determinism. In particular, he discusses the attitudes of Aristotle, Augustine, Aquinas, and Duns Scotus to determinism, and what their influence on Reformers like Calvin actually was.

In addition, there is also a great deal of *philosophical* literature on these issues, much of it devoted to whether and how various deterministic views like those listed above may nevertheless in some way be regarded as compatible with various ways of understanding human free will. It turns out that there are many different kinds of compatibilism and incompatibilism – and there are philosophers who reject both. The topic is both intriguing and complex and Kevin Timpe's two books: *Free Will: Sourcehood and its Alternatives* and *Free Will in Philosophical Theology* form an excellent introduction. In addition, the interested reader might also like to consult the aforementioned *Oxford Handbook of Free Will*.

Unfortunately, we cannot pursue these interesting and important issues any further here. For, whatever conclusions we come to about what Calvin and his successors actually believed about determinism and free will, it is surely reasonable to say that these theologians were at least instrumental in leading many people then and now to become determinists of one kind and another. Muller confirms this:

> *These assumptions about the deterministic nature of Calvinism have been absorbed both positively and negatively in much modern literature on the subject of divine will and its relationship to human free choice with the result that Calvinist or Reformed thought has been described, almost uniformly, by both opponents and advocates, as a kind of determinism, often compatibilism or soft determinism – with little or no concern for the possible anachronistic application of the terms.*
>
> *In short, an understanding of sixteenth- and seventeenth-century Reformed theology as a variety of fatalism or determinism, despite early modern Reformed claims to the contrary, became the dominant line in modern discussion.*[47]

---

47 *Ibid.*, pp. 21–22.

In light of this I see my main task in this book not to settle precisely historically what, for instance, thinkers from Calvin to Edwards taught, nor to attempt to analyse compatibilism from a philosophical viewpoint, but rather to see what Scripture teaches about free will and determinism. There is clearly no point in arguing for compatibility between view X on determinism and view Y on human freedom and responsibility, if view X or view Y or both are inconsistent with Scripture in the first place.

It is this prior question of *what Scripture teaches* that will principally concern us here. I use the word "concern" advisedly, since there is not just an intellectual but a pastoral dimension to be addressed, for theistic determinism troubles many.

None of us who believe in God can afford to give a wrong impression of God to the general public, especially one that causes people to call into question his goodness and love – and even his very existence.

Yet that is usually the first thing that happens. For the immediate reaction to the content of the sequence of quotations just listed does not normally first arise from a detailed knowledge of Scripture but from elementary logic and reasoning about morality. It is often put like this: if God micro-manages the entire universe in the manner outlined above, so that he even causes sin and disaster; if this is what is meant by the sovereignty of God; then his is surely the dictatorship of a moral monster. How is it possible for us to be moral beings, capable of performing morally significant acts, if our behaviour is completely predetermined by an absolute divine predestination? How can anyone believe that God is good, or that he is a God of love, if he fixes human destiny like a master chess-player or puppeteer, irrespective of the response of the humans involved? Some are created for eternal bliss and others for eternal torment? Indeed, if God causes sin in this direct way, how could the concept of a just God – or even the concepts of good and evil – retain any meaning?

At this point there is a striking similarity between the theistic and atheistic forms of determinism, in that each of them logically renders morality meaningless. We might call the atheist variant a *determinism from below*, since it regards human beings and their behaviour as nothing but products of the physics and chemistry of the basic stuff of the universe. The theistic form we might think of as a *determinism from above*, since it regards human beings and their behaviour as nothing but predetermined products of an inexorable and all-controlling divine will above them.

David Bentley Hart makes the following observation:

> *There comes a point when an explanation becomes so comprehensive that it ceases to explain anything at all because it has become a mere tautology. In the case of pure determinism this is always so. To assert that every finite contingency is solely and unambiguously the effect of a single will working all things – without any deeper mystery of created freedom – is to assert nothing but that the world is what it is, for any meaningful distinction between the will of God and the simple totality of cosmic eventuality has collapsed... Such a God at the end of the day is nothing but will and so nothing but an infinite brute event; and the only adoration that such a God can evoke is an almost perfect coincidence of faith and nihilism.*[48]

Not surprisingly, we find at both ends of the atheist-theist spectrum those who maintain that human free will is an illusion – an idea that at once leads not only to the moral difficulty already mentioned, but also to a major intellectual difficulty.

John Polkinghorne, physicist and Christian, explains:

> *In the opinion of many thinkers, human freedom is closely connected with human rationality. If we were deterministic beings, what would validate the claim that our utterance constituted rational discourse? Would not the sounds issuing from mouths, or the marks we made on paper, be simply the actions of automata? All proponents of deterministic theories,*

---

48   D. B. Hart, *The Doors of the Sea*, Grand Rapids, Eerdmans, 2005, pp. 29–30.

whether social and economic (Marx), or sexual (Freud), or genetic (Dawkins and E. O. Wilson), need a covert disclaimer on their own behalf, excepting their own contribution from reductive dismissal.[49]

The point is that causal determinism cannot even be meaningfully affirmed, since if it were true then the affirmation itself would be determined, and so would not be a belief freely formed on the basis of weighing the evidence for and against. The affirmation is therefore irrational. Furthermore, it is common for determinists to try to convince non-determinists to convert to determinism. But that assumes that the non-determinists are free to convert, and therefore their non-determinism is not determined in the first place. The cost of holding human free will to be an illusion would appear to be impossibly high, as it entails the invalidity not only of human morality but also of human rationality.

It is therefore to the moral problems raised by determinism that we now turn.

---

49   J. Polkinghorne, *Science and Theology*, London, SPCK, 1998, p. 58.

CHAPTER 3

Reactions to Determinism – The Moral Problem

Attitudes to determinism vary greatly. There are former atheists whose journey to Christianity has been triggered by the bleakness of atheistic determinism. On the other hand there are Christians who hold that absolute sovereignty is one of the most glorious of divine attributes and must be protected at all costs, even if it inexorably leads some to the (to my mind, appalling) conclusion that God is the direct cause of disasters, tragedies, and even sin itself.

Others, who may be inclined to agree, nevertheless shrink at what would seem to be the logical implications of their views. It is one thing to believe, as part of essential Christianity, that we live in a world in which nothing happens without God's permission and even foreknowledge. But it is entirely another thing to go way beyond that, and to believe that all that happens, including evil, is meticulously planned and its occurrence made certain by God, independent of any other considerations. It is hard to imagine that anyone could believe that such extreme deterministic ideas are even remotely Christian. They seem infinitely far away from describing the God of love revealed to us in Jesus Christ – or the God who condemns and says that we should avoid evil. Yet how can one condemn anything that God has predetermined ought to occur? Thus, as we have seen, this kind of determinism abolishes the very concept of evil.

It is not surprising that many instinctively sympathise with the passionate reaction of David Bentley Hart in saying that theological determinism

61

requires us to believe in and love a God whose good ends will be realized not only in spite of – but entirely by way of – every cruelty, every fortuitous misery, every catastrophe, every betrayal, every sin the world has ever known… It is a strange thing indeed to seek peace in a universe rendered morally intelligible at the cost of a God rendered morally loathsome.[50]

Bentley Hart's reference to the idea that somehow God's glory is enhanced by tragic events is reminiscent of what Ivan says to Alyosha in Dostoyevsky's masterpiece, *The Brothers Karamazov*:

Tell me yourself, I challenge you – answer. Imagine that you are creating a fabric of human destiny with the object of making men happy in the end, giving them peace and rest at least, but that it was essential and inevitable to torture to death only one tiny creature – that baby beating its breast with its fist, for instance – and to found that edifice on its unavenged tears, would you consent to be the architect on those conditions? Tell me, and tell the truth.

Ivan in the end maintains that he does not reject God; but in view of the hideous evil in the world, particularly the cruelty perpetrated on little children, he cannot bring himself to believe in the eventual reconciliation of all things and the universal harmony promised in the Bible. Nor does he wish to have any part in that harmony on the terms and conditions that (he imagines) the Bible lays down for it:

I don't want harmony. From love for humanity I don't want it. I would rather be left with the unavenged suffering. I would rather remain with my unavenged suffering and unsatisfied indignation, even if I were wrong. Besides, too high a price is asked for harmony; it's beyond our means to pay so much to enter. And so I hasten to give back my entrance ticket, and if I am an honest man, I am bound to give it back as soon as

---

50   D. B. Hart, *The Doors of the Sea*, Grand Rapids, Eerdmans, 2005, p. 99.

possible. And that I am doing. It's not God that I don't accept,
Aloysha, only I most respectfully return Him the ticket.[51]

It is not surprising to meet people who say they have become atheists because the version of theism presented to them was deterministic and contradicted their moral sense. Furthermore, there are more and more people within the Christian community who are disturbed if not repelled by such views.

For instance, concerned parents ask how they should respond to their son who says to them: "I am not going to bother with God since your church teaches me that if I am going to be saved I will be saved, and I can do nothing about it in either direction, so there is clearly absolutely no point in being concerned about it;" or the daughter who confronts them with: "I cannot believe in your God any more. How can I believe in a God who fixed my eternal destiny before I was born so that I can do nothing about it? How can I believe in a God who is actively involved in evil? Surely this is not only unfair but also immoral? Such a God, if he exists at all, is obviously neither loving nor good."

I agree. Having visited Auschwitz several times and been confronted with the evidence of consummate evil on an industrial scale, I could not believe in such a God either. In one sense that should be an end of the matter. The moral argument is surely entirely sufficient to invalidate theories of divine determinism. The problem is, however, that those theories are often so wrapped up in biblical quotations and Christian terminology that many of the clearly unacceptable logical implications of divine determinism are shrouded in mystery – a mystery that we are not allowed to question. It is even held by some that the solution lies in the fact that God has two wills: one is secret, and it is to save only those people he has unconditionally elected to salvation; and the other is revealed, and it is that he wills that all people be saved. Another, less charitable way of putting it is that the unacceptable implications of determinism get shrouded in intellectual fog and contradiction, in an intractable obfuscation.

---

51   F. Dostoyevsky, *The Brothers Karamazov*, transl. Constance Garnett, New York, Dover Publications, 2005, p. 222.

Christian utilitarianism

A further attempt to avoid the issue is to say that everything, including evil, is directly caused by God for the greater good. To make this plausible it is common to cite the contribution suffering can make to the development of character and so on – the so-called "greater good" argument. This view is a version of utilitarianism.

It is undeniable that we are taught in the New Testament that God does *permit* his people to suffer in order to learn of his grace. Paul was a case in point. But the use of that argument to say that God was the *direct cause* of the horrific abuse or murder of a child, as in Dostoyevsky's story and so often in real life, goes far beyond this biblical teaching and, from a moral perspective, is utterly reprehensible.

And what shall we say of those who try to vindicate God in such situations by suggesting that, although he causes people to do evil, they are in the end responsible for it – while, incredibly, God is not? How people can even get near to suggesting such things, without seeming to realise what a monster they are making of God, is beyond my capacity to imagine.

G. K. Chesterton was forthright in his assessment:

> The Calvinists took the Catholic idea of the absolute knowledge and power of God, and treated it as a rocky irreducible truism so solid that anything could be built on it, however crushing or cruel. They were so confident in their logic, and its one first principle of predestination, that they tortured the intellect and imagination with dreadful deductions about God, that seemed to turn Him into a demon.[52]

In another attempt to avoid the obvious negative implications of their views, some theological determinists, having stated that God causes everything down to the movement of the last atom and every

---

52   G. K. Chesterton, *The Collected Works of G. K. Chesterton*, vol. 3, San Francisco, Ignatius Press, 1990, p. 152.

human thought, proceed to contradict themselves by turning round and maintaining that, even so, evil is not directly caused by God. Rather, he only permits it. But this makes no sense whatsoever. There is a vast and critical difference between causation and permission. Imagine, as a parent, I permit my child to ride his/her bicycle on the road and he/she is killed in an accident. To hold me responsible for causing the accident would be monstrously unjust – and a burden too heavy to bear. No; we must be crystal clear about the fundamental distinction between causation and permission.

Not surprisingly, therefore, statements blurring that distinction may become misleadingly ambiguous and confusing, as, for example, when R. C. Sproul writes, "What God permits, he decrees to permit."[53] That could be interpreted as meaning that God has decreed that we are free moral beings and can ourselves decide to do good or evil. But that does not seem to be what Sproul believes. Such confusion may well be evidence of the internal conflict that arises when people see where the logic of their argument is leading them and they don't really like it.

John Piper, the most prominent contemporary defender of theological determinism, cites Jonathan Edwards with similarly confusing effect.

> God is, Edwards says, "the permitter... of sin; and at the same time, a disposer of the state of events, in such a manner, for wise, holy and most excellent ends and purposes, that sin, if it be permitted... will most certainly and infallibly follow."[54]

The depth of the resulting intellectual fog is shown by the astonishing position held by some that God directly causes the human evil that he expressly forbids. No amount of special pleading or theological sophistry can make such a view anything less than grotesque and completely unacceptable to a morally sensitive person. After all, one of the key biblical concepts is repentance from sin. It means a change

---

53   R. C. Sproul, *What Is Reformed Theology?*, Grand Rapids, Baker, 2016, p. 173.
54   "Is God Less Glorious Because He Ordained That Evil Be?", www.desiringgod.org

of mind, agreeing with God that what I have done is wrong. It carries with it the implicit recognition that I had (libertarian) freedom to do otherwise. Therefore repentance is without meaning if God caused me to sin. In any case, as it has often been put to me very bluntly, how can we say that God loves the world if he created a good portion of it to go to hell?

I can imagine that some of my readers will be thinking that surely this is exaggerated – no one could ever seriously suggest such things. Yet Calvin himself wrote:

> To sum up, since God's will is said to be the cause of all things, I have made his providence the determinative principle for all human plans and works, not only in order to display its force in the elect, who are ruled by the Holy Spirit, but also to compel the reprobate to obedience.[55]

That is, God's providence is equally determinative of good and evil. It is interesting to see that Calvin says that *he* has made God's providence the determinative principle for all human activity. A huge claim. Whether it is true to Scripture or not is another matter.

It is one thing to say *my times are in his hands* because Scripture teaches that (Psalm 31:15). If that is what is meant by God's sovereignty, it is true, wonderful, and very comforting. It is entirely another matter to include under the same concept of "sovereignty" what Gordon H. Clark says: "I wish very frankly and pointedly to assert that if a man gets drunk and shoots his family, it was the will of God that he should do so..." and yet Clark maintains that God is not responsible for sin even though he decrees it.[56] And the same applies to the holocaust, the killing fields, and ISIS, does it? Can this be the same God who says: *You shall not murder* (Exodus 20:13)?[57]

---

55 J. Calvin, *Institutes of Christian Religion*, I, xxvii, 2.
56 G. H. Clark, *God and Evil: The Problem Solved*, Unicoi, The Trinity Foundation, 2004, pp. 27, 40.
57 For a much fuller and more nuanced account of this, see R. Olson, *Against Calvinism: Rescuing God's Reputation from Radical Reformed Theology*, Grand Rapids, Zondervan, 2011.

Bentley Hart puts his finger on what is happening to produce such extreme views – the collapse of the important distinction between will and permission. He writes:

> But when any meaningful distinction between will and permission has been excluded, and when the transcendent causality of the creator God has been confused with the immanent web of causation that constitutes the world of our experiences, it becomes impossible to imagine that what God wills might not be immediately convertible with what occurs in time, and thus both the authority of Scripture and the justice of God must fall before the inexorable logic of absolute divine sovereignty.[58]

Hart traces this back to Calvin himself (*Institutes III*) who wrote that God predestined the Fall of man so as to show forth his greatness in both the salvation and the damnation of those he has eternally preordained to their several fates. Calvin added that this "ought not to appear absurd" – which shows that he rightly anticipated that it might!

John Piper makes the notion of God "showing forth his greatness" by his absolute sovereign control a cornerstone of what he calls "the vindication of God". He cites the view of Jonathan Edwards that God's greatness is shown by the exercise of his absolute and all-encompassing will:

> It is proper that the shining forth of God's glory be complete; that is that all parts of his glory should shine forth... Thus it is necessary that God's awful majesty, his authority and dreadful greatness, justice and holiness should be manifested. But this could not be unless sin and punishment had been decreed; so that the shining forth of God's glory would be very imperfect both because those parts of divine glory would not shine forth as the others do, and also the glory of his goodness, love and

---

58   D. B. Hart, *The Doors of the Sea*, Grand Rapids, Eerdmans, 2005, p. 90.

holiness would be faint without them; nay, they could scarcely shine forth at all.[59]

Piper then puts it this way: "God is more glorious for having conceived and created and governed a world like this with all its evil."[60] To say that this is hard to accept is an understatement. For instance, if evil ultimately occurs necessarily according to the inexorable decree of God, how could sin have any meaning? The deist Voltaire's trenchant exposure of the moral shock elicited by such a theodicy comes to mind. It is to be found in the poem he wrote after the horrific earthquake in Lisbon in 1755 that killed an estimated 60,000 people.

Tout est bien, dites-vous, et tout est nécessaire.
Quoi! L'univers entier, sans ce gouffre infernal,
Sans engloutir Lisbonne, eut-il été plus mal?

(All is well, you say, and all is necessary.
What? The entire universe, but for this infernal chasm
engulfing Lisbon, would have been worse off?)

For a more detailed evaluation of Piper's argument I refer the reader to the article by Thomas McCall that shows (convincingly, in my opinion) that Piper's views are not supported by Scripture.[61]

God's direct causation of evil is probably the most serious implication of theistic determinism. There are other implications, very practical matters of Christian faith and witness, that frequently come up in conversation. For instance, someone says to me: "You know, I wish I had your faith in God. But it just hasn't happened to me. Maybe God will give it to me one day, but in the meantime I have heard in church that there is nothing I can do about it." The impression given is that faith is something that either "happens" to

---

59 J. Piper, *The Justification of God*, Grand Rapids, Baker, 1993.
60 "Is God Less Glorious Because He Ordained that Evil Be?", www.desiringgod.org.
61 T. McCall, "I Believe in Divine Sovereignty", *Trinity Journal*, 29NS, 2008, pp. 205–26.

you or doesn't, without any action or input from your side. Whether you get it or not depends entirely on God. You may well also have been told that if salvation involved a response, then it could be said that you contributed towards it, and that would deny that salvation was altogether a work of God.

In a similar vein, some theological determinists accuse people like me, who engage in discussion and debate with atheists and agnostics, of wasting our time. "There is no point using argument to defend the Christian faith," they say. "After all, people who are not believers in God are 'dead in trespasses and sins' and so they can no more respond to your arguments than a dead dog could respond to a command to get up. In any case, unless God has chosen them for salvation, they will never respond, no matter what you do."

We must take such reactions very seriously. In the main this is not an argument between those who are theologically irresponsible and those who simply wish to pick holes in Christianity, but involves people who are wrestling with how to understand themselves, the world, and how God relates to it. People do think about the big topics of God's sovereignty and human freedom and responsibility, and it is important for those of us who claim to be Christians to make the effort to sit alongside them and listen hard to what they have to say.

Historical precedents

The in-house debate about these issues has a long and complex history, as is shown in particular by the controversies between: Augustine and Pelagius in the fifth century; Luther and Erasmus, Calvin and Arminius in the sixteenth century; and Whitefield and Wesley in the eighteenth century.

However, the debate is by no means confined to past history. In his 2009 book, *Young, Restless and Reformed: A Journalist's Journey with the New Calvinists*, Colin Hansen chronicles the rise of a movement that has arisen, in his view, partly because of the perceived superficiality of many churches, which has turned many to adopt what they see as the much more solid theology of past generations. This movement, which lays claim in particular to the legacy of Jonathan Edwards, is currently associated with influential authors and speakers like R. C. Sproul, John MacArthur, and John Piper. *Time* magazine in 2009 called this "New Calvinism" one of the "ten ideas changing the world right now".

It is certainly understandable that a theological system that seems to possess considerable intellectual and historical weight should appeal to many young people who long for something more glorious and godly. They are fed up with the ubiquitous, superficial kind of watered-down Christianity that has very little space for substantial biblical reflection and a great deal of space for comfortable, soft, self-centred schemes for human well-being that creates a god in its own image. I sympathise with their reaction. The lack of theological depth and biblical knowledge in many professedly Christian contexts is deplorable, so it is very encouraging to see young people taking Scripture seriously and spending time on finding out what it says.

However, when some of the core teaching that is presented to such young people moves so far towards the deterministic end of the spectrum that it appears to many to call into question the love and goodness of God, and in consequence alienates people who are beginning to think about Christianity, then we surely need to audit the validity of the interpretation of Scripture that lies behind such teaching. In this connection it is worth reading the book by Austin Fischer, *Young, Restless, No Longer Reformed*.[62] Fischer tells his story with clarity, honesty, and without bitterness.

Five-Point Calvinism

One legacy of the controversy between followers of Calvin and Arminius is the systematisation of some of the main issues into what has become known as the Five Points of Calvinism. They were discussed at the Synod of Dort in 1618–19, convened fifty-five years

---

62   A. Fischer, *Young, Restless, No Longer Reformed: Black Holes, Love, and a Journey In and Out of Calvinism*, Oregon, Cascade Books (Wipf and Stock), 2014.

after Calvin's death, to respond to the followers of Jacob Arminius (who were called Remonstrants). These points of doctrine are often referred to by the acronym TULIP:

T – Total Depravity
U – Unconditional Election
L – Limited Atonement
I – Irresistible Grace
P – Perseverance of the Saints.

These points are set out using slightly different terminology in what is regarded as a classic work on the subject, written in 1932 by Loraine Boettner, entitled *The Reformed Doctrine of Predestination*.[63]

Part of this acronym (TUI) can help at this stage to map out the main contours of some of the issues we shall meet in this book. The scheme begins with an analysis of the status of human beings after the entry of sin into the world. It is claimed that they are totally depraved, meaning that they are not only completely unable to merit God's salvation but they are totally incapable even of responding to God in any sense – like a dead man at the bottom of an ocean is incapable of even grasping and entrusting himself to a lifeline thrown to him.

Logically, therefore, in order for people to be able to respond and trust God, they must be given life – that is, they must be regenerated by an act of God. Faith must therefore be preceded by regeneration. The recipients of this regenerating act of God are chosen (elected) unconditionally by God in his predestining sovereignty without any involvement whatsoever on their part. The correlative of the predeterminateness of this sovereign act of God is that it is completely irresistible.

However, the fate of the non-elect is variously regarded as equally determined or blameworthy or both ("double predestination"). What is central to the whole scheme is the so-called *ordo salutis*, the order of salvation, on which it is based. The order proposed is: predestination and unconditional election, regeneration, faith, salvation.

---

63 L. Boettner, *The Reformed Doctrine of Predestination*, Phillipsburg, P & R Publishing, 1971.

The P in TULIP stands for the perseverance (or preservation) of the saints and raises a very important question that is part of the motivation for writing this book. Putting the issue in a sharper and perhaps more recognisable form, the question is: can a child of God be lost? For many Christians assurance is a matter of considerable concern, and even confusion, since here again opinion is divided. This division is sometimes expressed in terms of the differences between Calvinism and Arminianism. The doctrine of the perseverance of the saints (P) in the TULIP scheme is closely connected with the doctrine of unconditional election (U) – for obvious reasons: if God predetermines, if God elects, then (essentially by definition) the elect cannot become the non-elect; genuine believers cannot become non-believers. They will persevere. This is why some writers prefer the term "preservation of the saints" as a more accurate description of what is involved.

However, there is a problem. It is one thing to hold that the elect will persevere; it would appear to be entirely another to be personally sure that one actually belongs to the ranks of the elect. Indeed, history shows, rather paradoxically, that holding P and U does not necessarily lead to a genuine and deep assurance of salvation. It is one thing to believe that God predestines some to salvation and some to rejection; it is quite another to know where you yourself stand.

If we ask those who hold this view how a person might know whether they are one of the elect – chosen by God with no personal involvement on their part (certainly not of merit, but not even of their faith) – then we discover, again somewhat paradoxically, that their confidence does depend on their assessment of their own behaviour.

On the other hand, there are many people who hold that, if there is any real human freedom at all, then it must be possible for believers to opt out of their salvation and effectively lose it. They cite as evidence the famous "warning passages" in Hebrews 6 and 10. This is often held to be a characteristically "Arminian" view.

Blessèd assurance

This matter of what assurance and confidence we may have in our salvation is relevant to every area of personal Christian development and evangelism, because our thinking about it reflects what we believe the gospel really is. Today there are many external voices telling us that it is arrogant to be sure of anything, and arguing for the privatisation of the expression of a confident Christian faith. There is also the internal theological debate about the issue, which we will address in two ways in this book: first, we shall refer to it when it crops up naturally in the course of developing our main themes; and secondly, we shall devote our closing chapters entirely to it, so that the topic is not lost in the detailed discussion found in the rest of the book.

I am well aware that objections will be raised by people who will say that this or that is not quite what they believe. I take the point. However, these are the beliefs that I am constantly asked about and that I therefore wish to address, leaving readers to decide what relevance, if any, my responses have to their particular situation.

I am also aware that not all who would see themselves in what might broadly be called the Reformed tradition subscribe to all five of the points in the TULIP scheme. Many, for instance, do not hold with the third, and are sometimes called "four-pointers". Others disagree with some of the terms used. For instance, some use the term "total inability" rather than "total depravity", and some have replaced "limited atonement" with "definite atonement" or "particular redemption". Some think that in order to claim to be Calvinist a person needs to affirm much more than the five points, adding for instance the doctrine of infant baptism, regarding sacraments as means of grace, and holding to an amillennial eschatology. We shall occasionally refer to the TULIP acronym at relevant parts of the discussion; but since none of the terms is strictly biblical we shall be much more interested in the underlying doctrines and not the labels attached either to them or to the people who hold them.

There is a further important reason for this approach, to which we now turn.

CHAPTER 4

Weapons of Mass Distraction

The problem with labels

The mention of the names of famous scholars associated with the debate brings us to one of the main difficulties in the discussion, which is that for many people it really boils down to deciding whether one takes the label of Calvinist or Arminian (or Molinist or Reformed, or…). However, I would like to suggest that the very labels themselves are a big part of the problem, and this needs to be faced sooner rather than later if reasonable and productive discussion is to be at all possible. Human beings seem to have a propensity to use labels to define themselves and others, and those of theological inclination are no exception. As an immediate example of this, I suspect that some of my readers are already trying to shoehorn me into a pigeonhole, labelled, shall we say, Calminian.[64] They will then form an opinion of what I write, or even whether to go on reading at all, solely on the basis of that label. I would courteously ask them not to do that. Let me explain why.

Many years ago, on taking up a university appointment, I received what seemed at first to be intended as a welcoming visit from some fellow Christian academics. During the course of the conversation two things became clear. There was a question they wished to ask me, but they were not quite sure how to frame it. In the end they came out with it: "Are you a Calvinist?"

"You put me in great difficulty," I replied.

"How so, for that is the last thing we wish to do?"

"Well," I said, "when I think of Calvin I think of someone who

---

64 Calminius is, of course, a purely fictitious name formed by combining two familiar names in this debate!

had a huge effect in reforming the church in Europe and championing the centrality of Scripture. The value of that alone is immeasurable. And, like you I imagine, I am also greatly indebted to other great theologians of the past – Wycliffe, Tyndale, Luther, and many other luminaries stretching right back beyond the early church fathers to the apostles themselves. I have learned and continue to learn a great deal from them, and many of my friends would be happy to describe themselves as Calvinists or Lutherans.

"Yet, were I to survey the long list of eminent people to whom I am indebted and decide to call myself after one of them, I would actually be inclined to choose either Paul or Peter. I don't think either Luther or Calvin would regard that choice as insulting.

"But now comes my problem. I must not even do that, for the simple reason that Scripture forbids it. With full apostolic authority Paul lays it down that we must *not* say that I am of Paul, or Apollos, or Peter. We must not label ourselves, even if the names on the labels are attached to apostles. Why not? Paul gives the reason bluntly and directly: *Is Christ divided? Was Paul crucified for you? Were you baptised into the name of Paul?* (1 Corinthians 1:13). Paul is affronted by the very idea.

"Perhaps now you see my difficulty. Suppose I said to you that I was a Calvinist, how would you react? Would you have fellowship with me on that basis? If you did, I would have to ask you the question suggested by Paul's argument: was Calvin crucified for you? Suppose, on the other hand, I said that I was not a Calvinist. Would that diminish the possibility of our fellowship? If so, I would then ask the very same question: was Calvin crucified for you? Or were you baptised into the name of Calvin?

"So you should not be surprised that I am not going to answer your question in the way that you expect. What I am more than willing to do, however, is to discuss what the Bible has to say on particular points of common interest, and then we all might learn something."

But we didn't. They were only interested in pigeonholing me, and they had failed.

And that is perhaps the saddest thing of all. Such conversations about labels and systems are often conducted without Scripture even being mentioned, far less discussed. The objective is to label – to put someone in a box. The participants, having labelled each other, then completely fail to address the question: what exactly does Scripture teach about the issues subsumed under the labels?

Charles Simeon once wrote:

> *Calvinism is a system. God has not revealed his truth in a system; the Bible has no system as such. Lay aside system and fly to the Bible; receive its words with simple submission, and without an eye to any system. Be Bible Christians and not system Christians.*[65]

There is a further reason for refusing to take the label Calvinist or Arminian, or indeed any other similar label, because Paul himself indicates that the principle of rejecting labels applies much more widely, as we shall see later in this chapter. The fact is that there are many different shades of these views. For instance, there are people who call themselves Calvinists but don't agree with all that Calvin taught. There are also people who do not call themselves Calvinists, yet they agree with many things that Calvin taught. The same is true when it comes to Arminius, Luther, Augustine, Whitefield, Wesley, and so on.

Again, we hear of hyper-Calvinists (of at least four different types, so far as I can ascertain), neo-Calvinists, resurgent Calvinists, neo-Puritans and classic Arminians. We come across attempts to decide whether Arminians are semi-Pelagians or semi-Augustinians, and we even meet hybrids of Calvinists and Arminians (the aforementioned Calminians, no doubt!).

There are those who, by labelling themselves and others as Calvinists, hyper-Calvinists, ultra-Calvinists, or Arminians, or Reformed, or neo-Reformed, or any other of the many labels floating around, imagine that they have defined precisely what they or others believe. They suffer from the simplistic and false assumption that

---

65   A. W. Brown, *Recollections of Conversation Parties of Rev. Charles Simeon*, London, M. S. Rickerby, 1862, p. 269.

Calvinism and Arminianism, for instance, are two clearly defined systems that are polar opposites. So that, if one is true, the other is false. However, a moment's reflection will show that matters cannot be that simple. After all, we do not combat polytheism by denying the doctrine of the Trinity. There are nuances to be aired and discussed.

This is why labels are unhelpful.[66] Indeed, it may even lead to the banality of dismissive statements like, "You believe that because you are a Calminian." This is the so-called genetic fallacy, perhaps encountered more frequently in statements like, "You believe that because you are a woman, Irishman, banker, conservative, etc." The error lies in assuming that, if you can give some kind of causal explanation for a person holding a specific belief, you have thereby emptied that belief of any validity. In fact, you have not addressed the truth content of that belief at all. There is a deep irony in this kind of argument, especially when it is used by a determinist, since the argument is based on the assumption that a causally deterministic account of anything renders it meaningless.

When attempting to discuss these issues I am also aware that sometimes the reaction is: "But that is not what we Calminians think." Or, "But that does not represent classic Calminianism – it is more like the new Calminianism, and we don't accept that anyway." There is a deeply ingrained tendency to refer to some labelled theological system, rather than getting to grips with what Scripture actually says.

For instance, Smith could be studying Romans and may mention the importance of Paul's statements about predestination. "Ah, so Smith is a Calvinist!" Not necessarily. Smith may simply believe what Scripture says about predestination, and never would think that he has to see it within an overarching theological system. On another occasion the very same Smith could be discussing evangelism with friends, stressing that it is important to reason with people. "Ah, so Smith is an Arminian!" Not necessarily. Smith may simply be attempting to take seriously what Paul practised in the synagogues and market places.

---

66   For an example of the astonishing variety and complexity of labels in this area, see R. Olson, *Against Calvinism: Rescuing God's Reputation from Radical Reformed Theology*, Grand Rapids, Zondervan, 2011.

When reading books on these topics one gets the impression, from the sheer frequency of the use of labels, that it is the overarching system – the chosen theological paradigm – that is all important for many writers. The supreme irony is that the very apostles whose writings are being systematised *reject the use of any such labels* in the strongest possible terms. This can only mean that a wrong turning has been taken somewhere in theological space. It will become clear how serious this wrong turning is as we now consider in a little more detail why Paul did not regard this matter of labels as some "innocent convenience" (as I have heard it called).

The apostle Paul on labels

The initial striking thing is that Paul chooses to deal with this problem in a range of difficult issues facing the church at Corinth. Secondly, we notice the comparatively large space Paul devotes to the issue – no less than the first four chapters of 1 Corinthians. He repeatedly mentions it:

What I mean is this: One of you says, "I follow Paul"; another, "I follow Apollos"...

(1:12.)

For when one says, "I follow Paul," and another, "I follow Apollos," are you not mere men?

(3:4.)

So then, no more boasting about men! All things are yours, whether Paul or Apollos or Cephas [Peter] or the world or life or death or the present or the future – all are yours, and you are of Christ, and Christ is of God.

(3:21–23.)

Now, brothers, I have applied these things to myself and Apollos for your benefit, so that you may learn from us the

meaning of the saying, "Do not to go beyond what is written."
Then you will not take pride in one man over against another.

(4:6.)

This final statement shows that Paul is not simply concerned with the practice of following particular leaders, but of the underlying principle behind such a practice – divisions can be caused by differences over church practice, congregational form, ritual observance, and more. This is something that was of deep concern to John Bunyan (author of *The Pilgrim's Progress*) when he wrote:

> *You ask me next, how long is it since I was a Baptist? I*
> *must tell you that I know of none to whom that title is most*
> *proper than the disciples of John. And since you would know*
> *by what name I would be distinguished from others, I tell*
> *you I would be, and hope I am – a Christian, and choose*
> *if God should count me worthy to be called a Christian, a*
> *believer, or other such name which is approved by the Holy*
> *Ghost. And as for those titles of Anabaptists, Independents,*
> *Presbyterians and the like, I conclude that they came neither*
> *from Jerusalem, nor Antioch, but rather from hell and from*
> *Babylon, for they naturally tend to divisions. By their fruits*
> *you shall know them.*[67]

Bunyan's language is noticeably more intemperate than Paul's, but that should not put us off asking why Paul was so determined to resist these tendencies. The answer from these chapters in 1 Corinthians is that, far from being innocent, diversionary, peripheral issues, they detract people's attention from the preaching of the cross of Christ. They focus on natural thinking rather than on the Holy Spirit, and they cause people to have their confidence and boast in human leaders rather than in God. In short, Paul sees this development in the early church as imperilling people's perception of God the

---

67   J. Brown, *John Bunyan: His Life, Times and Works*, 3rd ed., Oregon, Wipf
      and Stock, 2007, p. 239.

Father, the Holy Spirit, the Son, and the gospel of his cross. He considers it to be maximally serious, since it affects our attitudes to the very Godhead. One dreads to think what Paul might have to say to us today, in the age of social media, where the interest is focused on how many followers we have.

Around twenty times in the New Testament our Lord is recorded as saying: "Follow me!" But none of the apostles ever uses these words. The nearest we get to anything like that is an appeal that Paul makes to the Corinthians at the end of the section we have just been considering. It is an appeal, not to follow him, but to imitate him:

> *I am not writing this to shame you, but to warn you, as my dear children. Even though you have ten thousand guardians in Christ, you do not have many fathers, for in Christ Jesus I became your father through the gospel. Therefore I urge you to imitate me. For this reason I am sending to you Timothy, my son whom I love, who is faithful in the Lord. He will remind you of my way of life in Christ Jesus, which agrees with what I teach everywhere in every church.*
>
> (1 Corinthians 4:14–17.)

Paul is very careful to emphasise that what should be imitated is his *way of life in Christ Jesus*, as he later explicitly says: *Follow my example, as I follow the example of Christ* (1 Corinthians 11:1).

And God gives all of us role models in godly leaders. We are instructed to remember those who brought the word of God to us and taught us. We are to consider not only their teaching but the outcome of their lives, and we are to imitate their faith:

> *Remember your leaders, those who spoke the word of God to you. Consider the outcome of their way of life and imitate their faith.*
>
> (Hebrews 13:7.)

We are to follow Christ, and any imitation of others is to be strictly controlled by comparing their life and teaching with that of Christ, so that he and he alone is the central focus.

So how can we resist pinning labels on others and ourselves? If Paul says it is not to be done, then it is not to be done. Not even in this book! That is a tall order, and realism tells me that I am likely to fail. Getting rid of labels is not going to be at all easy. For one group does not necessarily resent labels because they are pinned on it by another group. Far from it, many are convinced that labels are perfectly in order and very useful, so they happily accept and even proudly employ a great variety of labels to describe themselves. But surely we can at least try to avoid this tendency, and attempt to understand why Scripture is against it, rather than defining and labelling a particular system so that we can fit everything into it.

The power of paradigms

Now, this does not mean that I do not value systematic theology. Indeed, my academic background is in the mathematical sciences, and the essence of science is systematisation. Forming systems leads to the creation of frameworks of background assumptions, or paradigms, within which science is usually done and can be very useful.

However, there is a lesson we can learn from science. There is a danger, well recognised by philosophers of science, that a scientific system or paradigm can take on a life of its own, and end up essentially defining the reality that we are studying rather than being defined by it. The result is that, instead of questioning the paradigm, theories and even observations are trimmed to fit it. For example, for centuries Aristotle's view that the earth was physically fixed and unmoving in the centre of the universe dominated European thought. Therefore, any major advance in our understanding of the universe was difficult – witness Galileo and his experiences with the Roman Inquisition. Experience shows that it is often very hard to question a paradigm.

The power of paradigms is part of the reason that I am involved in the public defence of Christianity against the New Atheists. They are committed to spreading a naturalistic paradigm whose truth and adequacy I question, in the name of both science and my Christian worldview; I do this even though naturalism dominates the Western academy and is regarded as the default position.

There seems to be a parallel situation in theology. All of us are grateful – or should be – to theologians who have over the centuries systematised their knowledge in order to help us get a grasp of it. Yet, as in science, theological systems or paradigms can sometimes become so powerful that they end up defining what Scripture is or is not allowed to mean, so that "taking Scripture seriously" means accepting a particular theological system and fitting all Scripture into it. It is therefore wise to recall that, just as science did not create the universe, systematic theology did not produce the Bible. Our "isms" with their systems and paradigms are not infallible. Furthermore, although systems of theology can be of great help, the Bible itself was not in the main written in systematised form. So, just as we must be prepared to allow the universe to correct our scientific paradigms, we must also allow Scripture to control our theological systems.

It goes without saying that most of those reading this book will be convinced that their systems have been derived from Scripture in the first place. Yet we must all surely concede that, in the case of the Bible, just as in science, there is no such thing as a neutral or unbiased observer or commentator. Whether we recognise it or not, all of us come to Scripture with presuppositions and prejudices, both theological and philosophical. We must, therefore, be prepared to ask ourselves: do I read the text in this way because of what it says, or because of the colour of the spectacles (the nature of the paradigm) through which I am looking at it?

Of course, the issue is often simply about what is clear and what is less clear. Listening in on a typical discussion in which two sides are being taken, we often hear statements like: "Surely you can see that this whole raft of verses is absolutely clear, and the one or two verses that present a difficulty can easily be consistently resolved – so your position is not tenable."

It then becomes apparent that the other side takes exactly the same view. They also point to their own group of texts which they regard as completely clear, and they feel they can deal consistently with other texts that present the difficulty from their perspective. What is clear to one side presents a difficulty to the other, and vice versa. Each side looks at the texts that are problematic; but through each pair of glasses the text is clear and there is no problem.

I believe that this inevitability is more a reason for humility than for despair.

Motivations for writing

I shall presume that I am writing in the main to people who, like myself, take a high view of the inspiration and authority of the Bible. It is a sad spectacle when people with such convictions behave in an uncharitable way towards those with whom they have differences of opinion. It is surely axiomatic for fruitful discussion that we recognise that there have been and are servants of God who differ profoundly on these matters but whose effectiveness in bringing the gospel of Jesus Christ to the world is unquestioned: in connection with our present topic, think, for instance, of the evident spiritual blessing that accompanied the ministries of John Wesley and George Whitefield, or C. H. Spurgeon and Billy Graham.

We all, imperfect sinful men and women as we are, inevitably have blind spots in our theology (at least in the eyes of others, if not in our own – that is the definition of a blind spot!). Followed to their logical conclusion, these in practice might inhibit the communication of the gospel. Yet such is the grace of God and the power of the gospel that, when it comes to it, those blind spots get forgotten in our preaching, so that the message gets out in spite of them and God is gracious to bless it.

In New Testament times, when Paul observed that groups (factions, even) were beginning to form around leading teachers such as Apollos, Peter, and himself, he moved swiftly to try to put a stop to this divisive trend. One argument he used, as we saw above, was to embrace humility and major on the positives we all share:

> *So then, no more boasting about men! All things are yours, whether Paul or Apollos or Cephas [Peter]…*
>
> (1 Corinthians 3:21–22.)

We can therefore take it that if Paul were alive today he would say the same to us: "Whether Wesley or Edwards, Spurgeon or Graham – all are yours."

This is surely one of the keys to our discussion: the clear and conscious acknowledgment that there is a danger of grouping ourselves around our own special well-known preachers and teachers, and failing to recognise that all of these people are "ours". They are our fellow believers, whether or not we agree with them on all issues. We must therefore gladly acknowledge them as fellow members of the body of Christ, part of our rich and multifaceted Christian heritage. We must be humble enough to recognise what is, after all, sheer fact – that God has abundantly blessed men and women who hold very different views on these issues.

For that reason it is heartening to read statements like the following. The first is from a book entitled *Why I Am Not an Arminian*:

> *Heresy is such a corruption of the grace of God in Christ that it invalidates either Jesus as the Saviour or grace as the way of salvation. The Arminian tradition does neither… Whatever issues relevant to salvation we disagree upon, let us agree on this: the Calvinist and the Arminian are brothers in Christ…*
>
> *The issue of debate is not between belief and unbelief but rather which of two Christian perspectives better represents the biblical portrayal of the divine-human relationship in salvation and the contributions of both God and man in human history.*[68]

---

68   R. A. Peterson and M. D. Williams, *Why I Am Not an Arminian*, Downers Grove, IVP, 2004, p. 13.

We might just note in passing that for the author just cited only two perspectives come into consideration. That, too, may be part of the problem.

My second quotation is from a book entitled *Why I Am Not a Calvinist*:

> *We have enormous respect and appreciation for Calvin and the heritage he defined and engendered. Calvinism has for centuries represented a vital tradition of piety that is intellectually and morally serious… In their passion for the glory of God, Calvinists have played a leading role in the renewal of worship in this generation.*[69]

The very existence of such books shows that robust discussion is possible. Really valuable interchange can only occur where there is mutual respect, and an acknowledgment that people with different views are very likely to be motivated by the same concern for the reputation of God, so that they seek to uphold and promote his glory and holiness.

It is important for me as I come to this topic to realise that those who may disagree with me on some issues have just as much and maybe even more desire than myself to be faithful to Scripture. So let me try to summarise my stance. For the reasons I have given above, as far as is possible, I shall avoid terms like Calvinist, hyper-Calvinist, Reformed, radical Reformed, Arminian… I shall not be attempting to do the job of delineating the role of Calvinism (however defined) within the Reformed tradition (however defined), or even what the subtle differences are between the different strands of various theological traditions. Those are tasks for people much more competent in the relevant disciplines than I am.

I have learned a great deal from those traditions. I have read their books with profit and count many of their adherents as my friends. Indeed, I recall with pleasure how, during my student days at

---

69   J. L. Walls and J. R. Dongell, *Why I Am Not a Calvinist*, Downers Grove, IVP, 2004, p. 9.

Cambridge, I used to spend time with a friend reading and discussing Calvin's sermons in their original French. I share the concern for the glory and sovereignty of God who takes the initiative in salvation, and I also lament the loss of that sense of glory, holiness, and dignity of God in far too much of superficial, contemporary, feel-good preaching.

Indeed, it is precisely because I hold the glory of God to be supremely important that I am concerned here with theistic determinism, or anything approaching it, whatever it calls itself – anything that is perceived to misrepresent the glory, goodness, and love of God and the nature of the gospel to such an extent that it turns people away or confuses them.

What, for example, were readers to make of an article in the 23 March 2009 edition of *Time* magazine? What it calls the "New Calvinism" is described as

> *complete with an utterly sovereign and micromanaging deity,*
> *sinful and puny humanity, and the combination's logical*
> *consequence, predestination: the belief that before time's dawn,*
> *God decided who he would save (or not), unaffected by any*
> *subsequent human action or decision.*

Even if there is an element of caricature, this kind of publicity is very damaging to the gospel.

I am well aware, of course, that there are people in the traditions listed above who differ as to the degree in which this kind of determinism is central to or indeed required for their theology. For instance, Todd Billings, a pastor in the Reformed tradition from whom I got the *Time* magazine quote, writes:

> *TULIP does not provide an adequate or even accurate*
> *distillation of Reformed theology… The New Calvinists pick*
> *the TULIP from the Reformed field, overlooking the other*

flowers. There is much besides the TULIP in this spacious field that has grown from the seed of God's word.[70]

This once more serves to indicate that reducing beliefs to an acronym can create more problems than it solves. For instance, R. C. Sproul says that, although the TULIP acrostic has helped many people remember the distinguishing characteristics of Reformed Theology, "it has also caused great confusion and much misunderstanding". Sproul does not like the formulation of the concept of T = total depravity, because it is often confused with the idea of "utter depravity" – not surprisingly, I would have thought, since "total" and "utter" arguably cover roughly the same semantic ground. Sproul prefers the term "radical corruption". He also believes that the term "irresistible grace" is misleading and prefers the term "effectual grace" because, as he tells us, Calvinists do not believe that God's saving grace is literally irresistible. Indeed "Calvinists all believe that men can and do resist the grace of God".[71] This illustrates the minefield that we get into when we use unbiblical terminology to define what we believe is biblical teaching and then are forced by the popularity of the terminology to perform frequent re-definitions. More often than not these themselves are also couched in non-biblical terminology, thus adding to the confusion.

In light of all of this, and the fact that greater minds than mine have wrestled with these issues for centuries, it may well be asked, "What is the point of writing yet another book on the topic?" My response is that it is important for each generation to come to Scripture afresh. The instinct that led William Tyndale to translate the Bible into English, and Martin Luther to translate it into German, so that people could come directly to it without any ecclesiastical authority coming in between, is an instinct to be cultivated at the level of the understanding of Scripture as well.

---

70   Todd Billings, "Calvin's Comeback – The Irresistible Reformer", cover article for *The Christian Century*, December 2009.

71   R. C. Sproul, *Chosen by God*, Carol Stream, Tyndale House, 2011, p. 95.

It would, of course, be arrogant to ignore the vast contribution of those who have preceded us, but we would also be wise not to ignore the fact that history is littered by examples of "getting some of it wrong", as we now would see it. Indeed, I am sure that some of my readers will be persuaded that I am the one who has got it wrong. God is gracious and merciful, and sometimes even getting it wrong can serve to enrich the discussion and refine our understanding.

In order to do my best to avoid getting it wrong, I shall try as far as possible to deal with the broad context in which the relevant Scriptures occur. This will have the effect of lengthening the book, but I hope the gain in terms of facilitating clear appreciation of the logic of the biblical argument will be deemed worth the extra effort – and perhaps even lead readers into tangential pathways that encourage them to explore ideas unrelated to our main topic.

I simply offer to a wider audience what I have found useful in my own searching of Scripture, in the hope that it might prove of similar value to others – whether or not they agree with me in the end. In attempting to do so it is inevitable that I have to mention names of authors who are still alive – some of whom I regard as friends – with whom I do not agree. In one sense I find that difficult, and even distasteful, since it can so easily be read to mean that I disagree with everything they say. That is simply not the case. I shall be, as I said above, concentrating on the views of such people in so far as they relate to theistic determinism, and I feel as free to disagree with them as I imagine they would with me.

A personal anecdote comes to mind. On one occasion when I was sharing a conference platform with John Piper, if I recall it correctly, as we were discussing some of these issues in answer to public questions, he mentioned that his father disagreed with him. Well, in that spirit, I feel perfectly free to do the same!

Furthermore, in many cases I have profited greatly from the views of such authors on other topics. Therefore, in no case should my discussion of an idea, especially one with which I take issue, be construed as an attack on the person, any more than I would construe disagreement with my viewpoint as an *ad hominem* attack on me.

After all, these are my brothers and sisters in Christ, and I would like them to continue to think that I am their brother as well.

May our search be motivated by a desire to promote the glory of God alone.

PART 2

THE THEOLOGY OF DETERMINISM

CHAPTER 5

God's Sovereignty and Human Responsibility

There would be little discussion, let alone controversy, among Christians about God's sovereignty and human responsibility, if both of these concepts were not to be found in the Bible. Indeed, it sounds rather foolish putting it this way, for these are not peripheral issues in a grander story. In a real sense they are the story, for the biblical narrative is the story of God's sovereignty and human responsibility.

Take first God's sovereignty over history. Daniel the prophet, among many other biblical writers, addresses this topic. The opening statement in his book is:

> In the third year of the reign of Jehoiakim king of Judah, Nebuchadnezzar king of Babylon came to Jerusalem and besieged it. And the Lord delivered Jehoiakim king of Judah into his hand...
>
> (Daniel 1:1–2.)

Again, in that same book, one of the major lessons taught by God to the Babylonian monarch Nebuchadnezzar was a judgment on him because of his pride:

> You will be driven away from people and will live with the wild animals; you will eat grass like cattle and be drenched with the dew of heaven. Seven times will pass by for you until you acknowledge that the Most High is sovereign over the kingdoms of men and gives them to anyone he wishes.
>
> (Daniel 4:25.)

Through Daniel, God thus predicted seven years of discipline on Nebuchadnezzar.

More broadly, the Bible shows God's sovereign control of history in the major phenomenon of fulfilled prophecy – from the detailed predictions concerning the family lives of Abraham, Isaac, and Jacob, to the famous prophecies of Isaiah and Micah concerning the birth of Messiah, to the detailed prophecies in Daniel about the Hellenistic period.[72] In the New Testament, there are predictions made by Jesus regarding his death, resurrection, and ascension, the destruction of Jerusalem, and the dispersion of the Jewish nation, and many prophecies about Christ's return. Unique in all of literature, Scripture is full of prediction and fulfilment, a fact that must be factored in to any attempt to understand the nature of God's relationship to history and humanity.

We must put alongside this the complicating fact that the individuals who are the subject of these biblical predictions are not treated as puppets being manipulated by a master puppeteer. God holds them responsible for their behaviour. For example, Abraham and Jacob were two such individuals, to whose lives and experiences we shall return later.

Then we have instances in Scripture where God's sovereignty and human responsibility are brought directly together. In his speech at Pentecost Peter says of Jesus: *This man was handed over to you by God's set purpose and foreknowledge; and you, with the help of wicked men, put him to death by nailing him to the cross* (Acts 2:23). The crucifixion was therefore foreknown by God and occurred according to his set purpose; and yet the men who put him to death were wicked and therefore morally responsible.

Again, Jesus encourages people to come to him: *I am the bread of life. He who comes to me will never go hungry, and he who believes in me will never be thirsty* (John 6:35). He laments those who refuse to come: *You diligently study the Scriptures because you think that by them you possess eternal life. These are the Scriptures that testify about*

---

72   See the author's *Against the Flow: The Inspiration of Daniel in an Age of Relativism*, Oxford, Lion Hudson, 2015.

me, yet you refuse to come to me to have life (John 5:39–40). On the other hand he says: *No-one can come to me unless the Father who sent me draws him, and I will raise him up at the last day* (John 6:44). Thus we can see that two things hold:

1. God takes the initiative.
2. People are responsible to come to Jesus and capable of doing it or refusing to do so.

Or again, when Paul addressed the Athenian philosophers he said that God had *determined the times set for them and the exact places where they should live*. He then remarked that this had been done in order that they should *seek him and perhaps reach out for him and find him* (Acts 17:26–27). God has clearly determined certain limits, but that does not relieve men and women of the responsibility of seeking, feeling after, and finding him.

There is enough already in these texts to make us realise that these are very deep issues, and that we must not only approach them with humility but with a sense that, however profound our understanding may be, it will reach its limits and we shall be left with elements of mystery. As we noted earlier, no one has any real idea what human thought is, not to mention how it can trigger human action, so we are not likely to comprehend God's interaction with his creation any better. The best we can do is to try to understand what God has revealed about these things – what he wants us to know.

But even if we cannot fully understand, those of us convinced of the full authority and inspiration of Scripture must surely be prepared to believe what Scripture says. An analogy from science can help here. The universe that scientists study was not created by scientists but by God – so scientists study a given. They have to submit their theories to the universe, and not the other way round. Indeed, science was held up for centuries because certain influential thinkers like Aristotle made up their minds what the universe ought to be like and so tried to impose their structures on the universe. Similarly with Scripture. It is God-breathed. It is a given and we should submit our theories and systems to it and not it to our systems. We believe what Scripture says, we try to understand what it says, but we remain humble enough to realise that it is Scripture that is authoritative and inspired and not our interpretations of it.

That is especially so when we perceive a tension – as between God's sovereignty and human responsibility. Failure to reconcile everything in our minds is not a reason to give up believing one side or the other, nor is it a reason for emphasising one side to such a degree that the other side ceases to exist in a meaningful way.

Possibly one of the best known descriptions of God's initiative and our response is due to the late John Stott in the first chapter of his book *Why I Am a Christian*. The first chapter of that book is called "The Hound of Heaven", a metaphor taken from Francis Thompson's poem describing the relentless pursuit undertaken by God to reach a person. Describing his conversion Stott writes:

> On February 13, 1938, when I was a youth of nearly seventeen, I made a decision for Christ. I heard a clergyman preach on Pilate's question, "What shall I do with Jesus, who is called Christ?" Until that moment I didn't know I had to do anything with Jesus, who is called Christ. But in answer to my questions, the preacher unfolded the steps to Christ. In particular, he pointed me in the New Testament to Revelation 3:20, in which Jesus says, "Here I am! I stand at the door and knock. If anyone hears my voice and opens the door, I will come in and eat with him, and he with me." So that night, by my bedside, I opened the door of my personality to Christ, inviting him to come in as my Saviour and Lord.
>
> That also is true, but it constitutes only one side of the truth.
>
> The most significant factor lies elsewhere, and it is on this that I intend to concentrate in this first chapter. Why I am a Christian *is due ultimately neither to the influence of my parents and teachers, nor to my own personal decision for Christ, but to "the Hound of Heaven". That is, it is due to Jesus Christ himself, who pursued me relentlessly even when I was running away from him in order to go my own way. And*

if it were not for the gracious pursuit of the Hound of Heaven I would today be on the scrapheap of wasted and discarded lives.[73]

Stott then gives other examples of God's initiative in pursuing people, including Saul of Tarsus and C.S. Lewis, finally coming back to his own experience of conversion in terms of the imagery of the Stranger knocking at the door of his heart:

Yet through my sense of alienation and failure the Stranger at the door kept knocking, until the preacher I mentioned at the beginning of this chapter threw light on my dilemma. He spoke to me of the death and resurrection of Jesus Christ. He explained that Christ had died to turn my estrangement into reconciliation and had been raised from the dead to turn my defeat into victory. The correspondence between my subjective need and Christ's objective offer seemed too close to be a coincidence. Christ's knocking became louder and more insistent. Did I open the door, or did he? Truly I did, but only because by his persistent knocking he had made it possible, even inevitable…

If we become aware of the relentless pursuit of Christ, and give up trying to escape from him, and surrender to the embrace of "this tremendous lover", there will be no room for boasting in what we have done. There will only be room for profound thanksgiving for his grace and mercy, and for the firm resolve to spend time and eternity in his loving service.[74]

Three things are clear from this:

1. God took the initiative and knocked at John Stott's door.
2. Stott had to open the door. He had to "give up trying to escape" and "surrender".
3   Boasting is excluded.

---

73   J. R. W. Stott, *Why I Am a Christian*, Leicester, IVP, 2003, pp. 12–13.
74   *Ibid.*, pp. 27–28.

However, the last word of the penultimate paragraph above raises an important question: if Christ knocks at the door of someone's heart, is opening the door always "inevitable"? Some say yes because God's grace is irresistible and our response to it predetermined. To such questions we shall return in due course.

The Athenian philosophers would have found Paul's approach intriguing, since some of them were Stoics and essentially believed in the deterministic rule of fate; whereas others were Epicureans and took the view that chance was king and humans had therefore to take responsibility for their own destiny. Paul sided with neither but granted an element of truth in both. He told the Athenians that God had taken the initiative in setting up the boundary conditions of human lives, but men and women had a real responsibility (therefore an implied capacity) to seek God and feel their way towards him. This was neither Stoicism nor Epicureanism. It was Christian theism.

Acts 17 is also important historically as it reminds us of the pervasive influence of Greek thought on the ancient world. Many people in the early centuries of Christianity had a Greek education, and in order to communicate the Christian message to their contemporaries it was inevitable that they would employ Greek ideas and ways of thinking. Much of that was good, of course, as logical argument was high on the agenda of Greek classical education. However, there were deep currents of thought that left their mark on thinkers of all kinds – both pagan and Christian. For many people (especially Romans) the Stoic philosophy with its fatalism was attractive. The Christian thinking of those who had been exposed to a classical education, in both language and philosophy, was inevitably influenced to a degree that is not always appreciated. Many of the influential theologians of past centuries were educated in the classical ways of thinking before they studied theology, and Stoicism has left its mark on the more extreme forms of Christian determinism, where it is arguable that the concept of God appears more Greek than Christian.

By the same token Epicureanism, particularly in the writings of Lucretius, has left its mark throughout history. It was prevalent in the renaissance of classical thinking in the eighteenth century, and the doctrines of chance dominate the secular world of today.

According to the *Stanford Encyclopedia of Philosophy*,

> *One of the decisive developments in the western philosophical tradition was the eventually widespread merging of the Greek philosophical tradition and the Judeo-Christian religious and scriptural traditions. Augustine is one of the main figures through and by whom this merging was accomplished. He is, as well, one of the towering figures of medieval philosophy whose authority and thought came to exert a pervasive and enduring influence well into the modern period.*

The article goes on to say:

> *Augustine bequeathed to the Latin West a voluminous body of work that contains at its chronological extremes two quite dissimilar portraits of the human condition. In the beginning, there is a largely Hellenistic portrait, one that is notable for the optimism that a sufficiently rational and disciplined life can safely escape the ever-threatening circumstantial adversity that seems to surround us. Nearer the end, however, there emerges a considerably grimmer portrait, one that emphasizes the impotence of the unaided human will, and the later Augustine presents a moral landscape populated largely by the* massa damnata *[De Civitate Dei XXI.12], the overwhelming majority who are justly predestined to eternal punishment by an omnipotent God, intermingled with a small minority whom God, with unmerited mercy, has predestined to be saved.*[75]

Here we can recognise the contours of what later became the doctrines of total depravity and unconditional election – the T and the U of TULIP. With such deep historical roots it is obvious at once that our topic is not an easy one. Even at the surface level of thought

---

75   http://plato.stanford.edu/entries/augustine. It is important to point out that scholarly opinion is divided on Augustine's stance on these matters. See Muller, *op. cit.*, p. 104.

it is difficult to imagine God not being in control; and yet it is hard to see that morality has any meaning if human action is completely predetermined by God. To put it another way: if God has determined that x is going to happen, then it would seem to be impossible that x should not happen. How then can I be free to do other than x?

A theological spectrum

Scripture clearly teaches doctrines that can reasonably be described by the terms "God's sovereignty" and "human responsibility", even though neither of these expressions occurs in the Bible.[76] Our response to this apparent tension varies greatly and may be represented in terms of positions on a line, with God's sovereignty strongly emphasised at one end and human responsibility at the other.

God's sovereignty   *Human responsibility*

The spectrum then runs between those who emphasise divine sovereignty and those who emphasise human responsibility. The first hold that the "tension" may be resolved solely in terms of God's sovereignty, effectively denying any real role for human responsibility, as God is the direct cause of everything. This is theistic determinism. At the other end are those who maximise the role of human responsibility and minimise God's sovereignty. However, even if we only take into account the few texts we have already cited, it would seem that any attempt to obtain a complete resolution of tension by going to either end will not do justice to biblical teaching.

---

76   D. A. Carson helpfully collects together passages on both sides in his book, *Divine Sovereignty and Human Responsibility: Biblical Perspectives in Tension*, 2nd ed, Oregon, Wipf and Stock, 2002.

D. A. Carson writes about the way discussions on these topics often run:

> *Suppose, for example, that my opponent is so impressed with God's sovereignty that he constructs his theological system out of all the texts and arguments which support this important truth, and then with this grid filters out evidence which could be taken to call some of his theological system into question. My instant response is that his procedure is methodologically indistinguishable from the person who first constructs his theological system out of those texts and theorems which seem to support some kind of human freedom, and who then filters out election and predestination passages until he can safely defuse them by re-defining them. The name of the game is reductionism.*

Carson goes on to point out that such reductionism does not work; it only changes the shape of the sovereignty-responsibility tension. He argues that there is no escape from that tension itself,

> *except by moving so far from the biblical data that either the picture of God or the picture of man bears little resemblance to their portraits as assembled from the scriptural texts themselves.*

Carson concludes that, in his view,

> *It is no answer to tell me that my presentation of the sovereignty-responsibility tension still embraces certain unresolved tensions. Of course it does. But to correct me you must not claim to resolve all the tensions, for such delusion is easily exposed. Rather, if you wish to convince me that your theology is more essentially Christian than my own, you must show me how your shaping of the tension better conforms to the biblical data than mine does.*[77]

---

77   D. A. Carson, *Divine Sovereignty and Human Responsibility: Biblical Perspectives in Tension*, Oregon, Wipf and Stock, 1994, pp. 220-21.

Commenting on John 6:44 (*No-one can come to me unless the Father who sent me draws him, and I will raise him up at the last day*), Carson writes:

> *Yet despite the strong predestinarian strain, it must be insisted with no less vigour that John emphasizes the responsibility of people to come to Jesus, and can excoriate them for refusing to do so (e.g. 5:40).*[78]

Carson's view is that "John is quite happy with the position that modern philosophy calls 'compatibilism'".[79]

If what Carson means is that that John believes in both God's sovereignty and human responsibility, and that both must be held equally firmly, however paradoxical the resulting tension may appear to us, then that would be fine. However, the term "compatibilism", as we mentioned earlier, is normally used by philosophers who hold that human freedom and responsibility is compatible with determinism – a very different matter; unless, of course, one interprets sovereignty as determinism.[80]

Of course, what is meant by "each side in the discussion", or which version of which side is compatible with the other, is another matter! A further illustration of holding the views in tension is given by the seventeenth-century *Westminster Confession of Faith* (Section 3):

> *God from all eternity did, by the most wise and holy counsel of his own will, freely and unchangeably ordain whatsoever comes to pass; yet so as thereby neither is God the author of sin; nor is violence offered to the will of creatures; nor is the liberty or contingency of second causes taken away, but rather established.*

---

78   D. A. Carson, *The Gospel According to John*, Leicester, IVP, 1991, p. 293.
79   *Ibid.*, p. 291.
80   See the discussion in Tom McCall, *An Invitation to Analytic Christian Theology*, Downers Grove, IVP, 2015.

The second clause raises immediate questions as to what is really meant by the first. However, this statement has the considerable merit of clearly acknowledging that Scripture teaches both God's sovereignty and human responsibility, in which case all interpretations that press one side to the exclusion of the other must be incorrect, for the simple reason that *Scripture itself does not allow one side to override the other.* This elementary but vital principle is often overlooked by those who try to resolve the tension – an attempt that is thinly veiled in this Westminster statement that invokes some kind of theistic determinism.

The issues at stake are not simply questions of abstract theology. They have to do with our concept of God's person and character, and of ourselves as human beings, and they go to the very heart of the gospel itself. For example, one argument that is often used for placing virtually exclusive emphasis on God's sovereignty is that anything less means that God's glory is diminished if we concede that humans can have any part in their own salvation, even down to the exercise of faith. Human beings cannot even do that because of their "total depravity".

Thus, so we are told, before creating the universe God chose which ones he would save (the elect) and which ones would be lost (the reprobate). That is, the selection/rejection process had nothing whatsoever to do with the people involved but was solely governed by God's sovereign decision inscrutable to us. This view is often called "unconditional election".

Many react strongly against this view because, in their opinion, far from promoting God's glory, such determinism seriously diminishes and even eclipses it. They will say: how can you believe in a God who fixed your eternal destination before you were born, quite independently of what you do? If he chose to save you, he will give you the gift of faith so that you can believe and be saved. If he decided to condemn you, you will be condemned. There is nothing you can do about it. Surely this conflicts with any acceptable concept of morality and fairness and makes God out to be neither loving nor good, and therefore unworthy of our respect let alone our worship?

Nothing less than the character of God and his reputation in the world is at stake. So we must face the questions as fairly as we can.

One way to do this would be to research the origin of the various issues, give historical examples of how leading proponents on each side have handled them, and then relate them to the Bible. Another way would be to start with what the Bible says, and then bring in the difficulties that have been raised with its interpretation. Recalling Carson's advice, we shall adopt this second course. The first can easily get lost in an endless (and often fruitless) defining and redefining of systems of theology, wondering what X meant by his interpretation of Y and vice versa, rather than concentrating our attention on Scripture itself.

I deliberately re-emphasise what I wrote earlier: I shall not attempt to give definitions of the various kinds of hyper-Calvinism, as distinct from the various kinds of Calvinism, and then analyse who believes what and why. The most cursory glance at the literature shows that such efforts often lead to further confusion. What I shall try to do is to discuss Scripture and the validity of different interpretations, irrespective of what the people who hold those interpretations are inclined to call themselves. In other words, I shall be responding to the questions I have been asked by people from many points on the theological spectrum, and trying to analyse them in the light of Scripture with no attempt on my part to align them with this or that "ism".

What this means, for example, is that I shall not spend time on trying to answer questions like: are Calvinists determinists? Some who call themselves Calvinists distance themselves from determinism, whereas others seem to espouse a very explicit form of determinism. We shall be interested in what Scripture teaches about determinism, and consider the statements of others from that perspective.

This means that I shall avoid using the terms Calvinism, Arminianism, and so on, so far as is possible, although they will inevitably appear in quotations from various authors, many of whom are happy to employ such terms to describe their own positions. I shall leave my readers to judge whether or not I have succeeded in being fair in my attempt to understand the underlying biblical issues themselves.

CHAPTER 6

The Biblical Vocabulary

As a preliminary we shall need to look at the concepts that dominate this topic, some of which we have already mentioned. We shall try to examine them carefully, since it is very easy for any of us to make assumptions about the meanings of such terms that may not be in accord with biblical teaching.

We shall look first at three of the big ideas associated with God's sovereignty: foreknowledge, predestination, and election.

1. Foreknowledge

The Greek words here are *prognōsis* and *proginōskō*, and are only used on the following occasions in the New Testament. We recognise the first one, since it has come into English as a medical term – prognosis. The verb means, to know beforehand.

> *This man was handed over to you by God's set purpose and* **foreknowledge***; and you, with the help of wicked men, put him to death by nailing him to the cross.*
>
> (Acts 2:23.)

> *They have* **known** *me for a long time…*
>
> (Acts 26:5.)

> *For those God* **foreknew** *he also predestined to be conformed to the likeness of his Son, that he might be the firstborn among many brothers.*
>
> (Romans 8:29.)

God did not reject his people, whom he **foreknew.** *Don't you know what the Scripture says in the passage about Elijah – how he appealed to God against Israel...*

(Romans 11:2.)

... who have been chosen according to the **foreknowledge** *of God the Father, through the sanctifying work of the Spirit, for obedience to Jesus Christ and sprinkling by his blood: Grace and peace be yours in abundance.*

(1 Peter 1:2.)

He was chosen (literally, **foreknown***) before the creation of the world.*

(1 Peter 1:20.)

Therefore, dear friends, since you already **know** *this...*

(2 Peter 3:17.)

2. Predestination

The Greek word group here is *horizō* and *proorizō*. Verses marked with a star use the second of the two.

The Son of Man will go as it has been **decreed,** *but woe to that man who betrays him!*

(Luke 22:22.)

This man was handed over to you by God's **set purpose** *and foreknowledge; and you, with the help of wicked men, put him to death by nailing him to the cross.*

(Acts 2:23.)

They did what your power and will had **decided beforehand** *should happen.*

(Acts 4:28*.)

He commanded us to preach to the people and to testify that he is the one whom God **appointed** *as judge of the living and the dead.*

(Acts 10:42.)

The disciples, each according to his ability, **decided** *to provide help for the brothers living in Judea.*

(Acts 11:29.)

From one man he made every nation of men, that they should inhabit the whole earth; and he **determined** *the times set for them and the exact places where they should live.*

(Acts 17:26.)

For he has set a day when he will judge the world with justice by the man he has **appointed**.

(Acts 17:31.)

… and who through the Spirit of holiness was **declared** *with power to be the Son of God, by his resurrection from the dead: Jesus Christ our Lord.*

(Romans 1:4.)

For those God foreknew he also **predestined** *to be conformed to the likeness of his Son, that he might be the firstborn among many brothers. And those he* **predestined**, *he also called; those he called, he also justified; those he justified, he also glorified.*

(Romans 8:29–30*.)

No, we speak of God's secret wisdom, a wisdom that has been hidden and that God **destined** *for our glory before time began.*

(1 Corinthians 2:7*.)

*... he **predestined** us to be adopted as his sons through Jesus Christ, in accordance with his pleasure and will...*

(Ephesians 1:5*.)

*In him we were also chosen, having been **predestined** according to the plan of him who works out everything in conformity with the purpose of his will, in order that we, who were the first to hope in Christ, might be for the praise of his glory.*

(Ephesians 1:11–12*.)

*Therefore God again **set** a certain day...*

(Hebrews 4:7.)

This list will help us gain some idea of the range of meanings covered by "predestination". For instance, Acts 11:20 refers to the ordinary human act of deciding in advance to do something – in this case giving financial help to needy people. In Acts 17:31 God has appointed (predetermined) a man to judge the world. This is clearly an advance appointment in terms of our own understanding of a historical timeline. Similarly Hebrews 4:7.

In several of the passages cited the concepts of foreknowledge and predestination occur close together. One of the main questions that arises from this is: if God knows something beforehand, or if God predestines it, what implication does this have for the involvement, responsibility, and moral status of those people affected by the happening?

Is God's foreknowledge causative – i.e. does the fact that God knows that something will happen cause it to happen, and therefore relieve any participant from responsibility? Surely the answer is: not necessarily; if for no other reason than the fact that *the Bible itself does not regard God's foreknowledge or predestination as diminishing human responsibility.*

The very first quote under "foreknowledge" (which is the same as the second quote under "predestination") says that Christ's crucifixion was both foreknown and predestined, but that the men involved in it were wicked and therefore morally responsible. One could add to this that the death of Christ was actually predicted in Scripture centuries before it happened. However, Scripture itself tells us that this fact does not diminish the culpability of those involved in crucifying the Lord.

Also, the first quote under "predestination" says that the betrayal of Jesus was predestined, yet woe unto the betrayer. This is clearly implying that the betrayer was morally culpable and therefore accountable. Once again the implication of this is that, however we understand the terms, we may not interpret them in such a way that they negate human moral responsibility.

Of course on the human level foreknowledge – knowing something in advance – is not necessarily causative. If I see a horse rushing out of control, pulling a carriage across a field towards a cliff that the horse cannot see, I know in advance that there is going to be a disastrous accident. But the fact that I know in advance does not cause the accident. That said, it would of course be wise to be cautious with human analogies, since for the Creator and Sustainer of all things to know something in advance is hardly likely to be exactly the same as our knowing something in advance.

At the higher level there is another consideration. The idea that, because God knows about an event beforehand it must be predetermined, may rest on the assumption that God's relationship with time is the same as ours; that he sits, as we do, on a time line that stretches from the past to the future. However, Scripture indicates that God's relationship to time is not at all like ours. Jesus said, *before Abraham was, I am* (John 8:58 ESV). It could be, for instance, that God knew beforehand that I would trust Christ simply because he sees it in an eternal perspective, so that the issue of causation does not even arise.

We need, however, to be cautious here. Time is not an easy concept – indeed, no one admits to understanding what it actually is. It would therefore be wise to be sceptical of interpretations of God's foreknowledge that deny the freedom that, according to Scripture elsewhere, is possessed by the men and women God has created.

However, Scripture has more to say on the nature of God's knowledge. On one occasion Jesus denounced the cities where he had done many mighty works:

*Then Jesus began to denounce the cities in which most of his
miracles had been performed, because they did not repent.
"Woe to you, Korazin! Woe to you, Bethsaida! If the miracles
that were performed in you had been performed in Tyre
and Sidon, they would have repented long ago in sackcloth
and ashes. But I tell you, it will be more bearable for Tyre
and Sidon on the day of judgment than for you. And you,
Capernaum, will you be lifted up to the skies? No, you will go
down to the depths. If the miracles that were performed in you
had been performed in Sodom, it would have remained to this
day. But I tell you that it will be more bearable for Sodom on
the day of judgment than for you."*

(Matthew 11:20–24.)

This statement makes it clear that our Lord knew not only what *did*
happen in Tyre and Sidon in his day, and in Sodom centuries before,
but what *would* have happened had they been presented with different
evidence. And that knowledge will be used at the Day of Judgment.

This kind of knowledge was called "middle knowledge" by the
Spanish Jesuit Luis de Molina (1535–1600), and arguments based
upon it have (inevitably) produced yet another "ism" – Molinism.
Let me remind the reader that our approach is not to proceed from
"isms" but from Scripture, as there is a danger (and it lurks here once
more) that the moment we use the "ism" our attention is likely to be
drawn to a whole package of ideas and be diverted from the fact that
Scripture actually teaches that God has knowledge of what "would
happen if" – a kind of knowledge we may find it very hard to grasp.

The implications of this statement by our Lord are profound.
First of all, it supports our contention above that God's foreknowledge
is not causative, in the sense that it removes neither human freedom
of response nor human accountability.

It is interesting that it is in this very context that our Lord talks
about revealing to little children the things that are hidden from the
wise:

*I praise you, Father, Lord of heaven and earth, because you
have hidden these things from the wise and learned, and
revealed them to little children. Yes, Father, for this was your
good pleasure.*

*All things have been committed to me by my Father. No-
one knows the Son except the Father, and no-one knows the
Father except the Son and those to whom the Son chooses to
reveal him.*

*Come to me, all you who are weary and burdened, and I
will give you rest. Take my yoke upon you and learn from me,
for I am gentle and humble in heart, and you will find rest for
your souls. For my yoke is easy and my burden is light.*

(Matthew 11:25–30.)

Christ claims to be the sole source of knowledge of the Father,
revealing him to those he chooses. But that choice is far from
arbitrary, for in the very next sentence he shows that he chooses to
give rest to those who come to him – the presumption being that
they are capable of doing so freely.

The phrase "the doctrine of predestination" is usually taken
as shorthand for the view that some are predestined to salvation[81]
without any reference to their future co-operation, even if
foreseen by God. This often leads to the assumption that the word
predestination always refers to salvation. This, however, is not the
case. Indeed, only three of the fourteen references listed above are
even arguably related to the matter of salvation. They are repeated
for convenience below:

*For those God **foreknew** he also **predestined** to be conformed
to the likeness of his Son, that he might be the firstborn among
many brothers. And those he **predestined**, he also called;*

---

81   And, often, that others are predestined to condemnation – so-called
     "double predestination". However, it is hard to see how one can
     maintain so-called single predestination without logically affirming
     double predestination – indeed, Calvin thought it absurd to attempt to
     separate them. Later writers like Boettner and Sproul agree.

those he called, he also justified; those he justified, he also glorified.

(Romans 8:29–30.)

… he **predestined** *us to be adopted as his sons through Jesus Christ, in accordance with his pleasure and will…*

(Ephesians 1:5*.)

In him we were also **chosen**, *having been* **predestined** *according to the plan of him who works out everything in conformity with the purpose of his will, in order that we, who were the first to hope in Christ, might be for the praise of his glory.*

(Ephesians 1:11–12*.)

We shall look at the Ephesians passage under our next heading, and the Romans passages later when we consider God's dealings with Israel. But before we move on we should notice something rather striking. The list of Scriptures in which the Greek terms related to predestination occur is short and the topics are few. Three have to do with the death of Christ, two with his resurrection, two with his appointment as judge, one with God's determination of our places of habitation, three in connection with believers, and one in connection with social help.

In light of this it seems well-nigh incredible that the doctrine of predestination has been extrapolated to become an all-encompassing divine determinism that knows no bounds – as in the view of R. C. Sproul cited earlier:

The movement of every molecule, the actions of every plant, the falling of every star, the choices of every volitional creature, all of these are subject to his sovereign will. No maverick molecules run loose in the universe beyond the control of the Creator. If one such molecule existed, it could be the critical fly in the eternal ointment.[82]

82   R. C. Sproul, *What Is Reformed Theology?*, Grand Rapids, Baker, 2016, p. 172.

3. Elect, election, chosen

The word group here is *eklegomai, eklektos, eklogē* – from which we get the English "eclectic", "elect", and "select", and related words.

 In the majority of occurrences the term "elect" refers to God's people, believers. Our Lord uses it mainly in connection with his return. For instance:

> *And he will send his angels and gather his **elect** from the four winds, from the ends of the earth to the ends of the heavens.*
>
> (Mark 13:27.)

> *And will not God bring about justice for his **chosen** ones, who cry out to him day and night? Will he keep putting them off?*
>
> (Luke 18:7.)

Paul describes the Christians at Colosse as God's chosen people:

> *Therefore, as God's **chosen** people, holy and dearly loved, clothe yourselves with compassion, kindness, humility, gentleness and patience.*
>
> (Colossians 3:12.)

The apostle John speaks of a person to whom he writes (possibly a code word for the church) as the chosen or elect lady:

> *The elder, to the **chosen** lady and her children, whom I love in the truth – and not I only, but also all who know the truth...*
>
> (2 John 1.)

From these and many other references it is clear that "elect" or "chosen" was a common way in New Testament times of referring to Christian believers. So Peter describes the recipients of his letter:

> *Peter, an apostle of Jesus Christ, to God's **elect**, strangers in*

the world, scattered throughout Pontus, Galatia, Cappadocia, Asia and Bithynia...

(1 Peter 1:1.)

Furthermore, since "choose" and "elect" often carry with them the idea that a selection is being made from a group, it is also important to note that the words can be used without reference to any selection process whatsoever. For instance, in Luke 23:35 our Lord is referred to as *the Chosen One*; in 1 Peter 2:4–6 Christ is said to have been *rejected by men but chosen by God* as *a chosen and precious cornerstone*. And on the Mountain of Transfiguration God describes his Son as chosen:

*A voice came from the cloud, saying, "This is my Son, whom I have **chosen**; listen to him."*

(Luke 9:35.)

Obviously, the words "elect" or "chosen" here do not carry the idea of selection out of a group of candidates, since there were no other candidates – just as in Acts 17:31 Christ's appointment as judge did not involve him being selected from a group. Similarly, in ordinary conversation, we often use the word "choice" to denote "special" or "excellent", without implying that any selection process has been involved – for example, "Our orchards produce choice apples."

Contrast this with the following:

*Now it was the governor's custom at the Feast to release a prisoner **chosen** by the crowd.*

(Matthew 27:15.)

Pilate offered the crowd the choice between Jesus and Barabbas, and they chose Barabbas.

*Brothers, **choose** seven men from among you who are known to be full of the Spirit and wisdom. We will turn this responsibility over to them...*

(Acts 6:3.)

These are clear examples of selection from a group. Note that they were non-arbitrary choices that have to do with the character of the people involved. Also, these choices have nothing to do with salvation.

Israel is frequently described as "chosen" in the Old Testament. For instance:

> *For you are a people holy to the Lord your God. The Lord your God has* **chosen** *you out of all the peoples on the face of the earth to be his people, his treasured possession.*
>
> (Deuteronomy 7:6.)

However, the fact that God chose Israel did not mean that all Israelites were believers; or that all Gentiles were unbelievers. This opens up the idea of God choosing that there should be a group such as Israel to carry out his purposes, as distinct from his choosing the individuals who should be in it.

The idea of God choosing in advance who is to be a believer and who is not relates to the U (unconditional election) of the TULIP paradigm, so many people think that whenever the words "elect" or "choose" occur in Scripture they always carry this meaning. This is not the case.

In ordinary linguistic use, if I announce to someone, "You have been chosen," their immediate reaction will be to ask, "What for?" It is very important to ask that question in biblical contexts, rather than assuming the answer will inevitably be "chosen to be a believer". For instance, individuals in the Old Testament are said to have been chosen by God for varying reasons. Rebekah was chosen to be the wife of Isaac; Bezalel was chosen to be a craftsman; the Levites were chosen to serve as priests; Saul, David, and Solomon were chosen to be kings; and so on. In the New Testament our Lord chose the disciples "to be with him", though not all of them were believers. *Then Jesus replied, "Have I not chosen you, the Twelve? Yet one of you is a devil!* (John 6:70). None of these choices are focused on salvation.

In that connection we might add:

You did not **choose** *me, but I chose you and appointed you to go and bear fruit – fruit that will last. Then the Father will give you whatever you ask in my name.*

(John 15:16.)

Here the specific objective of the choosing and appointing was to bear fruit. How the people involved came to be fruit bearers is, logically speaking, another matter. Paul was chosen to carry God's name to the Gentiles (Acts 9:15). If we address the question "chosen – what for?" to each of these texts we shall clearly get several different answers, some of which have nothing to do with salvation or ultimate destiny.

Asking the "what for?" question is very important when considering the major theological passages that relate to our subject.

As we come to our key verses under this heading, we start with this one:

… who have been **chosen** *according to the* **foreknowledge** *of God the Father, through the sanctifying work of the Spirit, for obedience to Jesus Christ and sprinkling by his blood: Grace and peace be yours in abundance.*

(1 Peter 1:2.)

Chosen – what for? Here the answer is "for obedience to Jesus Christ". The context is the sanctifying work of the Spirit. Peter is not saying we are chosen to be believers, but explaining what God has chosen believers for. It is his intention to sanctify them, to make them increasingly holy, through their obedience to Jesus Christ.

A second key passage is from the beginning of Ephesians, where most of the text is quoted in order to get the context:

Praise be to the God and Father of our Lord Jesus Christ, who has blessed us in the heavenly realms with every spiritual blessing in Christ. For he **chose** *us in him before the creation of the world to be holy and blameless in his sight. In love he* **predestined** *us to be adopted as his sons through Jesus Christ, in accordance with his pleasure and will – to the praise of*

his glorious grace, which he has freely given us in the One
he loves. In him we have redemption through his blood, the
forgiveness of sins, in accordance with the riches of God's grace
that he lavished on us with all wisdom and understanding...
In him we were also **chosen**, *having been* **predestined**
according to the plan of him who works out everything in
conformity with the purpose of his will, in order that we, who
were the first to hope in Christ, might be for the praise of his
glory. And you also were included in Christ when you heard the
word of truth, the gospel of your salvation. Having believed, you
were marked in him with a seal, the promised Holy Spirit...

(Ephesians 1:3–8, 11–13.)

This is a magnificent hymn, praising God for his glorious initiative in providing untold spiritual blessings in salvation. Words like "chose", "predestined", "pleasure and will", tell us emphatically that our adoption, redemption, and forgiveness are all of God. We are also told that all these blessings are "in Christ". The subsequent repetition of phrases like "in him" indicates that being in Christ is of great importance. It is, in fact, a concept unique to Christianity. We never hear of pagans speaking of being "in Zeus" or "in Artemis". The opening paragraph of Ephesians unpacks for us some of the immense riches that God gives us in Christ. The first is:

For he chose us in him before the creation of the world to be
holy and blameless in his sight.

(Ephesians 1:4.)

This statement is often used as a major support of the view referred to above that before the creation of the world God selected those who should be Christians, and even (according to some) those who should not – that is, "election" is unconditional in the sense that it has nothing to do with anyone's individual response. However, this deduction arises from misreading the text – as if it said, "God chose us *to be* in him," meaning that God chose us to be Christians. But the words *to be* are not in the original text at this point. However, they

117

do appear at the end of verse 4, *to be holy*, where Paul is answering the question, what did God choose us for? The answer is not "to be in him" but *to be holy and blameless in his sight*. The text does not discuss here how we come to be in Christ; it discusses what God chooses for those who are in Christ. The difference is of critical importance.

A simple illustration may help to clarify. Suppose I have no children of my own and I go to an adoption agency and choose two children to become mine. That is very different from the situation where I now have these children and, on a sunny day, choose to take them to the sea rather than the mountains.

Choosing people to be in Christ is to be distinguished from choosing that those who are in Christ should be "holy and blameless in his sight". In the ancient world only the most important officials were allowed into the presence of a king (take the story of Esther for an example). What this text tells us is that God has chosen to dignify us with permission to be in his presence. This is a major honour and not to be taken for granted. God could have chosen to do something else – of lesser prestige, for instance.

We notice a similar feature in this passage in connection with the use of the term "predestined". We are told that the object of the predestination is that the Christians at Ephesus who first hoped in Christ would be to the praise of his glory. In other words, the passage is not concerned to tell us how they first came to hope in Christ but what God intended for those who are in Christ.

It is noticeable that when some authors quote the above passage in Ephesians they tend to omit the words *in him*. When I discover that they are among those who wish to minimise or exclude altogether a role for real human response in accepting salvation, I begin to wonder if paradigm pressure is gaining an upper hand over a sober consideration of what Scripture actually says, resulting in an attempt to resolve the tension in an unbiblical way.

Paul next turns to the question how people come to be in Christ, or how they came to hope in Christ. This shows that his preceding statement was not dealing with that question. His answer to this next question is: *And you also were included in Christ when you heard the word of truth, the gospel of your salvation. Having believed, you were marked in him with a seal, the promised Holy Spirit* (verse 13). There is no reference at this point to God's choosing, but rather to their response of hearing and believing.

Let us turn now to those biblical texts that do raise issues about who is and who is not "chosen". Many texts have already been mentioned that describe believers as "elect" or "chosen". The term is used without qualification and, as we have seen, it leaves open the question, chosen – what for?

There are also specific instances like Matthew 22:14 – *For many are invited, but few are chosen*. This statement was made at the conclusion of a parable Jesus told about a wedding banquet staged by a king, to which many people were invited. However, when they were informed that the feast was ready, they refused to come. Some preferred their agriculture and business activities, and others went to the horrific length of murdering the king's servants. The king sent more of his servants, this time out into the streets, to invite anyone they could find, and they filled the banqueting hall. The king provided the guests with wedding garments, as they could not appear in his presence in their own clothes. Yet one man thought he could and was summarily ejected. It is this parable that leads to our statement, which is often translated this way (e.g. the ESV): *Many are called, but few are chosen.*

The parable makes it clear that the choosing was neither arbitrary nor unconditional. The invited, the "called", included people who then refused to respond to the invitation – some of them even turned out to be murderers. This makes it clear that the reaction to the calling, and not simply the calling itself, determined who was eventually chosen. That is, although the word "chosen" is not qualified, the context makes clear that the choosing was done on the basis of certain clear criteria. The king chose to issue invitations, and when the recipients chose to ignore him, or worse, he chose to issue invitations to people on the streets. It is clear that their response in accepting the invitation was not a work of merit, indicating that they deserved to come. However, the fact that the guests were chosen did not mean that they were chosen unconditionally. And it is that capacity to respond that some would deny.

In the parable the King eventually turns to the streets in his search for guests. The New Testament gives us an instance of a similar kind of thing when Paul turns from the Jews to take the message to the Gentiles. Interestingly, a verse from that narrative in Acts is often quoted in support of the idea that God chooses some and rejects others, without regard to who they are:

> When the Gentiles heard this, they were glad and honoured the word of the Lord; and all who were appointed for eternal life believed.
>
> (Acts 13:48.)

It is important to read this text in its wider context. Paul had been speaking in the Jewish Synagogue in Pisidian Antioch and explaining the gospel message. He then appeals to them:

> "Therefore, my brothers, I want you to know that through Jesus the forgiveness of sins is proclaimed to you. Through him everyone who believes is justified from everything you could not be justified from by the law of Moses. Take care that what the prophets have said does not happen to you: 'Look, you scoffers, wonder and perish, for I am going to do something in your days that you would never believe, even if someone told you.'"
>
> As Paul and Barnabas were leaving the synagogue, the people invited them to speak further about these things on the next Sabbath. When the congregation was dismissed, many of the Jews and devout converts to Judaism followed Paul and Barnabas, who talked with them and urged them to continue in the grace of God.
>
> On the next Sabbath almost the whole city gathered to hear the word of the Lord. When the Jews saw the crowds, they were filled with jealousy and talked abusively against what Paul was saying.
>
> Then Paul and Barnabas answered them boldly: "We had to speak the word of God to you first. Since you reject it and do not consider yourselves worthy of eternal life, we now

turn to the Gentiles. For this is what the Lord has commanded us: 'I have made you a light for the Gentiles, that you may bring salvation to the ends of the earth.'" When the Gentiles heard this, they were glad and honoured the word of the Lord; and all who were appointed for eternal life believed.

(Acts 13:38–48.)

There was a bitter reaction on the part of some Jews to the huge crowd that assembled the following week wanting to hear the word of the Lord. Paul tells them straight that he had a responsibility to preach the message to them first, but now that they had made up their minds and come to a decision to reject the message, he would turn his attention to the Gentiles. Isaiah had predicted such a reaction, so we know that God knew about it beforehand. But that was not the cause of the reaction. It was their jealousy, for which they were responsible. And, as it turned out, the reaction of the listening Gentiles was very different: *When the Gentiles heard this, they were glad and honoured the word of the Lord; and all who were appointed for eternal life believed* (verse 48).

The Greek term translated *appointed* here is not one of the words in our earlier lists. It is from a verb whose root means "to cause someone to be in a state involving an order or arrangement" and is used in military contexts to describe troops lining up or getting into formation. The use of the word in this context is understandable – the Jews did not want the gospel and so the Gentiles lined up for it. The etymology of the word says nothing about how the lining up was done, but in the context it is clear that, just as the Jews made the conscious decision to get out of line, similarly the Gentiles made an equally conscious decision to get into line.

Once again it is to be stressed that God took the initiative in all of this. He sent them the messengers who preached to them in the power of the Spirit. In that sense God had worked on and in them, but in the end they were saved not because of some inscrutable fiat on God's part but because they responded to God's initiative. They lined themselves up and believed, and thereby received eternal life. I have very clear and moving memories of people, large crowds of them, lining up to respond to the gospel as preached by Billy Graham in the UK many years ago. I can imagine it was a bit like that in Pisidian Antioch.

We have now seen that the words "choose" and "chosen" and the like are used in different kinds of context in Scripture, not all of which are connected with ideas of selection for salvation (including some key passages used to support determinism). Yet when reference is made to the "doctrine of election" it is often only selection for salvation that is in view, which is of course the touchstone of the debate.

We recall the classic statement of this view given by John Calvin:

> *By predestination we mean the eternal decree of God by which he determined with himself whatever he wished to happen with regard to every man. All are not created on equal terms, but some are preordained to eternal life, others to eternal damnation; and accordingly, as each has been created for one or other of these ends, we say that he has been predestinated to life or to death.*[83]

A much more recent formulation is due to Loraine Boettner who is regarded as an authority in the field:

> *The Reformed Faith has held to the existence of an eternal, divine decree which, antecedently to any difference or desert in men themselves, separates the human race into two portions and ordains one to everlasting life and the other to everlasting death.*[84]

---

83 J. Calvin, *Institutes of Christian Religion*, III, xxi, 5.
84 L. Boettner, *The Reformed Doctrine of Predestination*, Phillipsburg, P & R Publishing, 1971, p. 102. We should note that this doctrine of double predestination is rejected by some theologians who would designate themselves as Calvinist; although, again, it seems logically rather hard to deny that, if God chooses some for salvation, then the others are effectively chosen for rejection.

Boettner holds that such an eternal divine decree is unconditional in the sense that it has nothing to do with the human objects of the decree – not even with their choices as foreseen by God.

The obvious rejoinder is that, if this is the case, it is difficult to see why God doesn't save everyone. The efforts of those committed to unconditional election to answer this question are not convincing. Sproul writes:

> *The only answer to this question is that I don't know. I have no idea why God saves some and not all. I don't doubt for a moment that God has the power to save all, but I know that he does not choose to save all. I don't know why... If it pleases God to save some and not to save all, there is nothing wrong with that. God is not under obligation to save anybody. If he chooses to save some, that in no way obligates him to save the rest.*[85]

I am not surprised that many people react against statements like this with anger. It sounds callous, hard, and even cruel to say, "I don't know the answer, but God can do what he likes and that is it." I am well aware that this view is often supported by appealing to Romans 9–11, and we shall devote several chapters to that later on. Sufficient to point out here that what appears to be missing in statements like Sproul's here is any sensitivity to any characteristic of God beyond his sovereignty. What about the love of God? And what about the love of Christians for their relatives and friends who are not believers? Is that all that can be said of them – if God chooses to save some and not others, what is wrong with that?

There is everything wrong with it if that selection is mysterious or even arbitrary. There is everything wrong with it if God is the God who so loved the world that he gave his Son that whoever believes in him should not perish but have eternal life. There is everything wrong with it if God is the God who inspired the apostle Paul to write, encouraging all believers to pray: *This is good, and it is pleasing*

---

85   R. C. Sproul, *Chosen by God*, Carol Stream, Tyndale House, 1986, p. 37.

in the sight of God our Saviour, who desires all people to be saved and to come to the knowledge of the truth (1 Timothy 2:3–4 ESV). There is everything wrong with it because it points to a God who hates rather than one who loves.

Thomas McCall gives an argument based on the love of God in order to highlight the problem with determinism here:

But consider:

1. God truly loves all persons.

2. Truly to love someone is to desire her well-being and to promote her true flourishing as much as you can.

3. The true well-being and flourishing of all persons is to be found in a right relationship with God, a saving relationship in which we accept the invitation of the gospel and come to love him and obey him.

4. God could determine all persons freely to accept the invitation of the gospel and come to a right relationship and be saved.

5. Therefore all persons will be saved.

Traditional Calvinists will agree that 5 is directly contrary to Scripture. But since 5 follows from 1–4 then there seems to be a problem here.[86]

McCall goes on to say that the obvious solution would be to deny 4 – but then divine determinism falls. For, in the final analysis, if God can determine some to be saved, he can determine all to be saved.

In light of these moral problems it is not surprising that the doctrine of unconditional election has been seen by many as a barrier to the free preaching of the gospel. Unconditional election assumes that humans are incapable of responding to

---

86 T. McCall, "I Believe in Divine Sovereignty", *Trinity Journal*, 29NS, 2008, pp. 205–26.

God, otherwise would it not mean that they are contributing to their salvation? Packer and Johnson in their introduction to their edition of Luther's *Bondage of the Will* put it this way:

> To the Reformers the crucial question was not simply whether God justifies believers without works of law. It was the broader questions whether sinners are wholly helpless in their sin and whether God is to be thought of saving them by free, unconditional, invincible grace, not only justifying them for Christ's sake when they come to faith, but also raising them from the death of sin by His quickening Spirit in order to bring them to faith. Here is the crucial issue: whether God is the author, not merely of justification but also of faith… What is the source and status of faith? Is it the God-given means whereby the God-given justification is received, or is it a condition of justification which it is left to man to fulfil? Is it part of God's gift of salvation, or is it man's own contribution to salvation?[87]

These are questions of central importance in the whole discussion, and we must now turn to consider them.

---

87   M. Luther, *The Bondage of the Will*, Grand Rapids, Baker, 1990, p. 59.

PART 3

THE GOSPEL AND DETERMINISM

C H A P T E R   7

Human Capacity and its Limits

The Gospel is good news because it is a message of salvation. It was that fact that motivated the apostle Paul to bring it to the world:

> *For I am not ashamed of the gospel, for it is the power of God for salvation to everyone who believes, to the Jew first and also to the Greek. For in it the righteousness of God is revealed from faith for faith, as it is written, "The righteous shall live by faith." For the wrath of God is revealed from heaven against all ungodliness and unrighteousness of men, who by their unrighteousness suppress the truth.*
>
> (Romans 1:16–18 ESV.)

> *Now we know that whatever the law says it speaks to those who are under the law, so that every mouth may be stopped, and the whole world may be held accountable to God. For by works of the law no human being will be justified in his sight, since through the law comes knowledge of sin.*
>
> *But now the righteousness of God has been manifested apart from the law, although the Law and the Prophets bear witness to it – the righteousness of God through faith in Jesus Christ for all who believe. For there is no distinction: for all have sinned and fall short of the glory of God, and are justified by his grace as a gift, through the redemption that is in Christ Jesus, whom God put forward as a propitiation by his blood, to be received by faith… For we hold that one is justified by faith apart from works of the law.*
>
> (Romans 3:19–25, 28 ESV.)

Paul tells us why it is that men and women need to be saved. Their situation is extremely serious. They are exposed to the righteous judgment of God because of their sin and unrighteousness. They therefore need to be put right with God. However, they cannot put themselves right with God as they have all sinned and fallen short of the glory of God. They cannot merit God's acceptance.

The wonder and glory of the gospel is that what humans cannot merit God offers as a free and gracious gift. He is prepared to declare them righteous – that is what the word "justify" means – through the redemption that is in Christ Jesus… to be received by faith. They are to be saved by the grace of God alone through faith in Christ alone.

The human condition is worse than many realise. It is surely evident to anyone who takes Scripture seriously that the entry of sin into the world has brought about major change and disruption. The consequences of and the damage due to the loss of Paradise are to be felt at every level. Humans are no longer what they once were. Alienated from God they cannot save themselves. To quote Paul, they are *dead in… trespasses and sins* (Ephesians 2:1 ESV). They can only be saved if God takes the initiative and provides salvation for them. On this, most if not all Christians will surely agree, whatever their position on determinism. If God did not provide salvation, no one could ever be saved.

The book of Genesis gives the account of how sin entered the world. That cataclysmic event is often called the Fall[88] and it occurred when the original humans were tempted first to question and then to disobey God's command not to eat of the tree of the knowledge of good and evil. That disobedience was precipitated by lack of trust in God and his word; it was a breakdown of faith.

It is therefore not surprising that the subsequent chapters of Genesis are devoted to the recovery of faith in God. Here, the major character Abraham is presented to us as the paradigm example of someone who learned to trust God. It was Abraham whose faith in God was credited as righteousness; Paul refers to this fact again and

---

88 An appropriate term, evidenced by Paul's reference to falling into temptation in 1 Timothy 6:9.

again in his explanation of what it means to have faith in Christ for salvation.

In one sense this is all – gloriously – plain sailing and is agreed by believers occupying a fairly broad theological spectrum. Yet difficulties begin when we try to go deeper, in order to grasp more fully what exactly it is that is wrong with humanity and how precisely it is to be put right. For instance, to what extent are we damaged by the Fall? The New Testament says we are dead in trespasses and sins, but what exactly does that mean? We clearly still possess many capacities, but is one of them the capacity to respond to God? What is the nature and status of the "faith" that Scripture talks about? Is it something that we produce? Is it something God gives us? And if so, does he do so mysteriously or even arbitrarily; or are we involved in some way? Why do some people "have faith" while others don't? It is to such questions that we now turn – important questions as they inevitably have implications for what we think of God.

The following are three of the major arguments advanced to promote the idea that humans are by nature incapable of any response to God.

Argument 1: Unconditional election

If human beings were capable of trusting God, they would be contributing to their salvation and therefore meriting it. Salvation would no longer be by grace and God's glory would thereby be diminished. For instance, J. I. Packer and O. R. Johnson in their introduction to Luther's *Bondage of the Will* say that, in Reformed eyes, "to rely on oneself for faith is no different in principle from relying on oneself for works".[89] Wayne Grudem similarly writes: "Election based on something good in us (our faith) would be the beginning of salvation by merit."[90] The only way out of this, he argues, is to hold that faith itself must be a gift of God distributed according to his sovereign will, completely independent of any attitude, desire,

---

89   M. Luther, *The Bondage of the Will*, Grand Rapids, Baker, 1990, p. 59.
90   W. Grudem, *Bible Doctrine*, Leicester, IVP, 1999, p. 287.

or behaviour on the part of those he elects to save. This view, as we have seen, is called "unconditional election" – an expression that does not actually appear in Scripture itself.

Argument 2: Total depravity

Human beings are incapable of believing because they are dead in trespasses and sins as a result of the sin that Adam introduced into the world. This view is often called the "total depravity" of man – although we note that this phrase too does not occur in Scripture. Just as dead creatures cannot respond to any stimulus, the argument runs, so men and women are constitutionally unable to respond to God. In order to be able to respond they must receive new life (they must be "born again"). Only then can they respond with the faith that God gives them. Without any action on their part (they are dead and therefore cannot act) God regenerates those he decides to regenerate by his Spirit; they are then, and only then, able to believe in Christ.

Argument 3: Original sin

Although human beings are incapable of believing in God, for the reason given under Argument 2, it is nevertheless their fault that they do not believe. God may justly condemn them. This has to do with their connection to Adam who brought sin into the world: when he sinned, they sinned.

I take these arguments very seriously. They, and variants of them, have been and are held by eminent and highly respected Christians, some of whom I know and value. I hope that the reader will grant me that I fully share their concern not to detract from God's glory in any way. Nevertheless, my contention is that, because of their strongly deterministic elements, all three arguments do detract from God's sovereign glory. I also hold that they are flawed.

Response to argument 1: Faith is a universal God-given ability

We first explore the idea that, if people had the capacity to believe in God, if they were capable of faith, their faith would itself be a meritorious work contributing to salvation. May I dare to suggest that this view arises from confusion about the nature of faith itself?

Some of the confusion arises from overlooking a simple logical point: *meriting something, and having to do something to obtain that thing, are not the same.* For instance, a distant relative may leave me a considerable sum in her will. I have done nothing to deserve it. She has gifted it to me as set out in a document held by her solicitor. He sends me a letter informing me of the fact. Now I have to decide whether I trust him and, indeed, her. I have to respond or I will not receive it. I could reject it. Clearly, the fact that I have to *do* something to make it my own does not mean that I have *merited* it or *contributed* to it in any way.

It is surely for that reason that our Lord can say to a woman on one occasion: *Your faith has saved you; go in peace* (Luke 7:50).

Consistent with this, when Paul is asked by a jailer at Philippi, who has just been terrified by an earthquake that freed the prisoners, *Sirs, what must I do to be saved?*, Paul does not understand the jailer to be asking how he can merit salvation. He does not respond by suggesting that the jailer can do nothing in view of the fact that his salvation depends entirely on the sovereign choice of God. On the contrary, he tells the jailer exactly what he is able to do – and should do: *Believe in the Lord Jesus, and you will be saved – you and your household* (see Acts 16:25–34).

Wayne Grudem, cited just above, says: "Election based on something good in us (our faith) would be the beginning of salvation by merit." What is striking here is the use of the adjective "good" used to qualify "faith" which is then linked with "merit". But does Scripture teach that faith is a good thing in this meritorious sense? I think not.

In his response to the jailer Paul was not denying that salvation was wholly by grace and unmerited. On the contrary, he was affirming it. For – and this is the critically important thing – *Paul regarded faith, the act of believing, as the opposite of merit.* This means that the personal act of believing in or trusting Christ for salvation is not a meritorious action that contributes to salvation. Salvation is all of God.

Paul was aware that the distinction between faith and meritorious work is a difficult concept for many to grasp, especially religious people, and consequently he goes to great lengths to explain it. One of his key arguments is to be found in his letter to the Romans, where he analyses the status of Abraham's faith. The first major statement is: *Abraham believed God, and it was counted to him as righteousness* (Romans 4:3 ESV). It is paralleled at the end of the chapter by the observation: *That is why his faith was "counted to him as righteousness"* (verse 22 ESV). Please note that the faith was Abraham's – *his* faith. The text does not say here that God "gave him the faith" (though we shall consider below how faith may be "given"), nor does it say that Abraham's faith was a meritorious contribution to his justification; it doesn't even say here that Christ's righteousness was imputed (reckoned) to Abraham as righteousness. No, Scripture says that it was Abraham's faith that was reckoned to him as righteousness.

Listen to Paul defining the essence of faith in God in verses 4–5 (ESV):

> *Now to the one who works, his wages are not counted as a gift but as his due. And to the one who **does not work** but **trusts** him who justifies the ungodly, his faith is counted as righteousness...*

Paul is using the concept of work here as an activity that merits wages. Faith in God, he says, is not like that at all: it is not to be taken as a meritorious action repaid by the reward of salvation – otherwise the person who has faith would be working.

We notice also that a person's faith in God is described as their own faith: the faith of an ungodly person is counted as righteousness.

Paul, then, is contrasting two possible actions or attitudes – working and trusting – on the basis of the tacit assumption that everyone is capable of performing both.

Now in writing this I am aware that some suggest that the background to his argument here in Romans was not the idea of earning salvation by amassing good works, but rather the danger of trusting peculiarly Jewish ritual and ceremony like circumcision and national privilege for salvation. However, my reading of Scripture would suggest that both are involved. Simon Gathercole has argued that

> many of Paul's Jewish contemporaries **did** hold to a doctrine of final salvation according to works, and that obedience to Torah was a criterion at the final judgment. Indeed, Paul makes it clear in Romans 2 that his interlocutor holds such a view.[91]

Furthermore, the emphasis in the New Testament is not on the *goodness* of faith but on its *rightness*, and it is noteworthy that it is often mentioned in connection with the righteousness of God because to have faith is to have the right attitude to God – hence Abraham's faith is *counted to him as righteousness* (Romans 4:3 ESV). And because the issue is rightness rather than goodness, Scripture is not embarrassed to commend people on their faith, as exemplified in the definition of faith given in Hebrews:

> Now faith is being sure of what we hope for and certain of what we do not see. This is what the ancients were commended for.
>
> (Hebrews 11:1–2.)

To commend someone for doing something that is not within their power to do is meaningless.

We observe in passing that one technical term for the claim that only God is involved in regeneration is "monergism". The alternative view, that human response is involved, is called "synergism". Unfortunately, these terms mean "one working" and "joint work" and

---

91   S. Gathercole, *Where Is Boasting?: Early Jewish Soteriology and Paul's Response Response to Romans 1–5*, Grand Rapids, Eerdmans, 2002, pp. 214.

beg the question as to whether *meritorious work* is involved. Paul's teaching is clearly that God alone does the work of regeneration, but we are responsible for trusting him *which activity is not a work*, such that regeneration is not in that sense synergistic. In addition, many who believe that regeneration precedes faith teach that regeneration is monergistic but subsequent salvation is synergistic since it involves our faith. For that reason the terms seem unhelpful and therefore best avoided.

In spite of the fact that Scripture explicitly says that it is Abraham's faith that is credited to him as righteousness, it will be objected that Paul explicitly says elsewhere that faith is a gift of God. The relevant passage is Ephesians 2:8–9 where Paul writes:

> *For it is by grace you have been saved, through faith – and this not from yourselves, it is the gift of God – not by works, so that no-one can boast.*

It is then argued that this verse is consistent with the view that the unregenerate person is incapable of believing, and unless God gives them the faith that person will never believe. However, in the Greek text the word for *faith* is feminine in gender, whereas the word for *it* (in the phrase *it is the gift of God*) is neuter. From a grammatical point of view it is therefore not faith that is the gift – the gift is salvation by grace. Paul is in fact here making the same point as in Romans 4, contrasting salvation by merit with salvation by grace through faith.

However, the matter is not to be left there at the grammatical level. There is a real sense in which faith can be seen to be a gift of God without denying it is also our faith. I am well aware that for many people the New Atheists have cleverly redefined the concept of faith, with the result that faith is now widely regarded by secular society (and, sadly, even by some professing Christians) as a purely religious concept that means believing where there is no evidence. This misrepresentation of faith is completely and dangerously false and needs constant refutation. Faith is not a specifically religious word, although it is used in religious contexts, for instance subjectively of "faith in God" and objectively in "the Christian faith".

According to the *Oxford English Dictionary* the word "faith" derives from the Latin *fides* (from which we get "fidelity"), so its basic meaning is "trust" or "reliance". The Greek etymological equivalent is *pistis*, which is found in the New Testament where it has the following principal senses:

1. belief, trust;

2. that which produces belief, evidence, token, pledge, engagement;

3. trust in its objective aspect, troth, observance of trust, fidelity.

So the main dictionary meanings given to "faith" are: belief, trust, confidence, reliance, and belief proceeding from testimony or authority. It is to be strongly affirmed that the faith in God described in the Bible is "reliance and belief proceeding from testimony or authority". Biblical faith is evidence-based.[92]

A famous passage explaining this is to be found towards the end of John's Gospel:

> *Now Jesus did many other signs in the presence of the disciples, which are not written in this book; but these are written so that you may believe that Jesus is the Christ, the Son of God, and that by believing you may have life in his name.*
>
> (John 20:30–31 ESV.)

John is stating here the purpose for which he wrote his book. It records a collection of signs. These were very special acts that Jesus did that pointed towards a reality beyond themselves, and thus bore witness to Jesus' identity as God incarnate. As we read John's Gospel, we find that is exactly what happened. Again and again John records how people believed because of the evidence that Jesus provided (see for example John 2:11; 3:2; 4:41; 4:53; 6:14). John clearly regarded

---

92   For more detail see the author's *Gunning for God*, Oxford, Lion Hudson, 2011.

that evidence to be sufficient also for those, like ourselves, who did not directly observe the events in question. According to John, the faith Christ requires is anything but blind. The blindness is on the part of the people who didn't believe and who don't believe, and we shall look at this in more detail shortly.

The signs were deliberately given by Jesus to stimulate faith in him. The signs preceded faith. Jesus drew out the faith of people by what he did, gaining their trust and affection. Now faith in Christ is faith in a person, and it is worth reflecting at this point on how trust between people is generated in everyday life.

In the commercial world, for instance, trust is of the essence. But how does trust actually arise in practice? Two people may meet in an office. Jones sees Smith as an open, honest person. He trusts Smith with a job. Smith does his work in such a way that Jones trusts him with even more. Jones hears from others that Smith represents him with great integrity, even if it costs him to do so. Jones begins to find that Smith inspires him with confidence, and so he comes to trust him even more, and a solid business relationship is established. Where does the trust that Jones has in Smith come from? In a sense Smith has given it to Jones, in that he has drawn it out of him. But that does not alter the fact that the faith is Jones' faith. Jones has the capacity to trust. Because of what Smith is and does, Jones gives his trust to Smith.

Similarly in the marriage relationship, the trust, faith, and commitment of each partner is drawn out by the other. And that does not alter the fact that the faith of each partner is their own subjective response to the other – it is their faith.

In that sense we can certainly regard faith as a gift of God. God draws it out of us by his grace and love. If God did not initiate it himself, we would never experience it. But he regards the faith as ours – just as he did with Abraham.

That brings me to another point. In ordinary life, whether we believe in God or not, each of us exercises faith in many things. We trust some of what we read; we trust friends; we trust experts like surgeons and airline pilots with our very lives. Each day we are called upon to exercise faith in something or someone, and most of us intuitively believe that we are free to do so. This capacity to trust is related to our freedom of will and is part of our nature, created by God whether or not we believe in him. It is a wonderful gift of God's grace to us as his creatures. It creates the possibility of love and genuine relationship, and is part of the image of God stamped in our nature. To suggest that humans do not have that capacity, but that their fate is determined by their possessing or not possessing some special and very different kind of "saving faith" – one that it is the prerogative of God alone to give arbitrarily – massively diminishes rather than enhances the glory of God's character, to say nothing of its dehumanising effect on us.

The biggest issue facing human beings is surely this: will we use this magnificent gift of the capacity to trust (which we all possess) to trust the source of that gift, God himself? The crucial thing here is faith's location, not its quantity: in *whom* do we place our faith; not *how much* faith do we have? We use the capacity daily to exercise trust in a myriad of areas. But are we prepared to use that capacity to trust God? That is the central challenge of the gospel message.

Paul tells us where humanity went wrong:

> *For, although they knew God, they neither glorified him as God nor gave thanks to him...*
>
> (Romans 1:21.)

Their wrong consisted in their refusal to express their dependence on God, for that is what being thankful involves. They would not trust him, so they descended into a rebellious moral darkness. If that is where things went wrong, then it is utterly appropriate that the way back will involve learning to trust God – learning to use God's gift of the capacity to believe, to trust him and what he has done for human salvation.

The apostle John wrote:

> *We accept man's testimony, but God's testimony is greater because it is the testimony of God, which he has given about his Son.*
>
> (1 John 5:9.)

All of us, whether regenerate or not, are capable of and do accept the testimony of others. We should therefore be prepared to accept and trust the much greater and more powerful testimony of God, accompanied as it is by the power and grace of God poured out in our hearts through the Holy Spirit.

When our Lord offered to come to the home of a Roman centurion in Capernaum to heal his paralysed servant, the man said: *Lord, I do not deserve to have you come under my roof. But just say the word, and my servant will be healed.* Christ's reaction was: *I tell you the truth, I have not found anyone in Israel with such great faith.* (Matthew 8:8–10.) If theological determinism is true, then surely it would have been much more accurate if our Lord had said, "To no one in Israel have I given such great faith." But he did not. Furthermore, if faith has nothing to do with the one exercising it, how can it be great or little?

I am aware that Argument 2 is waiting impatiently in the wings and we must now come to it.

Response to argument 2: Faith precedes regeneration

The contention here is that human beings do not have the capacity to believe and respond to God because they are by nature dead in trespasses and sins as a result of the sin that Adam introduced into the world (as per the doctrine of total depravity or total inability). Hence, in order to be able to believe, they must first be given new life – that is, they must be born again by the power of God's Holy Spirit. This view has been held by some seriously heavyweight and respected thinkers from the time of Augustine.

Arthur W. Pink writes:

> *A man is not regenerated because he has first believed in Christ, but he believes in Christ because he has been regenerated.*[93]

---

93   A. Pink, *The Widsom of Arthur W. Pink*, vol. 1, Zeeland, Reformed Church, 2009, p. 65.

R. C. Sproul puts it this way:

> *Unless regeneration takes place first, there is no possibility of faith.*[94]

He also writes:

> *We do not believe in order to be born again; we are born again that we may believe.*[95]

John Piper writes:

> *New birth is a miraculous creation of God that enables a formerly "dead" person to receive Christ and so be saved. We do not bring about the new birth by our faith. God brings about our faith by the new birth.*[96]

In a more recent popular book Ben Peays writes:

> *Repentance and faith flow infallibly and inseparably from regeneration… we cannot believe unless we are born again.*[97]

However, the order affirmed by these writers – regeneration before faith – is the exact opposite of the order given in Scripture. For instance, in John 3:14–15 Jesus says: *the Son of Man must be lifted up, that everyone who believes in him may have eternal life.* He does not say, "so that everyone who has eternal life may believe." The very next verse says: *whoever believes in him shall not perish but have eternal life.* It does not say, "Anyone who has eternal life believes in him and shall not perish."

---

94 R. C. Sproul, "Regeneration Precedes Faith", *Tabletalk*, February 1997, p. 35.
95 R. C. Sproul, *Chosen by God*, Carol Stream, Tyndale House, 2011, p. 73.
96 "What We Believe About the Five Points of Calvinism", desiringgod.org
97 K. DeYoung (ed.), *Don't Call It a Comeback: The Old Faith for a New Day*, Wheaton, Crossway, 2011, pp. 90–91.

Again, two verses later: *Whoever believes in him is not condemned, but whoever does not believe stands condemned already because he has not believed in the name of God's one and only Son* (verse 18). Finally, at the end of the chapter: *Whoever believes in the Son has eternal life, but whoever rejects the Son will not see life, for God's wrath remains on him* (verse 36). It does not say, "whoever has eternal life believes in the Son."

By what authority, then, do the above-quoted writers reverse the biblical order in a classical example of putting the cart before the horse? One suggestion is that they use the term "regeneration" more widely than Scripture to describe any work of God in a person's life before they come to believe the gospel. However, there is no warrant in the New Testament for such a use of the word.

The idea that human beings can initiate their own salvation, or respond to God independently of his grace, is a heresy often called Pelagianism, named after the Celtic monk Pelagius who in the fourth and fifth centuries propounded a strong view of the believer's role in salvation. So let us underline that, according to Scripture, there would be no salvation unless God provided it and poured his grace out on the world. Paul writes:

> For the grace of God has appeared, bringing salvation for all people.
>
> (Titus 2:11 ESV.)

The coming of the Saviour into the world is a prerequisite for salvation. God is the author and initiator of salvation. Elsewhere we read that the Word is the true light that enlightens everyone (see John 1:9). We also read of Christ "drawing" and of the Holy Spirit coming to *convict the world of guilt in regard to sin and righteousness and judgment* (John 16:8).

It was God's grace that led Paul initially not to claim his Roman citizenship to avoid prison in Philippi, yet clearly he made that decision of his own free will. It was God's grace that shook the prison in Philippi and with it the jailer's heart. However, this "prevenient grace"[98] did not amount to regeneration and salvation. As we have already noted, there was something the jailer had to do. He asked what he should do and Paul told him: *Believe in the Lord Jesus* (Acts 16:31).

There is, therefore, much of God's grace to be experienced before someone comes to trust Christ, but this should not be confused with regeneration. Scripture is very careful in its use of terms, and none of the divine activities mentioned above is equivalent to regeneration. Indeed, they are things that precede regeneration. And, however we interpret them, we must never interpret them in such a way as to undercut human free will, thereby making God ultimately responsible for sin and evil. The jailer was free to believe or not to believe. God would not make the decision for him. That would be to remove his human moral integrity and value.

Perhaps an illustration can help, although it remains only an illustration. All large vehicles (and many smaller ones nowadays) have power-assisted steering. I would not have the strength to turn the steering wheel of a large articulated vehicle. But power-assisted steering means that, the moment I touch the steering wheel, the power is supplied and the wheels turn. If I do not touch the steering wheel nothing will happen; yet I can do nothing without the power being supplied. The servo mechanism does not decide to move the wheels, I do; but I cannot do it without the power.

I sense this may be something like what lies behind the famous and honest prayer: *I believe; help my unbelief!* (Mark 9:24 ESV). God will do everything in his power to help us, but he cannot decide for us. It also lies behind the notion of the Holy Spirit as Comforter, or Paraclete, who comes alongside us to help. He has the power, but makes it available to us only as we avail ourselves of it.

To sum up then: John 3 tells us no fewer than three times that the condition for obtaining eternal life is faith in Christ; and it also tells us that the person who believes in (has faith in) Christ is not condemned. Conversely, John tells us that the person who does not

---

98 Augustine used this term to describe any activity of God's grace that precedes the moment of conversion.

believe is condemned already. The reason is given explicitly: *because he has not believed in the name of God's one and only Son* (verse 18). This verdict is repeated at the end of the chapter: *whoever rejects the Son will not see life, for God's wrath remains on him* (verse 36). That is, the charge against such a person is that they have failed or refused to believe in the Son, and so rejected him.

The criterion expressed here has nothing to do with a person's merit in terms of works or good behaviour. The criterion is solely whether or not a person has believed in the Son of God. Faith comes before regeneration.

We should note that this repeated emphasis in John 3 is not contradicted by a later statement by John:

> *Everyone who believes that Jesus is the Christ is born of God…*
>
> (1 John 5:1.)

Piper says:

> *This means that being born of God comes first and believing follows. Believing in Jesus is not the cause of being born again; it is the evidence that we have been born of God.*[99]

However, this verse does not reverse the order laid down in John 3 but is entirely consistent with believing being the ground of the new birth – the grammar of the statement does not imply that the being born precedes the believing.

Interestingly, Piper seems at once to reverse his position by citing John 1:13, that those who do receive Christ *"were born, not of blood nor of the will of the flesh nor of the will of man, but of God."* In other words, *it is necessary to receive Christ in order to become a child of God*, but the birth that brings one into the family of God is not possible by the will of man. Only God can do it.

This leads to a further reversal:

---

99   "What We Believe About the Five Points of Calvinism", desiringgod.org

The two acts (new birth and faith) are so closely connected that in experience we cannot distinguish them. God begets us anew and the first glimmer of life in the newborn child is faith.

There is no doubt, of course, that faith and regeneration are closely connected, but that is not an argument on which a reversal of the biblical order can be based.

We note also that there is not the slightest hint of: "if God decided before the foundation of the world to save you, you will be saved; if he decided to condemn you, you will be condemned – and there is nothing you can do about it." Rather the opposite: "granted that God has taken the initiative in providing salvation, there is something you can and indeed must do. You must respond to the offer of salvation by trusting Christ as Lord."

Yet there are theologians like E. H. Palmer who hold that:

Reprobation as condemnation is conditional in the sense that once someone is passed by, then he is condemned by God for his sins and unbelief. Although all things – unbelief and sin included – proceed from God's eternal decree, man is still to blame for his sins. He is guilty; it is his fault and not God's.[100]

It is sad to read of Palmer's own reaction to this. Elsewhere in the same work he freely – and rather oddly – admits that his view is "illogical, ridiculous, nonsensical and foolish".[101] He then takes refuge in saying, "This secret matter belongs to the Lord our God and we should leave it there."[102]

To ascribe views that are illogical, ridiculous, nonsensical, and foolish to God and his word sounds like the language of unbalanced extremism. After all, if an argument – and Palmer uses his reason all through – leads to illogical, ridiculous, nonsensical, and foolish

---

100 E. H. Palmer, *The Five Points of Calvinism*, Grand Rapids, Baker, 2009, pp. 105–106.
101 *Ibid.*, p. 85.
102 *Ibid.*, p. 87.

conclusions, then the first thing to look for are flaws in the argument – either in its logic or its premises. Yet Palmer, astonishingly, encourages us blindly, and purely on the basis of his own personal authority, to "leave it there". But God does not leave it there. Christ does not leave it there. The New Testament does not leave it there. As we have seen, and will further explore, a long and detailed argument in John's Gospel is geared precisely to establish the very opposite of Palmer's contention. God justifies his ways to us and repeatedly asks us, as his creatures, to use our moral judgment to grasp that his will and actions are the exact opposite of illogical, ridiculous, nonsensical, and foolish. Simply to "leave it there" risks undermining the credibility of Scripture.

Using our God-given moral judgment is very important. For instance, the most elementary moral logic surely tells us that, if someone is going to be condemned because they personally failed to do something (in this case, to believe), then they must have been capable of doing it in the first place. Otherwise no guilt could attach to their action, and their condemnation would be unjust. Attempts like Palmer's to dismiss this point by saying that this belongs to the secret counsel of God are singularly unimpressive and cannot be correct, as the Lord himself makes it clear that guilt implies responsibility and moral capacity.

In his discussion with the religious leaders about his healing of the blind man, Jesus makes the point:

> If you were blind, you would not be guilty of sin; but now that you claim you can see, your guilt remains.
>
> (John 9:41.)

According to Christ, then, people will never be condemned for not seeing what they cannot see. Therefore, if they are to be judged for not believing, they must have been capable of believing. To suggest otherwise is to run the risk of representing God as a moral monster, and that is unthinkable.

To this moral deduction it is sometimes objected that, even in human law courts, people are sometimes condemned for doing what they were incapable of not doing. Irish people enjoy telling the story of a man who was arrested on a drink-driving charge. As evidence the judge cites the fact that, when the police asked him to walk along the white line in the middle of the road, he failed to do it and tottered all over the place. The man objects: "Your Honour, you can't blame me for that, since I just couldn't walk straight that night. You cannot condemn me for not doing what I couldn't do." The judge, of course, makes the obvious reply that the man was responsible for getting drunk and gives him a hefty fine. The guilty man's failure to walk straight was a consequence of his love for alcohol. We notice, however, that the man in the story was not actually condemned for not doing what he couldn't do. His failure to walk straight was a symptom, not a cause. The cause was his drunkenness, for which he was directly and culpably responsible.

Similarly, the analysis of unbelief in John 3 places strong emphasis on human responsibility:

> *This is the verdict: Light has come into the world, but men loved darkness instead of light because their deeds were evil. Everyone who does evil hates the light, and will not come into the light for fear that his deeds will be exposed. But whoever lives by the truth comes into the light, so that it may be seen plainly that what he has done has been done through God.*
>
> (John 3:19–21.)

Here John explains the criterion that God will use in judgment. Notice its moral reasonableness. First of all, *Light has come into the world*. Once again we see that God takes the initiative. He provides men and women with evidence. The question is, how do they react to that evidence? They *loved darkness instead of light*. That is, they have seen the light, rejected it, and hence have merited judgment.

It is important that we constantly remind ourselves what is at stake here: the morality and credibility of God's judgments. This is an immensely serious matter, and it is no wonder that people take exception to any idea that God will judge people for failing to do what they couldn't do, or failing to see what they couldn't see.

Scripture therefore goes to great lengths to champion the justice of God's judgments. To present God's judgments as contradictory to biblically based moral intuition is to risk undermining people's confidence in the authority of the Bible and the character of God.

It is important that we stay with our response to Argument 2 (the unbiblical view that regeneration must come before faith); we shall come to Argument 3 later, in Chapter 10.

CHAPTER 8

The Human Condition – Diagnosis and Remedy

God's righteousness and justification by faith

This is a topic of such importance that Paul devotes the first part of his letter to the Romans to it. Here is the argument in a nutshell, taken from the first three chapters. Paul is

> ... not ashamed of the gospel, for it is the power of God for salvation to everyone who believes, to the Jew first and also to the Greek. For in it the righteousness of God is revealed from faith for faith, as it is written, "The righteous shall live by faith."
>
> (Romans 1:16–17 ESV.)

This is the beginning of Paul's lengthy explanation of how human beings can be justified through faith in him.

It is important to know that the term "to justify" means "to declare righteous or right". It does not mean "to make righteous". I mention this because Augustine, working from a defective Latin translation, thought that the verb meant "to make right" – a translation error that caused considerable theological confusion in subsequent years. Alister McGrath makes the observation:

> Although this is a permissible interpretation of the Latin word, it is unacceptable as an interpretation of the Hebrew concept which underlies it.[103]

---

103 A. E. McGrath, *Iustitia Dei*, CUP, 1998, p. 31. See also the article "Justification" in W. A. Elwell (ed.), *Evangelical Dictionary of Biblical Theology*, Grand Rapids, Baker, 1996.

The underlying Hebrew concept is, of course, that of Abraham's justification by faith. The Greek word that translates this concept means "to declare righteous". For example, the Greek of Luke 7:29 says that tax collectors "justified God" which clearly cannot mean "make God right". The ESV correctly translates *declared God just*.

It is worth taking some time thinking about justification, because it is the central distinguishing glory of the Christian message, and no believer should tire of being reminded of the story of God's salvation.

Paul's first task is to show that such salvation is necessary because all are guilty before God. He proceeds to establish this in detail:

> *The wrath of God is being revealed from heaven against all the godlessness and wickedness of men who suppress the truth by their wickedness.*
>
> (Romans 1:18.)

They suppress the truth, for there is truth to be known. In particular,

> *… what may be known about God is plain to them, because God has made it plain to them.*
>
> (Romans 1:19.)

That is, they are perfectly capable of seeing what God has taken the initiative to show them. What has God shown them?

> *For since the creation of the world God's invisible qualities – his eternal power and divine nature – have been clearly seen, being understood from what has been made.*
>
> (Romans 1:20.)

God has built a signature message into the created universe. This is part of what is often called his "common grace" to mankind. Men and women can perceive, through what he has made, that there is a Creator God of great power. The assumption here is clearly that human beings have the capacity to do so. Not only that, but Paul adds that the evidence supplied by creation is so strong that they are *without excuse* (verse 20). Men and women are not intellectually blind and so will be held accountable if they refuse the evidence of creation.

But there is more evidence than that supplied by the created world. There is, in addition, the evidence of our human moral sense. Paul next outlines the steep moral decline that results from rejecting God, and yet he makes it clear that men and women are morally responsible for their actions, for they still retain moral awareness.

> *Although they know God's righteous decree that those who do such things deserve death, they not only continue to do these very things but also approve of those who practise them.*
>
> (Romans 1:32.)

Nor does the moralist who condemns such behaviour escape:

> *You, therefore, have no excuse, you who pass judgment on someone else, for at whatever point you judge the other, you are condemning yourself, because you who pass judgment do the same things.*
>
> (Romans 2:1.)

Paul faces such people with the question:

> *Or do you show contempt for the riches of his kindness, tolerance and patience, not realising that God's kindness leads you towards repentance?*
>
> (Romans 2:4.)

The implication is that they could have repented had they wished to. God had certainly been patient and given them plenty of time to repent. However, they did not repent but hardened their hearts. Paul tells them,

> *… you are storing up wrath against yourself for the day of God's wrath, when his righteous judgment will be revealed.*
>
> (Romans 2:5.)

It is they who are storing up wrath for themselves. God's judgment is righteous because it has been deserved.

Paul goes on to point out that such moral awareness is not restricted to Israel who have received the written law of God. He now argues that all men and women are morally responsible beings, as can be seen from their behaviour. Even though they do not have the law in its formal written form,

> ... they show that the requirements work of the law are written
> on their hearts, their consciences also bearing witness, and
> their thoughts now accusing, now even defending them...
> on the day when God will judge men's secrets through Jesus
> Christ, as my gospel declares.
>
> (Romans 2:15–16.)

Whether or not they believe in God, all men and women behave as moral beings because they have been created as such. All possess a conscience as part of their God-given constitution. When Smith accuses Jones, or when Smith excuses his actions before Jones, it is clear that Smith expects Jones to adhere to a moral standard that is independent of both of them. Paul uses this as further evidence to be used (ultimately by God) to demonstrate that his judgment is deserved. Men and women are not morally blind.

The aim of this part of Paul's argument is to establish that all men and women are guilty before God. He gives a devastating indictment of the sinfulness of human beings, be they pagan or religious, and shows that no one has any excuse for their sin because of the evidence God has given them in creation, in conscience, and in his revealed word.

All will therefore be held accountable:

> Now we know that whatever the law says, it says to those who
> are under the law, so that every mouth may be silenced and
> the whole world held accountable to God. Therefore no-one
> will be declared righteous in his sight by observing the law,
> rather, through the law we become conscious of sin.
>
> (Romans 3:19–20.)

The grand conclusion is:

> ... *all have sinned and fall short of the glory of God.*
> (Romans 3:23.)

So far this makes moral sense. Personal guilt is incurred by personal sin and so judgment is merited. What is also abundantly clear is that salvation cannot be initiated, engineered, or merited by human beings. The great question that Paul now answers is: how, then, can men and women, all of whom have sinned and come short of the glory of God, be put right with God?

The wonder of salvation

Paul explains the wonder of God's salvation. What humans cannot deserve, engineer, or merit, God is prepared to give as a gracious gift. Men and women can be

> ... *justified by his grace as a gift, through the redemption that is in Christ Jesus, whom God put forward as a propitiation by his blood, to be received by faith.*
> (Romans 3:24–25 ESV.)

God's provision for salvation involves no less than the death of his Son, the Lord Jesus Christ. The reason for this is that we live in a moral universe in which we have incurred the wrath of God by our sin.

The word "propitiation" is key here. It is a sacrificial term meaning something that holds back the wrath of God. What Christ did on the cross is foreshadowed (as Paul says in 3:21) by the Old Testament sacrifices. God cannot simply wave a wand, as many think, and say, "I forgive you". The cross is necessary, as it provides a just basis for declaring righteous the sinner who believes. Speaking about the death of Christ, Paul says:

> ... *he did it to demonstrate his justice at the present time, so*

as to be just and the one who justifies those who have faith in Jesus.

(Romans 3:26.)

The cross and redemption through Christ have become a major target of atheist critics, as a result of which some Christians are tempted to feel ashamed of the message of Christ's death and resurrection. The atheists say that it is absurd and immoral to claim that Christ could die for our sins. Paul, however, is not ashamed of this message. Far from being immoral, it is the only possible moral basis on which God could forgive repentant believing humans.[104]

The objective side of the story is that God has taken the initiative. In his grace, Christ has been set forth by God as a propitiation. He has died and provided the basis for redemption. In that sense salvation is all of God – without him there would be none. Yet salvation is not automatic; it has to be received individually by faith in Jesus as redeemer. Four times over in this short section Paul emphasises the need for response:

> through faith in Jesus Christ
>
> for all who believe
>
> to be received by faith
>
> God is the justifier of the one who has faith in Jesus.

Most Christians will of course agree that the Bible teaches that salvation is by faith. But some will say that we can only exercise this faith because we have first of all been regenerated by God. This would mean, logically, that salvation is by faith but not regeneration. My contention is that the New Testament teaches that both are by faith alone. Incidentally, it is very hard to maintain in any case that regeneration is to be distinguished from salvation, to such an extent that one could be regenerate without being saved; and yet that is a possible implication of the idea of regeneration preceding faith.

---

104 For more on the atheist critique of the atonement, see the author's *Gunning for God*, Oxford, Lion Hudson, 2011.

Paul describes salvation itself as the *washing of regeneration* (Titus 3:5 ESV).[105]

This being so, if regeneration precedes faith, a serious logical problem confronts us. If a person is regenerate by an act of God, are they not therefore a member of the kingdom of heaven and already in receipt of salvation? What then would be the point and purpose of subsequent repentance and faith? C. H. Spurgeon once commented:

> *If I am to preach the faith in Christ to a man who is regenerated, then the man, being regenerated, is saved already, and it is an unnecessary and ridiculous thing for me to preach Christ to him, and bid him to believe in order to be saved when he is saved already, being regenerate.*[106]

Dead in trespasses and sins: The case of Adam

In spite of what would seem to be overwhelming evidence that faith is the ground of regeneration and not its fruit, it is maintained that this cannot be so since men and women are dead in trespasses and sins. It follows, so the argument runs, that they cannot respond in faith until they are first regenerated. However, those who use this argument to reverse the explicit and oft-repeated order given in Scripture have not understood the biblical expression "dead in trespasses and sins" correctly. In fact that expression can be readily understood in a manner consistent with the assertion that faith precedes regeneration.

---

105 Paul is not here speaking of baptism, but it is perhaps worth mentioning that those who hold to the doctrine of baptismal regeneration for infants must by definition hold that regeneration precedes faith. However, discussion of the reasons for believing that this doctrine is not biblical would go beyond the scope of this book and, in any case, baptismal regeneration is not often used as an argument by those who hold that regeneration precedes faith.

106 C. H. Spurgeon, *C. H. Spurgeon's Sermons: Metropolitan Tabernacle Pulpit*, Pasadena, Pilgrim Publications, 1970, p. 532.

Now it is certainly the case that men and women are dead in trespasses and sins, for that is stated explicitly in the New Testament. Paul reminds the church at Ephesus of their former state: *you were dead in the trespasses and sins in which you once walked* (Ephesians 2:1–2 ESV). Secondly, it is also true that dead bodies are incapable of reacting – that is, physically dead bodies. But is this what Scripture is talking about here?

Let us start with the claim that the human incapacity to respond results from the sin that Adam introduced into the world. Since Adam was the one who committed that sin, he is by definition the paradigm case of what it means to be dead in trespasses and sins.

Some theistic determinists put a confusing gloss on what happened in Eden. They say that, yes, Adam fell into sin by using his freedom, but what they mean by freedom is not what most people typically understand by that term. They mean only the freedom of spontaneity. They hold that Adam was free to do what he wanted to do, but they believe that he was not free to do anything other than he actually chose to do, since he was predestined to disobey God's command.

For instance, Calvin writes:

> *God not only foresaw that Adam would fall, but also ordained that he should… I confess it is a horrible decree; yet no one can deny but God foreknew Adam's fall, and therefore foreknew it, because he had ordained it so by his own decree.*[107]

J. M. Frame writes:

> *the Bible teaches theistic determinism that is "soft" in James' sense. It teaches that human beings sometimes have moral freedom, usually have compatibilist freedom, but never have libertarian freedom.*[108]

107 J. Calvin, *Institutes of the Christian Religion*, III, xxiii, 7.
108 "Determinism, Chance and Freedom" in W. C. Campbell-Jack and G. J. McGrath (eds), *New Dictionary of Christian Apologetics*, Leicester, IVP, 2006, p. 220.

This contradicts the biblical account of what is involved in temptation. Paul writes:

> No temptation has seized you except what is common to man. And God is faithful; he will not let you be tempted beyond what you can bear. But when you are tempted, he will also provide a way out so that you can stand up under it.
>
> (1 Corinthians 10:13.)

It sometimes happens that a believer gives in to temptation. According to this verse, at the time of the temptation a way of escape was available to him. That implies that he could have done other than he did. Thus even a believer has libertarian freedom. The text just cited refers to temptation that is *common to man* and so is the same as is experienced by non-believers.

An example of this is given in the story of Ananias and Sapphira in Acts 5. The context is the distribution of wealth by the early Christians to help those of their number who were needy. It was a spontaneous response to their experience of the power of the gospel. Ananias also responded; however, with the connivance of his wife Sapphira he brought only part of the proceeds of the sale to the apostles, while pretending that it was the whole amount. Peter said to Ananias:

> ... how is it that Satan has so filled your heart that you have lied to the Holy Spirit and have kept for yourself some of the money you received for the land? Didn't it belong to you before it was sold? And after it was sold, wasn't the money at your disposal? What made you think of doing such a thing? You have not lied to men but to God.
>
> (Acts 5:3–4.)

Peter clearly believed that Ananias had libertarian freedom to do other than he did.

In this connection the record of the first human temptation is also very instructive. What actually happened, according to the biblical account, was that the first humans disobeyed God by taking and eating the forbidden fruit. At once they experienced a sense of shame, unease, and alienation from God that impelled them to hide from him. To get around the obvious question as to what God meant by commanding Adam not to eat of the tree of the knowledge of good and evil, some take recourse to the exotic notion that God has two wills: his so-called "prescriptive will", by which he says to Adam that he should not eat; and his "decretive will", by which he has determined that Adam should eat the fruit. However, the second makes the first completely disingenuous and unreal, and negates any form of true freedom. And with freedom goes responsibility. Once more, excessive extrapolation of the biblical teaching on predestination leads, not to paradox, but to patent contradiction, both logical and moral. How can God, whose love and justice are impeccable, hold guilty those who were incapable of doing what he commanded them to do?

This kind of contradiction can make it difficult to understand what people really believe. For instance, in a book authored by fourteen people from the Reformed tradition, we read:

> *God created Adam upright. He possessed what we might call original righteousness. This was a probationary period in which Adam and Eve were exposed to temptation and capitulated to it. It was possible for them not to sin, and it was also possible for them to sin. God gave to man the power of contrary choice. Man of his own will, by no external compulsion or determination, used that power in the commission of sin. There was no necessity arising from his physical condition, nor from his moral nature, nor from the nature of his environment, why he should sin. It was a free movement within man's spirit.*[109]

---

109 Reddit Andrews III, in D. A. Carson and T. Keller (eds), *The Gospel as Center*, Wheaton, Crossway, 2011, pp. 10–11.

This sounds unexceptionable. But two short paragraphs after it we read this:

> God sovereignly decreed that sin would enter the world, and
> Adam was responsible for freely sinning.

Apart from the flat self-contradiction within this sentence, it negates the preceding paragraph. How can Adam's acting "by no external compulsion or determination" be squared with God's sovereign decree that Adam should sin? In addition, the statement "God gave to man the power of contrary choice" contradicts a prior comment by one of the editors of this book, where he says that he aligns himself with those

> who do not hold that human freedom, as power to contrary, is
> logically defensible in light of divine sovereignty.[110]

This inconsistency does not make it easy to understand what is going on. Of course, it may well represent a change of mind, in which case it would be helpful to read the reasons behind it.

It should be noted that these statements just quoted (apart from the last) appear in a book that is written against the following background claim:

> Important aspects of Christianity are in danger of being
> muddied or lost as relativism takes root in our churches today.
> What was historically agreed upon is now readily questioned
> and the very essentials of the Christian faith are in jeopardy.
> It's time to reclaim the core of our beliefs.

If "what was historically agreed" refers to the central claims of the New Testament regarding the person and work of Christ, and the authenticity of the Scriptures, then I support the authors' desire to combat this trend wherever found. However, if "what was historically

---

110 D. A. Carson, *Divine Sovereignty and Human Responsibility: Biblical Perspectives in Tension*, Grand Rapids, Baker, 1994, pp. 208–209.

agreed" refers to times subsequent to the New Testament, and includes theological determinism, then it needs to be questioned, because it is a real issue as to whether it does or does not belong to the core of Christian belief.

Another example of shrouding the issues in impenetrable mists of secret and mystery appears in a well-known work on God's sovereignty by A. W. Pink:

> *That God had decreed sin should enter this world through the disobedience of our first parents was a secret hid in His own mind. Of this Adam knew nothing, and that made all the difference so far as his responsibility was concerned... Though nothing contrary to holiness and righteousness can ever come from God, yet He has for His own wise ends, ordained His creatures to fall into sin... God never tempts man to sin, but he has by His eternal counsels (which He is now executing)* **determined its course...** *though God has decreed man's sins, yet is man responsible not to commit and is to blame because he does.*[111]

It is hard to know how to react to this kind of convoluted and self-contradictory language.

William Lane Craig says:

> *There's nothing wrong with mystery per se... the problem is that some Reformed theologians... try to resolve the mystery by holding to universal, divine, causal determinism and a compatibilist view of human freedom. According to this view, the way in which God sovereignly controls everything that happens is by causing it to happen, and freedom is reinterpreted to be consistent with being causally determined by factors outside oneself. It is this view, which affirms universal determinism and compatibilism, that runs into... problems.*

---

111 A. W. Pink, *The Sovereignty of God*, Newberry, Bridge Logos, 2008, pp. 351–54.

Making God the author of evil is just one of the problems this neo-Reformed view faces.[112]

But back to the Genesis account. Upon eating the fruit of the tree of the knowledge of good and evil, Adam and Eve did not die physically at once. They would eventually die physically, but physical death is the lowest form of death, corresponding to the lowest or first level of life, physical life. The Genesis narrative makes it clear that the highest level of life is a relationship with God involving moral obedience to his word. When they disobeyed they died in the profoundest sense – they died spiritually, such that their relationship with God was broken. Eventually, in consequence of this breach, other forms of "death" would follow in all of those spheres that gave life its meaning – the "deaths" of morality, of the life of the mind, of work, of the family, of aesthetics… and eventually physical death.

Adam and Eve were now dead in trespasses and sins, and we need to look carefully at the text of Genesis to see what faculties they still possessed. The immediate result of their transgression was that *the eyes of both of them were opened, and they realised that they were naked* (Genesis 3:7). From this we can conclude that they were not simply physically alive, they were conscious – they were alive mentally. They at once attempt to cover up their nakedness by stitching fig leaves together. From this we see that they were morally alive – they were experiencing guilt.

They then hear the sound of the Lord God and they hide themselves. Yet God does not leave them to their own devices. In his grace God takes the initiative, calls to Adam and says: *Where are you?* (Genesis 3:9). According to Argument 2, Adam should not have been able to hear God's voice and respond to him. Yet he could and did respond. He was perfectly able to hear and react to God's voice and enter into conversation with him. Adam says: *I heard you in the garden, and I was afraid because I was naked; so I hid* (Genesis 3:10). Here we see that Adam, though "dead in sins", could hear God's voice and could run away from it through guilt-driven fear.

112 www.reasonablefaith.org/molinism-vs-calvinism#ixzz3Q63gy7HU

God asks him if he has eaten of the forbidden tree, and he replies by blaming Eve. So he was not morally dead. No man who blames his wife is morally dead!

In order to avoid the obvious implications of this, some suggest that the unregenerate can register the words that are being said in the gospel but they cannot hear at a depth that is necessary for salvation (distinguishing the "general" call and the "effectual" call). This is just not good enough. Adam heard God's voice at the deepest level of his being. It shook him into reality and led to his admission of guilt.

The deterministic idea held by some, that Adam's sin was caused by God's decree, and therefore Adam could not have done otherwise, is grotesque. Morality would thereby be emptied of all coherent meaning, and the problem of evil would cease to exist (because we could simply blame God for everything). We have seen that Calvin calls his deterministic view "horrible", but if his view were true, a moral concept would have no meaning.

Adam was certainly dead as a result of his trespass – spiritually dead. Yet he was capable of responding to God's word. God then graciously provided salvation in the form of garments for them to cover their sense of shame. Thus, whatever damage Adam and Eve sustained as a result of their sin, and whatever concomitant damage was sustained by the world through them, they still retained a real capacity to respond to God.

In light of all of this, the term "totally depraved" seems a very strange phrase to use for the human post-Fall state. Indeed, according to the dictionary, the word "depraved" on its own means perverted, debased, or corrupt; so to add the adverb "totally" to it is even worse. Having just seen what happened with Adam and Eve, it seems a singularly inappropriate and misleading theological term to describe their state.

C.S. Lewis warns of the dangers lurking in such thinking:

Or could one seriously introduce the idea of a bad God, as it were by the back door, through a sort of extreme Calvinism? You could say that we are fallen and depraved. We are so depraved that our ideas of goodness count for nothing; or worse than nothing – the very fact that we think something good is presumptive evidence that it is really bad. Now God has in fact – our worst fears are true – all the characteristics we regard as bad: unreasonableness, vanity, vindictiveness, injustice, cruelty. But all these blacks (as they seem to us) are really whites. It's only our depravity that makes them look black to us...

Finally, if reality at its root is so meaningless to us – or, putting it the other way round, if we are such total imbeciles – what is the point of trying to think either about God or about anything else? This knot comes undone when you try to pull it tight.[113]

The Genesis account shows why.

The flaw in the argument

It should now be apparent where Argument 2 goes wrong. Its premise is flawed, since it uses the analogy of a *physically dead body* – the very thing that is *not the case in the biblical account*. This is a classic case of theological misinterpretation arising from the use of an unbiblical and, in fact, irrelevant analogy.

One sad consequence of this is that Argument 2 is sometimes taken to the extreme that C.S. Lewis represented – that there is no point in reasoning, discussing, or even preaching to the unregenerate, since they are dead and cannot hear. Christ and his apostles emphatically show where they stand on that matter by their constant appealing, reasoning, discussing, and preaching to the unregenerate (as did Luther and Calvin and many who follow them).

Boettner uses the term "total inability" rather than "total depravity". That may sound less offensive, but the adjective "total" once more conveys the impression that, after the entry of sin into

---

113 C.S. Lewis, *A Grief Observed*, New York, Bantam, 1976, p. 38.

the world, human beings became incapable of doing anything.[114] We have seen that this is false, but it is important to add that there are certain very important things of which human beings are incapable – the major one being that they are incapable of saving themselves.

The second part of Argument 2 is that, in order for someone who is dead in trespasses and sins to be able to respond, they must first receive new life (they must be *born again*, John 3:3). After all, it would be absurd to ask a dead dog to look at you or come to heel. In order to react, the dog needs life. Similarly, so the argument runs, since people who are dead in trespasses and sins cannot react, God regenerates them by his Spirit without any action on their part. Only then are they able to believe in Christ. Thus regeneration precedes faith.

We have just seen that this argument is wrong because it is based on an unbiblical analogy involving *physical death*, and we therefore have no warrant whatsoever to reverse the explicit order that is stated many times in Scripture.

This point is so important that we illustrate it by considering R. C. Sproul's argument for the contrary. Sproul proceeds by emphasising the scriptural fact that all human beings are dead in trespasses and sins. They are, in his words, "spiritually dead". He then cites analogies that he has heard used by evangelists to communicate the gospel. One of these concerns a drowning man who is utterly helpless and about to go down for the third time, when someone throws him a lifeline. The man reaches out, grasps the lifeline, and is saved. Sproul admits that the illustration takes seriously the utter helplessness of sinful man to save himself, but he rejects it nonetheless:

> *The drowning man is in a serious condition. He cannot save himself. However he is still alive; he can still stretch out his fingers. His fingers are the crucial link in salvation. His eternal destiny depends on what he does with his fingers. Paul says the*

---

114 L. Boettner, *The Reformed Doctrine of Predestination*, Phillipsburg, P & R Publishing, 1971.

man is dead. He is not merely drowning, he has already sunk to the bottom of the sea. It is futile to throw a life-preserver to a man who has already drowned.[115]

The problem with this is that, although Sproul correctly claims that all men are spiritually dead, and although he knows that spiritual death and physical death are not the same, he is, perhaps unwittingly, suggesting that Paul says the man is as good as *physically dead*. This is precisely what is not true in the biblical situation, as we have seen from Genesis. We could equally well have seen it in the very context where the phrase "dead in trespasses and sins" occurs. Just look at the wider context:

> *And you were dead in the trespasses and sins in which you once* **walked**, *following the course of this world,* **following** *the prince of the power of the air, the spirit that is now at work in the sons of disobedience – among whom we all once* **lived** *in the passions of our flesh,* **carrying out** *the desires of the body and the mind, and were by nature children of wrath, like the rest of mankind.*
>
> (Ephesians 2:1–3 ESV.)

I have highlighted the words indicating that those dead in trespasses and sins were far from physically or mentally or morally dead – they were extremely active in all kind of directions. Sproul's argument is invalid.

Furthermore, the original analogy of the drowning man is meant to illustrate human helplessness and the fact that salvation is all of God. To say with Sproul that the man's eternal destiny depends on what he does with his fingers is misleading. Nothing he did with his fingers could merit the salvation he is offered by the throwing of the lifeline. However, it is clear that he can reject the salvation by pushing the lifeline away. His fingers were not of his own creation,

115 R. C. Sproul, *Classic Teachings on the Nature of God*, Peabody, Hendrickson, 2010, p. 221.

they are part of the gift of God to him as a human being. It is his responsibility to use them.

Tim Keller's example is better:

> *Faith is simply the attitude of coming to God with empty hands. When a child asks his mother for something he needs, trusting that she will give it, his asking does not merit anything. It is merely the way he receives his mother's generosity.*[116]

Quite so. The child is *doing* something (showing its faith in its mother), but it is not *meriting* anything. Free will is that gift of God that gives us the capacity to come to God with empty hands.

Returning to the biblical teaching on salvation, let us say it once more: we cannot merit salvation, it is all of God. But when God has offered that salvation as a free gift, we can receive it or reject it. Since we are finally to be judged on the basis of whether we believed or not, it shows that, although we are *dead in trespasses and sins*, we still possess the capacity to accept or reject what God offers. This is a matter of basic morality.

The serpent lifted up

Christ himself gives us a biblical analogy to help us understand the point clearly. Jesus said to Nicodemus:

> *Just as Moses lifted up the snake in the desert, so the Son of Man must be lifted up, that everyone who believes in him may have eternal life.*
>
> (John 3:14.)

The background is Numbers 21 where Israel, on their way to the promised land through desert terrain, became impatient and spoke against God and against Moses. The result was that God sent snakes

---

116 T. Keller, *Romans 1–7 for You*, Epsom, Good Book Company, 2014, p. 81.

among them, causing many to die. The people then repented and asked Moses to pray to God to remove the threat. This was God's response:

> Make a snake and put it up on a pole; anyone who is bitten can look at it and live.

Moses did precisely that, with the result that when anyone was bitten by a snake and looked at the bronze snake, he lived (Numbers 21:8–9).

We notice the twice-repeated order of events: first look and then live. Now Jesus makes the application:

> Just as Moses lifted up the snake in the desert, so the Son of Man must be lifted up, that…

What follows? According to Argument 2 it should read, "… whoever has eternal life may now believe". But it doesn't. It reads:

> … everyone who believes in him may have eternal life.
> (John 3:14.)

One day Jesus would be lifted up like that serpent, and if people looked to him they would live. First look, then live. The reverse would make no sense. There would be no point in looking if they already had new life. Therefore, this biblical analogy reinforces what John says: faith (looking) precedes regeneration (living). Furthermore, by looking, the smitten people were neither contributing to their salvation nor meriting it in any way. They were simply doing what God told them to do, in order to receive a salvation that they could never have engineered or merited for themselves.

In light of this, insistence on reversing the order and treating our Lord's statement as if it read, "whoever is regenerate believes in him" is entirely without warrant. Indeed, I find it hard to imagine how serious theologians can imagine that they are at liberty to do this kind of thing with the word of God. It would seem that very powerful, non-biblical presuppositions must be at work in what is a classic example of paradigm pressure. Surely, as a principle, it makes far more sense to start with what Scripture actually says rather than with unbiblical interpretative analogies?

Putting this another way, Scripture says two things:

1.   Whoever believes in him has eternal life.

2.   Human beings are dead in trespasses and sins.

The problem here is that a certain interpretation of the second phrase clashes with what the first actually says. One would expect that those with a high view of the authority and inspiration of Scripture would at once question the validity of their interpretation of the second phrase. After all, it is one thing to interpret Scripture, it is entirely another to rewrite it and thus to undermine its authority.

The aged Abraham

There is a further biblical analogy given to us by Paul in order to help us understand what faith means, and this analogy does involve a physical body – if not a dead one, then certainly one too old and decrepit to generate new physical life. It is the story of Abraham:

> *That is why it depends on faith, in order that the promise*
> *may rest on grace and be guaranteed to all his offspring –*
> *not only to the adherent of the law but also to the one who*
> *shares the faith of Abraham, who is the father of us all, as it*
> *is written, "I have made you the father of many nations" – in*
> *the presence of the God in whom he believed, who gives life to*
> *the dead and calls into existence the things that do not exist.*
> *In hope he believed against hope, that he should become the*
> *father of many nations, as he had been told, "So shall your*
> *offspring be." He did not weaken in faith when he considered*
> *his own body, which was as good as dead (since he was about*
> *a hundred years old), or when he considered the barrenness*
> *of Sarah's womb. No distrust made him waver concerning*
> *the promise of God, but he grew strong in his faith as he gave*

glory to God, fully convinced that God was able to do what he had promised. That is why his faith was "counted to him as righteousness". But the words "it was counted to him" were not written for his sake alone, but for ours also. It will be counted to us who believe in him who raised from the dead Jesus our Lord, who was delivered up for our trespasses and raised for our justification.

(Romans 4:16–25 ESV.)

So far as the prospect of children was concerned, both Abraham's body and Sarah's were *as good as dead*. Yet God had promised them a child from those dead bodies. The challenge for Abraham was whether or not he would believe what God had said regarding a child. Could he believe that God had the power to "regenerate" him. Abraham believed God and his faith was counted as righteousness. Note that God did not first regenerate Abraham's body, leading to his faith. It was the other way round. But note also that neither did Abraham's faith regenerate his body – that was impossible and Abraham knew it. God did the regenerating in response to Abraham's faith. At the spiritual level, as Paul points out, it is exactly the same for us.

CHAPTER 9

Drawn by the Father and Coming to Christ

John's Gospel provides us with even more ways to help us understand what it means to believe in Christ. He uses the metaphor of hearing to illuminate what it means to believe in Christ. Jesus said:

> *I tell you the truth, a time is coming and has now come when the dead will hear the voice of the Son of God and those who hear will live.*
>
> (John 5:25.)

Note once more the order. The text does not say that those who live will hear, but that those who hear will live. This is completely consistent with the fact that the spiritually dead Adam could hear the voice of God. Hearing and believing come together:

> *I tell you the truth, whoever hears my word and believes him who sent me has eternal life…*
>
> (John 5:24.)

Once again the order is crystal clear: hearing and believing are the conditions on which eternal life is given.

Later in that same chapter John adds the metaphor of coming to as a way of helping us grasp what believing means. Jesus says to the Jewish authorities:

> *… you refuse to come to me to have life.*
>
> (John 5:40.)

Note once more that coming precedes the reception of life. Jesus did not say, "You refuse to have life so that you can come to me." Note also that the word translated *refuse* means "will not" and refers to a deliberate action of the human will. The implication is that they were capable of coming, if only they willed to do so.

John 6 is universally regarded as a key chapter in connection with the debate about determinism, and in it there is further detailed discussion of what coming to Christ involves. Christ miraculously feeds five thousand, withdraws, and crosses the Lake of Galilee. He is followed by large crowds and expresses suspicion of their motives:

> *Jesus answered, "I tell you the truth, you are looking for me, not because you saw miraculous signs but because you ate the loaves and had your fill. Do not work for food that spoils, but for food that endures to eternal life, which the Son of Man will give you. On him God the Father has placed his seal of approval."*
>
> *Then they asked him, "What must we do to do the works God requires?"*
>
> *Jesus answered, "The work of God is this: to believe in the one he has sent."*

> (John 6:26–29.)

Jesus points them away from physical bread to a spiritual source of eternal life, and tells them to "work for it". On their enquiring what that means he replies that the work of God is to believe in the one he has sent. They profess to be interested in doing what God requires. What God requires is that they believe in Christ.

This provokes the crowd to challenge him to do a sign – even though they had already seen the spectacular miracle of the feeding of a large crowd.

> *So they asked him, "What miraculous sign then will you give that we may see it and believe you? What will you do? Our forefathers ate the manna in the desert; as it is written: 'He gave them bread from heaven to eat.'*

> *Jesus said to them, "I tell you the truth, it is not Moses who has given you the bread from heaven, but it is my Father who gives you the true bread from heaven. For the bread of God is he who comes down from heaven and gives life to the world."*
>
> *"Sir," they said, "from now on give us this bread."*
>
> (John 6:30–34.)

Jesus is quick to correct their mistake: *it is not Moses… but my Father.* He is the Father's Son, and the major emphasis in the discourse that follows is to get his listeners to make the connection between him and his Father, God – the God in whom they professed belief. That connection is profound – it is the key to understanding and receiving salvation. Christ is the bread that is given by the Father for the life of the world.

His audience professes to want the bread of God. Now Jesus explains how they can possess it.

> *Then Jesus declared, "I am the bread of life. He who comes to me will never go hungry, and he who believes in me will never be thirsty."*
>
> (John 6:35.)

In order to have their hunger and thirst for life assuaged, they must come to him, they must believe in him. The two terms *come* and *believe* are clearly synonymous. Yet there is a problem:

> *But as I told you, you have seen me and still you do not believe.*
>
> (John 6:36.)

The sad thing is that they have seen Jesus; they have seen his wonderful acts; indeed, they have been fed by his supernatural power. And in spite of all that, many still did not believe. He is clearly suggesting to them that they have had enough evidence on which to base the step of faith in him.

What of those who do come? Jesus says:

All that the Father gives me will come to me, and whoever comes to me I will never drive away. For I have come down from heaven not to do my will but to do the will of him who sent me. And this is the will of him who sent me, that I shall lose none of all that he has given me, but raise them up at the last day. For my Father's will is that everyone who looks to the Son and believes in him shall have eternal life, and I will raise him up at the last day.

(John 6:37–40.)

How are we to understand this? Does this mean that their failure to come to Jesus is explained by their not having been chosen by the Father, with the implication that unless the Father decides to do so they will never come? Such an interpretation of the phrase taken on its own is superficially plausible. However, if such is the case, then what we read in the previous chapter of John seems disingenuous. There Jesus said:

… you refuse to come to me to have life.

(John 5:40.)

Whatever it means to be "given by the Father", we cannot argue that it eliminates human responsibility, since such responsibility is exactly what Christ affirms three sentences later. And, as we have seen, it is not good enough simply to assert that humans are responsible, not if we then proceed to portray God as holding people responsible for something they did not have the power to do.

The statement, *Whoever comes to me I will never drive away,* is a direct guarantee from the Lord Jesus that he will never cast out anyone who comes to him. That is, our assurance lies first of all in the authority of the word of Christ. Humanity went wrong because the first humans disobeyed the word of God, and we have seen that the way back to God involves learning to reverse that attitude and coming to trust him and what he has done for our salvation. On the authority of Christ's word, then, we can know that if we have come to him, he will never drive us away.

Some sensitive people, more aware than others, perhaps, of their own weaknesses and failures, sometimes react by saying. "Yes – I can understand and accept that Jesus will never drive me away or cast me out. But I am a weak person and I don't know what is round the corner. How can I know that I will not myself choose to wander away from Jesus' care? Am I not free to wander away? So yes, he will not drive me away; but if I go it will be my fault entirely." This view is common among Christians who think that human freedom must include the possibility that a believer may walk away from Christ and so lose their salvation. Inevitably they lack assurance of salvation.

We shall look at this extensively in our last chapter, but for now we note how Jesus himself addresses this concern. To avoid this misinterpretation Jesus now claims once more that he has come down from heaven; but this time he says that it is not to do his own will but the will of the Father who sent him. He then explains what that will is – that he should *lose none of all that* the Father *has given* him.

An analogy may help. Suppose a shepherd asks me to look after his sheep for an hour with the instruction, "Please don't drive away any sheep that comes to you." He comes back and finds me alone.

"What has happened?" he says.

"Well, I did what you said. I didn't drive any sheep away – they went on their own." It would be an entirely different matter if the shepherd had said, "Don't lose any sheep that comes to you." And that is precisely what the Father has said to Jesus, the Good Shepherd.

This passage is therefore a source of great assurance for the believer. It teaches us not only that Christ will never cast out anyone who comes to him, but also that he explicitly commits himself to losing none of those whom the Father has given him. He will raise them from the dead. In other words, he will keep them eternally, because it is inconceivable that he should fail to do the will of his Father. The believer can be utterly confident not only in the love of God in Christ, but also in the provision made by the sovereign will of the Father for the Son.

This is so important that it is stressed in two parallel statements:

And this is the will of him who sent me, that I shall lose none of all that he has given me, but raise them up at the last day.

For my Father's will is that everyone who looks to the Son and believes in him shall have eternal life, and I will raise him up at the last day.

(John 6:39–40.)

The double reference to the Father's will suggests that the second statement explains the first. The emphasis in the first is on the Father's giving, and in the second on human responsibility to look and believe. That is, those whom the Father has given him are precisely those who have looked to the Son and believed in him. The giving is not an arbitrary act of divine determinism. God is determined that those who come, look, and believe will never be lost.

John later gives us a further example of people being given by the Father to the Son:

I have revealed your name to those whom you gave me out of the world. They were yours; you gave them to me and they have obeyed your word. Now they know that everything you have given me comes from you. For I have gave them the words you gave me and they accepted them. They knew with certainty that I came from you, and they believed that you sent me.

(John 17:6–8.)

The context is that Jesus is speaking to his Father about his disciples, and so the expression *they were yours* (not "yours they are") means that they had been true and genuine Jewish believers in God. A whole host of such people is named in the New Testament – Zechariah, Elizabeth, John the Baptist, Anna, Simeon, the disciples, and so on. *You gave them to me* involved them coming historically to believe in Jesus as the Son of God – a momentous transition for an orthodox

Jew. John tells us how it happened. God took the initiative and sent his Son into the world, and he revealed God's name to them. They came to believe as a result of him giving them the very words that the Father had given him. He then goes on to say that he has kept them and not lost one of them, except Judas (whom we shall consider in Chapter 18).

Once more we observe that the statement *you gave them to me* does not override the responsibility of the individuals involved actively to receive Christ's words and believe in him. We are much more familiar with the idea of someone giving something to another, like a birthday present, rather than a person being given by one person to another. However, there is one ceremony where this is precisely what is done, when, in some traditions, the father of the bride gives his daughter to the bridegroom at a wedding. This recognises that there is a sense in which she belongs to her father; she is her father's daughter. Now she is being given to the bridegroom. Of course, there are arranged weddings where this giving has a strong deterministic element in it, since the bride has no say in the matter. However, most weddings that occur in the West are not arranged by the parents but by the mutual free decisions of the bride and groom. I would not wish to push this analogy but merely mention it to indicate that even at the human level matters are not as simple as we might imagine.

A universal offer of salvation

There is more to be said about John 6. Jesus' claims about doing the will of the Father result in his audience becoming restive and giving vent to what is really on their mind:

> At this the Jews began to grumble about him because he said, "I am the bread that came down from heaven." They said, "Is this not Jesus, the son of Joseph, whose father and mother we know? How can he now say, 'I came down from heaven'?"
>
> "Stop grumbling among yourselves," Jesus answered. "No-one can come to me unless the Father who sent me draws

him, and I will raise him up at the last day. It is written in the Prophets: 'They will all be taught by God.' Everyone who listens to the Father and learns from him comes to me. No-one has seen the Father except the one who is from God; only he has seen the Father. I tell you the truth, he who believes has everlasting life. I am the bread of life."

(John 6:41–48.)

Instead of facing the mounting evidence before them pointing to Jesus' deity, they argue about his origin. Jesus tells them to stop grumbling and continues to explain what is involved in coming to him. He now uses a new metaphor – not that of the Father giving, but that of the Father drawing people. The key idea is that, in order for someone to come to Christ, the Father must draw him. Once more the emphasis is on God taking the initiative in salvation. But, as before, no deterministic inference should be drawn, since Jesus goes on to explain how such drawing is evidenced – listening to the Father and learning from him. And that is precisely what many in his audience were failing to do. They were not really listening to him. But he had spoken; he had taken the initiative in speaking to them. Indeed, Jesus cites the prophets to say, *They will all be taught by God.* There is no exclusivism here. The teaching is open and accessible to *all*.

However, some theologians ascribe to the term "draw" a compelling, if not coercive, dimension. That is, they regard the drawing as irresistible (the I of TULIP). But this cannot be, for Christ uses the same term later in John's Gospel in this way:

… I, when I am lifted up from the earth, will draw all men to myself.

(John 12:32.)

If the drawing is compelling and irresistible, this would mean that all would be saved, which is not the case. A more reasonable understanding of the situation is that, on the one hand, no one comes to Christ unless the Father draws him (God always takes the initiative in salvation), but on the other hand his drawing is accessible to all who are willing to listen, learn, and trust. (We should also note that there is no suggestion that those who have not yet been drawn by the Father are necessarily permanently barred from salvation. They can still be drawn to him if they are prepared to listen and learn.)

This understanding of accessibility to all is reinforced by Paul:

> I urge, then, first of all, that requests, prayers, intercession
> and thanksgiving be made for everyone – for kings and all
> those in authority, that we may live peaceful and quiet lives
> in all godliness and holiness. This is good, and pleases God
> our Saviour, who wants all men to be saved and to come to a
> knowledge of the truth. For there is one God and one mediator
> between God and men, the man Christ Jesus, who gave himself
> as a ransom for all men – the testimony given in its proper
> time. And for this purpose I was appointed a herald and an
> apostle – I am telling the truth, I am not lying – and a teacher
> of the true faith to the Gentiles.
>
> (1 Timothy 2:1–7.)

This is an unequivocal statement that God's desire is that all might be saved. Some seek to mitigate the force of this statement by altering it to mean all kinds of men rather than all individual men. But this has no warrant. The emphasis is repeated in the next sentence, that Jesus has given himself as a ransom for all. Paul rams it home very unusually by saying that he is not lying but telling the truth. We have no liberty to interpret this as saying anything else: Christ has made provision for all, and this is the public confirmation of God's will that all should be saved.

This also resonates completely with several other texts. For instance, Peter says:

> The Lord is not slow in keeping his promise, as some
> understand slowness. He is patient with you, not wanting
> anyone to perish, but everyone to come to repentance.
>
> (2 Peter 3:9.)

John tells us that Jesus was *the true light that gives light to every man* (1:9); that Jesus is *the Lamb of God, that takes away the sin of the world* (John 1:29); and that *God so loved the world that... whoever believes him shall not perish* (John 3:16).

Of John 1:29 Luther wrote:

> *You may say: "who knows whether Christ also bore my sin?"... Don't you hear what St. John says in our text: This is the Lamb of God who takes away the sin of the world? And you cannot deny that you are also a part of this world for you were born of a man and a woman. You are not a cow or a pig. It follows that your sins must be included as well as the sins of St. Peter or St. Paul... Don't you hear? There is nothing missing from the Lamb. He bears all the sins of the world from its inception; this implies that He also bears yours, and offers you grace.*[117]

And what could be clearer than John's magnificent statement in his first letter?

> *He is the propitiation for our sins, and not for ours only but also for the sins of the whole world.*
>
> (1 John 2:2 ESV.)

Luther's comment on this verse is noteworthy:

> *The offering was for the sins of the whole world, even though the whole world does not believe.*[118]

Reinforcing that we could also mention:

---

117 J. J. Pelikan (ed.), *Luther's Works*, vol. 22, St Louis Concordia: 1957, 22:169.
118 *Ibid.*, 26:38.

We know that we are from God, and the whole world lies in
the power of the evil one.

(1 John 5.19 ESV.)

That is, none of these statements imply that all will be saved, but that
the offer of salvation is there for all – and not just for a special class
chosen by God without reference to their faith. This is one of the
basic motivations for preaching the gospel. Without it no evangelist
could honestly say to his hearers: "Christ died for your sins."

Indeed, evidence is given to all: a point that is crucial at the
beginning of the Paul's letter to the Romans in establishing that all
are guilty. Paul explains:

For since the creation of the world God's invisible qualities –
his eternal power and divine nature – have been clearly seen,
being understood from what has been made, so that men are
without excuse.

(Romans 1:20.)

As we have seen, the evidence comes not only from creation but also
from conscience. God has placed his moral law on the human heart,
and our attempts to accuse one another and excuse ourselves are also
evidence that constitutes us as guilty sinners (Romans 2:1–16).

All of this invalidates the L of TULIP – "limited atonement" –
the view that Christ did not actually die for all but only for the "elect".
In fact, not only Luther but many of the other reformers, including
Calvin, did not subscribe to limited atonement. For an interesting
historical survey that points out that this view of the atonement
was not even introduced until the second or third generation of
Reformers, see David Allen's book, *Whosoever Will*.[119]

It is a serious matter to deny the plain teaching of Scripture in
the interests of maintaining a theological paradigm, or to try to get
round it by special pleading that Christ's death brings some kind of
non-specific temporal benefit to all, or that God has different kinds

---

119 D. Allen, *Whosoever Will*, Nashville, B & H Academic, 2010, pp. 67ff.

of love for the elect and non-elect. To say to people, as some do, that Christ died for them in some vague unexplained sense, rather than telling them that Christ died for their sins and that they may be saved by trusting him, is not only insulting to the intelligence, it is insulting to the message of the cross.

At this point we return to pick up the argument of John 6. Let us remind ourselves once more of the point we had reached. Jesus is speaking.

> It is written in the Prophets: "They will all be taught by God." Everyone who listens to the Father and learns from him comes to me. No-one has seen the Father except the one who is from God; only he has seen the Father. I tell you the truth, he who believes has everlasting life. I am the bread of life. Your forefathers ate the manna in the desert, yet they died. But here is the bread that comes down from heaven, which a man may eat and not die. I am the living bread that came down from heaven. If anyone eats of this bread, he will live for ever. This bread is my flesh, which I will give for the life of the world.
>
> (John 6:45–51.)

We have mentioned the universality of the statement, *They will all be taught by God*. Its provenance is also important. Our Lord is here quoting Isaiah 54:13, which is immediately followed by one of the most powerful appeals to people who are hungry and thirsty to come to the Lord for spiritual satisfaction. To such people God says:

> Give ear and come to me… Seek the Lord while he may be found; call on him while he is near; let the wicked forsake his way and the evil man this thoughts. Let him turn to the Lord, and he will have mercy on him, and to our God, for he will freely pardon.
>
> (Isaiah 55:3, 6–7.)

This, then is the way in which the Father draws people to him, by appealing to them to "listen, come, seek, call, and return". It is open to anyone to respond, and if they do, says Jesus, they will come to him and receive eternal life by believing in him.

Yet there were some Jews in the crowd listening to Jesus who did not respond in this way, but lacking in any kind of imagination or willingness to understand began to argue with each other: *How can this man give us his flesh to eat?* (John 6:52). He has just said:

> whoever believes has eternal life
>
> he is the bread of life
>
> if anyone eats this bread he will live for ever
>
> the bread he will give for the life of the world is his flesh.

This makes it completely obvious that "eating this bread" is not to be understood literalistically but metaphorically, as "believing" in him. Indeed, crude literalism is now completely ruled out, as Jesus presses on with his key message:

> *I tell you the truth, unless you can eat the flesh of the Son of Man and drink his blood, you have no life in you.*
>
> (John 6:53.)

Jews were prohibited from eating literal blood; so by introducing blood as well as flesh Jesus was pushing them away from wooden literalism, to get the message that the only way for them to receive the eternal life they professed to desire was by feeding on him – in the sense of believing in him as the Son of God. Jesus further explained:

> *Just as the living Father sent me and I live because of the Father, so the one who feeds on me will live because of me.*
>
> (John 6:57.)

It was clear that there was no sense in which Jesus was literally feeding from the Father – after all, as Jesus has already said, *God is Spirit* (John 4:24). Jesus meant that he lived in humble trust in and dependence on the Father, and that is what his listeners were required to do in order to receive eternal life. We should also note that verse 51 indicates that the giving of the bread of life would involve his death.[120]

Some of his disciples thought it was all too tough:

This is a hard teaching. Who can accept it?

(John 6:60.)

The term "disciples" here is broader than the Twelve. In John 8:31 the Lord explains that only those who continue in his word are truly his disciples. Here were people who were beginning to react against what Jesus said. What they found "hard" about his message is seen from his final reply to them:

"Does this offend you? What if you see the Son of Man ascend to where he was before! The Spirit gives life; the flesh counts for nothing. The words I have spoken to you are spirit and they are life. Yet there are some of you who do not believe." For Jesus had known from the beginning which of them did not believe and who would betray him. He went on to say, "This is why I told you that no-one can come to me unless the Father has enabled him."

(John 6:61–65.)

Firstly, they had already found it hard to accept his claim to have come down from heaven. If they were scandalised by that, what would they make of the ascension when he would bodily ascend to where he was before?

Secondly, they had stumbled at Jesus' metaphorical use of language, and he now plainly told them that such a literalistic approach was useless in this context. They needed to grasp that it was the Spirit that gave life, and that the words that he had spoken were spirit and life.

---

120 For discussion of suggested relationships between this passage and the Lord's Supper, see D. A. Carson, *The Gospel According to John*, Leicester, IVP, 1991, pp. 296–98. Carson's conclusion: "John 6 does not directly speak of the eucharist; it does expose the true meaning of the Lord's supper as clearly as any passage in Scripture."

Thirdly, he informed them directly that the real problem was that some of them did not believe. John then adds in parentheses that Jesus knew from the beginning who those were who did not believe – including the identity of the traitor, Judas.

Fourthly, and finally, Jesus reminded them of the fact that he had earlier told them that no one could come to him unless it was granted to him by his Father.

It was a turning point for many of them:

From this time many of his disciples turned back and no longer followed him.

(John 6:66.)

The question is: how are we to understand it? Perhaps even more importantly, how were they meant to understand it?

Were they to conclude that the reason they did not believe was entirely due to the inscrutable decision of God, entirely unrelated to their attitude and therefore not culpable? Well, as we have seen before, this is certainly a logically possible way of understanding the statement taken on its own, but it would clash head-on with the entire tenor of John's message. If Jesus' audience had understood it that way, they might reasonably have replied: "So that is it, is it? You are telling us, are you, that the reason we don't believe in you is that God has ordained it that way – he has decided we shouldn't become believers and so we do not believe – in fact, cannot believe? So be it then – we don't want to believe anyway. In any case, if that is really true, why have you gone to such lengths to try to persuade us, when such attempts are entirely disingenuous as the matter has already been settled?"

Of course, we do not know what they said, if anything. We are simply told that many of them turned away. That was their decision and their response. We note that John does not say that they all turned away. There may well have been some who understood and believed.

All of this is reason enough to look at our Lord's statement in the entire context of his lengthy discourse.

The audience that Jesus was addressing consisted largely of people who claimed to believe in God. What they found very difficult was establishing the essential link between Jesus and God upon which he insisted – that he was the unique Son of the Father – the Father who had taken the initiative to send Jesus down from heaven to give salvation and life to the world. The crowd had seen unmistakable evidence of God's power in him; they had eaten the loaves and that is why they had followed him. But they were not prepared to draw the deeper conclusion, that it was not only God himself speaking through Jesus, but that Jesus himself was God the Son.

Christ's earlier explanation of their unbelief, to which he here refers, was framed in terms of their failure not to respond to God's voice. Let us recall that statement:

> *No-one can come to me unless the Father who sent me draws him, and I will raise him up at the last day. It is written in the Prophets: "They will all be taught by God." Everyone who listens to the Father and learns from him comes to me.*
>
> (John 6:44–45.)

The initiative was God's; his was the drawing voice, and theirs was the responsibility to listen to him. The conclusion with which our Lord was facing his listeners was that they hadn't listened to God. They had not responded to his drawing power. If they had done so, they would have received Christ.

The chapter concludes with Jesus asking his immediate disciples: *You do not want to leave too, do you?* (verse 67). Peter is swift to reply:

> *Lord, to whom shall we go? You have the words of eternal life. We believe and know that you are the Holy One of God.*
>
> (John 6:68–69.)

But Peter was not quite correct – there was a traitor amongst the Twelve, a sobering fact that Jesus now pointed out. (Note here that the use of the word "chosen" clearly does not refer to salvation.)

Have I not chosen you, the Twelve? Yet one of you is a devil!
(John 6:70.)

The battle would continue.

CHAPTER 10

The Irreversibility of Regeneration

It is convenient to start the discussion of this topic by considering Jesus' claim to be the bread of life, which he makes in the chapter of John's Gospel that we have just been studying.

> *Everyone who listens to the Father and learns from him comes to me. No-one has seen the Father except the one who is from God; only he has seen the Father. I tell you the truth, he who believes has everlasting life. I am the bread of life. Your forefathers ate the manna in the desert, yet they died. But here is the bread that comes down from heaven, which a man may eat and not die. I am the living bread that came down from heaven. If anyone eats of this bread, he will live for ever. This bread is my flesh, which I will give for the life of the world.*
>
> (John 6:45–51.)

Once more there is emphasis on faith as the pre-condition for receiving eternal life (*he who believes has everlasting life*). The passage then goes on to give a further answer to the question we raised above – what is to stop people using their freedom (on the assumption that God does not remove it completely) to opt out of salvation and eventually be lost? Putting this another way, what is to stop people availing themselves of the bread of life but then opting out and eventually dying spiritually?

We might dare to go further: what about heaven? If we retain our free will, what is to stop us using it to opt out of heaven itself?

The answer is that, if that were the case, then the true bread of life would be no better than the manna in the wilderness which, as Jesus reminded his hearers, the fathers ate and died. But the bread of life is not like that: *If anyone eats of this bread, he will live for ever* (verse 51).

For ever means for ever. Genuine regeneration is irreversible – both in this life and in the one to come. This is confirmed by Peter's statement that we have been *born again, not of perishable seed, but of imperishable, through the living and enduring word of God* (1 Peter 1:23). Regeneration is for ever since it results from the implantation of imperishable seed.

Therefore, receiving new life through Christ is not to be thought of as putting us back into the original state of humanity in the Garden of Eden – otherwise what would prevent the whole sorry history of human sin and failure repeating itself in the world to come? No, when we use our gift of freedom to trust Christ for salvation, something irreversible occurs. Indeed, in ordinary experience, we may choose, say, to undergo an irreversible medical procedure without it ever occurring to us that we have somehow curbed our freedom. In the case of regeneration it is its irreversibility that prevents the ruining of heaven by human sin. It is not like the old creation; in fact Scripture tells us that it is a new creation:

> *Therefore, if anyone is in Christ, he is a new creation; the old has gone, the new has come!*
>
> (2 Corinthians 5:17.)

The irreversibility of regeneration is supported by a legal consideration – the fact that the Final Judge has pronounced his verdict. Indeed, in the preceding chapter of John Jesus says:

> *I tell you the truth, whoever hears my word and believes him who sent me has eternal life and will not be condemned; he has crossed over from death to life.*
>
> (John 5:24.)

Regeneration brings with it an irreversible change in our legal standing before God, for the Final Judge says that we shall not come into judgment – that is, we shall never be condemned, we pass (permanently) from death into life. That verdict could not be issued if it were possible to opt out of eternal life at any stage, either in this life or in the one to come.

At the beginning of his Gospel John uses a further synonym for believing – receiving. Speaking of Jesus he says:

> *He came to that which was his own, but his own did not*
> *receive him. Yet to all who received him, to those who believed*
> *in his name, he gave the right to become children of God –*
> *children born not of natural descent, nor of human decision or*
> *a husband's will, but born of God.*

> (John 1:11–13.)

In the old creation we were made creatures of God; in the new we become children of God. Clearly, one does not become what one already was. We note once again that receiving (believing) is the condition for the new birth and not a consequence of it.

John also says here of the new birth that it is not *of human decision*. Some have taken this to mean that the human will is nowhere involved in the process. Surely the emphasis is that it is God who takes the initiative. Regeneration is something only God can do and humans cannot will it into being. But humans can and must receive it – *to all who received him…* The process of reception (or rejection) involves our will, as we have just seen where Jesus says to some of the unbelieving Pharisees, *you refuse to come to me to have life* (John 5:40). The refusal lay with them and not with any determination on God's part to deny them salvation. Therefore, their will was involved in responding to a salvation that God's will had provided.

The same order – faith preceding regeneration – is also laid down in John's key statement of the purpose of his writing, which we cited earlier in another connection. Such is its importance we now refer to it for a second time.

> *Jesus did many other miraculous signs in the presence of the*
> *disciples, which are not recorded in this book. But these are*
> *written that you may believe that Jesus is the Christ, the Son*

of God, and that by believing you may have life in his name.
(John 20:30–31.)

Believing leads to life, and not the reverse. What specifically stimulates the believing here are the signs that Jesus did. There would have been no sense in providing the signs if people were inherently incapable of responding to them.

The fact that human beings have the capacity to believe, and the fact that faith precedes regeneration, are therefore a constant refrain in the Gospel of John. We recall that they underline the fairness and justice of God's judgments, and in particular his condemnation of those who refuse to believe. The final verdict of that judgment will turn on whether a person believed or not:

> *Whoever believes in the Son has eternal life, but whoever rejects the Son will not see life, for God's wrath remains on him.*
> (John 3:36.)

This is a very solemn statement. In light of our argument so far, it is very hard to imagine how it could have been made if men and women did not possess the capacity to believe. Yet, in spite of the wealth of consistent Scriptural evidence that faith is the precondition for regeneration, we still read statements like this:

> *The idea that regeneration comes before saving faith is not always understood by evangelicals today. Sometimes people will even say something like, "If you believe in Christ as your Saviour, then (after you believe) you will be born again.* **But Scripture itself never says anything like that.** *This new birth is viewed by Scripture as something that God does within us to enable us to believe".*[121]

Surely the reason that many evangelicals understand that faith precedes regeneration is precisely because Scripture, not once

---

121 W. Grudem, *Bible Doctrine*, Leicester, IVP, 1999, p. 303. Emphasis mine.

but over and over again, says exactly that. As we have seen, this is especially so in John's Gospel, where we are assured that *God so loved the world that he gave his one and only Son, that whoever believes in him shall not perish...* (John 3.16); it does not say, "whoever has eternal life believes in him." D. A Carson writes:

> *The verb "to believe" is used absolutely (i.e. without an object) elsewhere in John as the condition or ground of eternal life.*[122]

Objections

1. LOGICAL AND TEMPORAL PRIORITY

Sometimes an attempt is made to avoid the consistent sequence – first faith, then regeneration – by saying that, while regeneration and faith are essentially simultaneous, we must distinguish logical priority from temporal priority. For instance, R. C. Sproul writes:

> *Similarly when Reformed theology says regeneration precedes faith, it is speaking in terms of logical priority, not temporal priority. We cannot exercise saving faith until we have been regenerated, so we say faith is dependent on regeneration, not regeneration on faith.*[123]

However, his phrase "we cannot exercise faith until" shows that he is thinking of temporal order; so his statement about logical priority does not appear to make sense. And then consider these verses in John's Gospel:

---

122 D. A. Carson, *The Gospel According to John*, Leicester, IVP, 1991, p. 202.
123 R. C. Sproul, *Grace Unknown: The Heart of Reformed Theology*, Grand Rapids, Baker, 2000, p. 195. Calling this "Reformed doctrine" does not fit with my experience. There are many people who would describe their theology as "Reformed" but who do not subscribe to the view that regeneration precedes faith. Yet another example of the misleading effect of labels?

Yet to all who received him, to those who believed in his name,
he gave the right to become children of God.

(John 1:12.)

... yet you refuse to come to me to have life.

(John 5:40.)

These involve a temporal priority that is simultaneously logical. According to our Lord, believing, looking, hearing, coming, all precede regeneration, both in the logical and the temporal sense, because the logical priority is temporal. Faith is both a logical and a temporal precondition for regeneration.

2. REGENERATION AND BIRTH

Sometimes the suggestion is made that, just as in the physical realm there is a difference between the generation of life (of which we are completely unconscious) and birth (of which we are conscious); so in the spiritual realm God begets us by his Spirit (we are unaware of it) and then some time later we are brought to birth (we consciously repent and believe).

However, this cannot be the case, since once more it reverses the biblical order of belief first and then regeneration. When Paul is writing to the Corinthian Christians he describes himself as their spiritual father: *in Jesus Christ I became your father through the gospel* (1 Corinthians 4:15). That is, Paul preached the gospel to them, they responded and were regenerate. Peter describes the same thing when he writes,

For you have been born again, not of perishable seed, but of
imperishable, through the living and enduring word of God...
And this is the word that was preached to you.

(1 Peter 1:23, 25.)

Since Martin Luther was one of the leading Reformers it is worth citing him on this matter. In his commentary on Galatians he wrote:

Paul as a true apostle of faith always has the word "faith" on the tip of his tongue. By faith, says he, we are the children of God. The Law cannot beget children of God. It cannot regenerate us. It can only remind us of the old birth by which we were born into the kingdom of the devil. The best the Law can do for us is to prepare us for a new birth through faith in Christ Jesus. Faith in Christ regenerates us into the children of God. St. John bears witness to this in his Gospel: "As many as received him, to them gave he power to become the sons of God, even to them that believe on his name" (John 1:12).[124]

There is scarcely any clearer statement of the order of salvation (ordo salutis) than this one. Also, whereas John Calvin states in his commentary on 1 John 5:1 that "no one can have faith, except he is born of God," he also begins his commentary on that passage saying that "God regenerates us by faith." Sometimes it is hard to tell exactly what some people believe!

Argument 3: Original sin

Although some writers in this field are convinced that human beings are incapable of believing in God, they hold that it is nevertheless people's fault that they cannot believe, so God may justly condemn them.

It is claimed that this has to do with their involvement with Adam, who brought sin into the world. What we have already said regarding Argument 2 makes this look very implausible.

However, out of fairness to those who advance it, we should consider some of the issues it raises. The argument is expressed by Phillip Johnson as follows:

… man's own inability is something he is guilty for, and that inability cannot therefore be seen as something that relieves the sinner of responsibility.[125]

---

124 M. Luther, *Commentary on the Epistle to the Galatians*, new abridged translation by T. Graebner, Milton Keynes, Authentic Media, 2012, Galatians 3:26 (online version).
125 P. R. Johnson, "A Primer on Hyper-Calvinism", romans45.org/articles/hypercal.htm

That guilt, according to Johnson's argument, is something that all human beings are born with; and it was their own fault that they were born with it. The reason for that is that they were "in Adam" when he sinned. Adam is the federal head of humanity, and so when he sinned they sinned. (Adam's sin is sometimes said to be "imputed to them".) They are therefore blameworthy for their inability to respond to God.

This argument is based on Romans 5:

> *Therefore, just as sin came into the world through one man,*
> *and death through sin, and so death spread to all men because*
> *all sinned – for sin indeed was in the world before the law was*
> *given, but sin is not counted where there is no law. Yet death*
> *reigned from Adam to Moses, even over those whose sinning*
> *was not like the transgression of Adam, who was a type of the*
> *one who was to come.*
>
> (Romans 5:12–14 ESV.)

The argument depends on interpreting the statement *because all sinned* (ESV and NIV) as "because all sinned in Adam", therefore all are guilty of Adam's sin. There are two issues of exegesis here. The first has to do with the Old Latin translation where the phrase is rendered *in quo omnes peccaverunt* – "in whom all (have) sinned". Augustine used this translation, so it is understandable that he came to the conclusion that all had sinned in Adam. Augustine's view has had widespread influence. However, the Latin *in quo* ("in whom") is a mistranslation of the original Greek *eph ho*, which means "because" or "since". Therefore the overwhelming majority of commentators have subsequently settled for the translation "because" or "since" – "because all (have) sinned".

Secondly, the tense of the Greek verb translated "sinned" here in Romans 5:12 is aorist. It may or may not be translated as an English past definite. This is because the aorist tense in Greek covers a different range of possible meanings from a past definite in English. This can be seen from the fact that in Romans 3:23 the very same word in Greek is translated as *all have sinned* (ESV and NIV). In that case, the translators used an English perfect tense ("have sinned") to translate the Greek aorist. Translating it by a past definite would not convey the right sense. The perfect tense does.

So the question arises as to what considerations should guide translators in Romans 5:12. As far as grammar is concerned, there are at least two possibilities, and theological presuppositions are also likely to play a role in deciding preference for one over the other. If one believes that Paul is intending here to convey the idea that all sinned when Adam sinned, then the past definite translation will be preferred. However, it is equally possible that he intended to convey the idea that death passed upon all because all have individually sinned, in which case the translation using the perfect tense is correct. (The King James Version used this translation.)

In his authoritative work on Romans, C. E. B. Cranfield makes a detailed investigation of all the main interpretations of Paul's statement and comes to this conclusion:

> There is on the other side the important consideration that there is nothing in the context or in this verse to suggest that hemarton [the Greek word translated "sinned"] is being used in an unusual sense and that in every other occurrence of this verb in the Pauline epistles the reference is quite clearly to actual sin. We conclude that pantes hemarton [the Greek words translated "all sinned"] has the same meaning here as it has in [Romans] 3:23.[126]

We should also remember that the argument we are considering is not being used in this case to prove that people are incapable of responding to God, but that people are culpable in spite of that incapacity. Of course, if the case for incapacity cannot be biblically sustained, culpability follows automatically, without having to decide on the translation of an aorist tense.

---

126 C. E. B. Cranfield, *Romans 1–8*, vol. 1, Edinburgh, T & T Clark, p. 279. See also the discussion on this passage in Michael Bird's commentary in *The Story of God Bible Commentary: Romans*, Grand Rapids, Zondervan, 2016.

Some religions teach that if a child is born with some disability it is the child's fault, in the sense that the child has sinned in a previous incarnation or has somehow inherited the sin of its parents. The disciples may well have had something like that in mind when they asked Jesus about the man born blind: *Rabbi, who sinned, this man or his parents, that he was born blind?* (John 9:2). Jesus at once disabused them of any such thought: *It was not that this man sinned, or his parents...* (John 9:3 ESV). In light of this, it would surely be wise to be cautious about teaching that it is our fault that we were born sinners – the result of a sin committed by us in the distant past when we were "in Adam".

We can explore this idea further by imagining a situation that sadly occurs in some parts of the world today. A pregnant woman is arrested and sentenced to death for drug smuggling. She gives birth to a child in prison as she awaits execution. That child was in her when she committed the crime. Would it be morally right that the child should therefore be regarded as guilty of her sin and executed as well? Clearly not. However, her son may well have been born damaged because of the mother's own drug habit. He may never quite recover and might even eventually become an addict himself, or even a dealer. If he were to be tried and sentenced for dealing, the lawyers might plead for more lenient treatment because it was not his fault that he had a bad start in life. Yet he would be held responsible, tried, and sentenced for what he personally had done. Furthermore, no lawyer would argue that he should be given the same sentence as his mother, just because he was in her womb when she committed her crime.

Oliver Crisp gives a slightly different analogy that is helpful:

> *If a person inherits a vitiated condition, like the child born a heroin addict because its mother is a heroin addict, we do not blame the child for being in this state as we do the parent. For plainly an agent cannot be culpable for being generated and born in a state with which it did not concur or condone. Similarly, if a person is born with a disposition to alcoholism, we would not think that agent morally responsible or culpable for possessing such a disposition,*

though we would normally think the agent is morally responsible for taking the steps that lead toward alcohol dependency because in the latter case the agent chooses to act on the basis of a disposition. It seems to me that something similar can be said for fallen human beings. They all possess the moral corruption inherited from their parents, and their parents, and so on, going back through the generations to some original human community. Being born in such a state is not something for which one can reasonably be said to be responsible or culpable. But acting upon such a disposition (if, indeed, it is a disposition) is something for which a person may be morally responsible and culpable.

There is, in other words, a distinction to be made between original sin and actual sin. Whereas original sin is that inherited moral corruption with which we are all generated, and for which we are not responsible or culpable, actual sins are those particular things we are disposed to do because we are born in a morally vitiated state. The person born with a disposition to substance abuse is liable to become an alcoholic; the fallen human being is liable to commit actual sin. Does this mean only that it is **very likely** *that those born with the moral corruption of original sin will commit actual sin? Is it possible to* **avoid** *actual sin as (we might think) it is possible for the person disposed to alcoholism to avoid becoming an alcoholic? Following others in the Reformed tradition, I do not think so. Rather, the moral corruption of original sin makes it inevitable that all fallen human beings will actually sin on at least one occasion* **if they live long enough and are the proper subject of moral states and properties.**[127]

There are some who suggest that there is a parallel passage in Hebrews that throws light on the issue:

---

127   O. Crisp, "On Original Sin", in *International Journal of Systematic Theology*, vol 17, no. 3, July 2015 doi:10.1111/ijst.12107, p.261. Emphasis mine.

One might even say that Levi, who collects the tenth, paid
the tenth through Abraham, because when Melchizedek met
Abraham, Levi was still in the body of his ancestor.

(Hebrews 7:9–10.)

However, this passage is talking about status. By paying tithes to Melchizedek, Abraham was acknowledging that he was inferior to him in status. The argument is that if the founder of the Hebrew race had a lower status than King Melchizedek, his descendants would also have lower status. There is no suggestion anywhere that Abraham's faith is imputed to his physical descendants – far from it, *it is those of faith who are the sons of Abraham* (Galatians 3:7 ESV) – even though they were in that same sense "in his body" when he *believed God, and it was counted to him as righteousness* (Romans 4:3 ESV). Nor, on the negative side, was Levi or anyone else imputed with blame for something Abraham did.

To believe that Adam's sin damaged his posterity and constituted them sinners is one thing; to believe that all of his posterity are guilty of his sin is quite another. And to believe that all humans have Adam's sin imputed to them – that they are guilty of Adam's sin because they sinned in Adam – cannot be reconciled with what Paul says a little later in the very same passage:

Yet death reigned from Adam to Moses, even over those whose
sinning was not like the transgression of Adam...

(Romans 5:14 ESV.)

Here we are told unequivocally that there are people whose sin was *not like the transgression of Adam.*

How could Paul have written this if he had intended us to deduce the exact opposite from the earlier statement? If we are all guilty of Adam's sin because we sinned in Adam, then there is no one whose sin was not like Adam's. Or, putting it another way, if Adam's sin is imputed to all, then all are guilty of it since that is the meaning of the word "impute". According to Paul that is not the case. This is surely decisive. It means that, while death is universal because of Adam, guilt is not – guilt is universal because all humans commit sin.

Sometimes people argue that if we are not all guilty by imputation of Adam's sin, then why do babies die when no one can seriously suggest that they have personally sinned? The answer to this question lies in the Genesis account. One consequence of the first sin was that God removed access to the fruit of the tree of life (Genesis 3:22–24). We are told that this took away from human beings the possibility of physical immortality. With that gone, all of Adam's descendants would inevitably be born as mortals.

The salient fact here is that the tree of life was external to Adam and Eve. There is no suggestion that mortality came upon humans by some internal (genetic) process, but rather that their access to a very special food was cut off.[128] In other words, human beings from the beginning may well have been dependent on this food in order for physical life to continue indefinitely; so that all humans after Adam are liable to physical death simply because they live in a world where that source no longer exists.

Finally, in Romans 5 Paul also draws a parallel between Adam and Christ:

> For as by the one man's disobedience the many were made
> sinners, so by the one man's obedience the many will be made
> righteous.
>
> (Romans 5:19 ESV.)

If one is going to argue that when Adam sinned we sinned and therefore earned God's judgment, then the parallel would suggest that when Christ obeyed we obeyed, and were therefore contributing to earning our salvation. It is hard to imagine anyone being happy with that conclusion, not least who believe that all sinned in Adam.

Oceans of ink have been used to try to explain exactly to what extent human beings were damaged by the entry of sin into the world.

---

128 Could this possibly be a source of the many stories and legends hinting at the existence of an "elixir of life"?

I am under no illusion that I can shed any more light on the subject. However, certain things would seem to be fairly clear. Adam's sin has made us all sinners and brought us under the domination of death. But this cannot mean that we are incapable of hearing God's voice, of seeing evidence given by him, and of responding to the gospel by repenting and believing in the Lord Jesus.

All of these things are explicitly taught in Scripture. Since we have the capacity to do them, we incur guilt if we refuse to do so and will rightly be condemned by God. It is surely not unreasonable to conclude, therefore, that we are all damaged by Adam's sin but we are not all guilty of it.

In other words, Romans teaches original sin but it does not teach original guilt. Crisp gives the following helpful summary: "Fallen humans are not culpable for the primal sin either. That is, they do not bear original guilt (i.e. the guilt of the sin of some putative first human pair or human community being imputed to them along with original sin)."[129] Incidentally, Crisp points out that such a view has a distinguished pedigree including such Reformed theologians as Zwingli.

It is important to emphasise that this understanding of Scripture does not commit the heresy of Pelagianism, that human sinfulness is a matter of imitation not imputation, and is not in principle a foregone conclusion for any particular individual. Nor does it fall into semi-Pelagianism, which teaches that humans beings are able to exercise free will quite independently of divine grace in order to co-operate with that grace to effect their own salvation.

Finally, it should be mentioned that an interesting *philosophical* case has been made by Michael Rae that commitment to original guilt need not involve determinism.[130] However, since I do not think that a *biblical* case can be made for original guilt I shall say no more about it.

---

129   O. Crisp, "On Original Sin", in *International Journal of Systematic Theology*, p.261.

130   See Michael C. Rea's essay "The Metaphysics of Original Sin," in *Persons, Divine and Human*, Dean Zimmerman and Peter van Inwagen (eds), OUP, Clarendon Press, 2007, pp. 319–356

CHAPTER 11

The Gospel and Human Moral Responsibility

Quite apart from the effects of Adam's sin, there is the question whether we human beings can render ourselves less able to respond to God through our own sinful behaviour and attitudes. The answer to that is undoubtedly in the affirmative. Consciences can become seared to such an extent that men and women no longer hear its voice.

Jesus spoke trenchantly to those who were seeking to kill him. They claimed to know God, but Christ tells them straight that the evidence that they do not know him is seen in the fact that they *do not believe the one he sent* (John 5:38). Jesus continues:

> *You diligently study the Scriptures because you think that by them you possess eternal life… yet you refuse to come to me to have life.*
>
> (John 5:39–40.)

They are morally responsible for their refusal. Worse than that, their behaviour is beginning to close the door against God on the inside:

> *How can you believe if you accept praise from one another, yet make no effort to obtain the praise that comes from the only God?*
>
> (John 5:44.)

The more evidence they rejected, the less they became morally capable of responding to Jesus' message.

Another example is to be found in John 12:

*Even after Jesus had done all these miraculous signs in their
presence, they still would not believe in him. This was to
fulfil the word of Isaiah the prophet: "Lord, who has believed
our message, and to whom has the arm of the Lord been
revealed?" For this reason they could not believe, because,
as Isaiah says elsewhere, "He has blinded their eyes and
deadened their hearts, so they can neither see with their eyes,
nor understand with their hearts, nor turn – and I would heal
them." Isaiah said this because he saw Jesus' glory and spoken
of him.*

*Yet at the same time many even among the leaders
believed in him. But because of the Pharisees they would not
confess their faith for fear that they would be put out of the
synagogue; for they loved praise from men more than praise
from God.*

(John 12:37–43.)

This statement of our Lord does not occur in the early days of his
ministry but towards the end. Over the previous three years he had
done many signs and preached the word of God to the people. Many
had believed, but there were others who, in spite of the evidence of
the signs and the power of Christ's message, wilfully rejected him.
They had reached a point of no return and God stepped in and
hardened their hearts.

God's hardening of the human heart is a serious matter; we shall
look at it in more detail in due course in connection with Romans
9–11. Here, however, we concentrate on the scriptural teaching of a
position being reached in a person's heart that cannot be reversed –
there is a point of no return.

We see this elsewhere in the Gospels. On one occasion Jesus
cured a demon-oppressed man who was blind and dumb. There were
two reactions to this spectacular cure:

All the people were astonished, and said, "Could this be the Son of David?" But when the Pharisees heard this, they said, "It is only by Beelzebub, the prince of demons, that this fellow drives out demons."

(Matthew 12:23–24.)

These Pharisees were unregenerate men, yet Jesus does not speak to them as if they were devoid of moral perception. On the contrary, he responds with a series of powerful arguments that appealed to their moral judgment, showing the absurdity of their position.

Every kingdom divided against will be ruined... If Satan drives out Satan, he is divided against himself. How then can his kingdom stand? And if I drive out demons by Beelzebub, by whom do your people drive them out? So then, they will be your judges.

(Matthew 12:25–27.)

Their moral obtuseness is culpable, since it is a wilful rejection of the obvious conclusion to be drawn from the healing of the demon-possessed man. Jesus himself points out:

But if I drive out demons by the Spirit of God, then the kingdom of God has come upon you.

(Matthew 12:28.)

He then pronounces his judgment:

And so I tell you, every sin and blasphemy will be forgiven men, but the blasphemy against the Spirit will not be forgiven. Anyone who speaks a word against the Son of Man will be forgiven, but anyone who speaks against the Holy Spirit will not be forgiven, either in this age or in the age to come.

(Matthew 12:31–32.)

Jesus clearly expected these unregenerate men to understand the logic of his ethical argument. They could not deny that the man had been healed by supernatural power; but against all logic and common sense they resolved not to admit that Jesus had acted by the power of God. They would have had to acknowledge that he was the Son of God, the Messiah, so they perversely attributed the miracle to the devil. Christ solemnly told them that this amounted to culpable blasphemy against the Holy Spirit that would put them beyond the possibility of ever being forgiven.

This was not all that he had to say to them. His final word in this discourse was:

> I tell you, on the day of judgment people will give account for every careless word they speak, for by your words you will be justified, and by your words you will be condemned.
>
> (Matthew 12:36–37.)

There was a very real sense in which these Pharisees had, without realising it, just experienced what the Day of Judgment would be like. They had been standing before the Judge, who had called them to account for their foolish and perverse words. In the same way God's ultimate judgment will be fair, and seen to be fair.

It is important to point out here that this is no tyrannical verdict, somehow proving that God is not a God of love after all. There is only one gospel – salvation through repentance and faith in Jesus as the Son of God. It is witnessed to by the power of the Holy Spirit, and if people ultimately reject that witness and attribute it to the devil, then, in the very nature of things, God has no alternative gospel to offer. It is apparent from Scripture that, by their own behaviour, human beings can irreversibly damage their capacity to repent and believe.

No one reading the New Testament can fail to see that the gospel is an appeal by God to men and women. Indeed, the Gospel of John has been described as one long appeal from beginning to end. Christ and his apostles preached, taught, reasoned, discussed, and persuaded their audiences. The apostle Peter tells Christians:

Always be prepared to give an answer [apologia, a defence] to everyone who asks you to give the reason [logos] for the hope that you have.

(1 Peter 3:15.)

Yet we sometimes meet people who hold that reasoning about the gospel is useless. "You cannot argue someone into the kingdom of God," they say. As we saw earlier, this line of reasoning is sometimes used on the basis of an incorrect understanding of what it means to be dead in trespasses and sins.

There is, however, another aspect to this. Many of us, especially those who have had the privilege of higher education, are sometimes tempted to trust our minds first and only turn to God when we get into difficulty. That is certainly not what the apostles did; their attitude was the very reverse. They trusted God, and used their minds, their talents, and gifts in God's service. Trusting the mind and using God is tantamount to idolatry: trusting God and using the mind is Christian. Once we get this clear we can see that our intellect is no different from our other talents. It is a gift of God to be used in his service with his help, and not to be trusted as an idol or God-substitute.

It is bordering on the irreverent to suggest that Christ and his apostles were "wasting their time" teaching, arguing, and reasoning with people in the meeting places of the ancient world. Far from it! As we shall see from chapters 7–10 of John's Gospel, this was God's own strategy to reach the world. Since these chapters contain a passage that is frequently used to support theistic determinism, they are of particular relevance to our main theme. Christ said to the religious leaders listening to him:

... but you do not believe because you are not my sheep. My sheep listen to my voice; I know them, and they follow me. I give them eternal life, and they shall never perish; no-one can snatch them out of my hand.

(John 10:26–28.)

This text is often used to argue that becoming one of Christ's sheep is a matter of God's unconditional election. He selects some to be his sheep and others not, without any reference to them. The chosen will believe in Christ; those who are not chosen to be his sheep will never believe, so they will be lost eternally. We shall consider whether this amounts to a defensible interpretation, bearing in mind the much wider context of John's Gospel in which it occurs. This section falls into four major parts, conveniently defined by its chapter divisions:

John 7 – Jesus teaches at the Feast of Tabernacles in Jerusalem;

John 8 – Jesus forgives the woman taken in adultery;

John 9 – Jesus heals the man born blind;

John 10 – Jesus reveals himself as the Shepherd of the sheep and teaches at the Feast of Dedication.

Jesus is revealed in this part of John's Gospel as the Light of the world, and each of these four chapters is dedicated to a different aspect of the way in which he communicates his good news to the world. Two important Jewish festivals are involved – the Feast of Tabernacles at the start, and the Feast of Dedication at the end. Each of these festivals involved a special lamplight illumination of the temple. At the Feast of Tabernacles (*Sukkot*) Jerusalem was like a great sheepfold filled to overflowing with Jewish pilgrims from all over. One of the features of that feast was a magnificent ceremony of the illumination of the temple. It involved the lighting of four golden, oil-filled lamps in the Court of Women. It is said that these huge menorahs were over twenty metres high. They shed a brilliant light over Jerusalem through the night, acting as a symbol of the pillar of fire that once guided Israel on their journey to the promised land.

The climax of this section of John is reached in a scene in Part 4 that took place in the temple court area of Jerusalem on the twenty-fifth day of the Hebrew month Kislev. It was a celebration of the Feast of the Dedication (*Hanukkah*, Feast of Lights), which was not one of the biblical feasts but still of great historical importance to the Jews. The Maccabees added it to their calendar in the second century BC to celebrate the cleansing and rededication of the temple. The festival lasted eight days and nights, and it involved the lighting of the lamps on the special nine-branched Hanukkah Menorah: one on the first night, two on the second, and so on until a total of eight had been reached. The additional light was for practical purposes of illumination. Every home had a light in the window, and Jerusalem must have looked wonderful in the glow of thousands of them shining all over the city.

Thus our section of John's Gospel is bracketed at the beginning and end by two festivals, each of them lasting a week and each involving the illumination of the city. It is to these festivals that Jesus comes as the Light of the world. In the first part we read of Jesus *going up* to Jerusalem, and in the fourth part John uses the same Greek term (*anabaino*) to describe the thief's approach to the fold of the sheep (where he *climbs in*, literally "goes up", John 10:1). This is one of the key issues in the section: how are people to distinguish between the approach of the true shepherd, who has the sheep's best interests in view, from the approach of the false "shepherd" who plans to exploit and destroy the sheep? How do the sheep know which is which? How does the true shepherd approach them in order to gain their trust? The answers to these questions will further help us to understand the nature of human responsibility and its relationship with the sovereignty of God's initiative.

The middle parts 2 and 3 also contribute to the theme of Jesus' approach to men and women as the Light of the world. In John 8 we find the religious leaders illuminating a woman's sin, whereas it is their sin that Jesus brings to the light of day. In chapter 9 we have the healing of a blind man who, through no sin of his own or his parents, hadn't been able to see from birth and therefore could have no conception of what light was. Jesus enables him to see and uses him as a parable for the blindness of the religious leaders.

Our treatment of this section will be somewhat uneven, for the simple reason that some parts are more relevant to our main theme than others; and we must resist the temptation to give a detailed exposition.

We start with the Feast of Tabernacles.

John 7: Jesus at the Feast of Tabernacles

After this Jesus went around in Galilee, purposely staying away from Judea, because the Jews there were waiting to take his life. But when the Jewish Feast of Tabernacles was near, Jesus' brothers said to him, "You ought to leave here and go to Judea, so that your disciples may see the miracles you do. No-one who wants to become a public figure acts in secret. Since you are doing these things, show yourself to the world." For even his own brothers did not believe in him.

(John 7:1–5.)

The vast crowd attending the Feast of Tabernacles represented a unique opportunity, at least in the eyes of his brothers, for Jesus to get his message across to the world. The logical thing in their opinion was to go to the largest concentration of people and show them what he could do.

It was not quite so simple, however, as Jesus pointed out to them. His was no ordinary message with instant popular appeal. It involved him telling the world that its works were evil. Exposing sin in that way was very likely to stir up resentment, and this feature had to be taken into account in Jesus' approach to men and women. Therefore he did not go up to the Feast with his brothers at that time. No doubt, in their unbelief, they would have advertised his presence to the crowds in an unhelpful manner. Jesus waited some days until the feast was well under way, and only then did he go up to Jerusalem in secret. Meanwhile the city was abuzz with gossip about him, and the crowds were divided as to whether he was good or a deceiver.

How was he to approach them in order for his message to have its maximum impact?

Not until halfway through the feast did Jesus go up to the temple courts and begin to teach. The Jews were amazed and asked, "How did this man get such learning without having studied?"

(John 7:14–15.)

His strategy – startlingly simple as it is – is now revealed. He went to the temple courts and publicly started to teach anyone who would listen to him, immediately captivating the audience by his profound wisdom and learning. The temple experts were amazed. They would have known all the teaching staff at the temple and in the rabbinic schools, and it was clear that, whoever this teacher was, he had not studied in the approved way in their schools. They did not regard him as acceptably accredited therefore. Yet his teaching was nothing short of stunning in its reach and depth.

On this occasion we are not given any detail as to the content of Jesus' teaching. The listeners' focus was on the source of his teaching – where did he get it?

> Jesus answered, "My teaching is not my own. It comes from him who sent me. If anyone chooses to do God's will, he will find out whether my teaching comes from God or whether I speak on my own. He who speaks on his own does so to gain honour for himself, but he who works for the honour of the one who sent him is a man of truth; there is nothing false about him. Has not Moses given you the law? Yet not one of you keeps the law. Why are you trying to kill me?"
>
> (John 7:16–19.)

Jesus was speaking to unregenerate people, yet he expected them to follow his logic and understand exactly what he was saying. He claimed his teaching was from God and that they could verify this by *choosing* to do God's will. In other words, Jesus demanded a moral response; for such knowledge will not be granted to satisfy mere intellectual curiosity. In order to know, his hearers would have to exercise their own moral will and be prepared to do God's will. Christ treated them as responsible moral agents who were capable of making moral decisions. This suddenly becomes clearer as he presses the moral case and asks why they are trying to kill him. That awakens in them the realisation that they may well have come across him before:

"You are demon-possessed," the crowd answered. "Who is trying to kill you?"

Jesus said to them, "I did one miracle, and you are all astonished. Yet, because Moses gave you circumcision (though actually it did not come from Moses, but from the patriarchs), you circumcise a child on the Sabbath. Now if a child can be circumcised on the Sabbath so that the law of Moses may not be broken, why are you angry with me for healing the whole man on the Sabbath? Stop judging by mere appearances, and make a right judgment."

At that point some of the people of Jerusalem began to ask, "Isn't this the man they are trying to kill? Here he is, speaking publicly, and they are not saying a word to him. Have the authorities really concluded that he is the Christ? But we know where this man is from; when the Christ comes, no-one will know where he is from."

Then Jesus, still teaching in the temple courts, cried out, "Yes, you know me, and you know where I am from. I am not here on my own, but he who sent me is true. You do not know him, but I know him because I am from him and he sent me."

At this they tried to seize him, but no-one laid a hand on him, because his time had not yet come. Still, many in the crowd put their faith in him. They said, "When the Christ comes, will he do more miraculous signs than this man?"

(John 7:20–31.)

Jesus was reminding them that the last time he had been in Jerusalem he had healed a man on the sabbath (John 5). He invites them now to make a moral judgment on the comparison between his making a person whole on the sabbath and their activity of circumcising infants on the sabbath. He points out, as a matter of simple logic, that their anger against him is misplaced.

We must not fail to see the implications of this for our topic. Remember, this is our Lord's strategy to communicate his message. It begins by him telling his hearers to use their moral and logical faculties to assess both his teaching and his deeds. He does not say to them that God's thoughts are way beyond them on this issue, or that they cannot be expected to understand what is going on because they are intellectually and morally dead in trespasses and in sins.

That cannot be the case. Even though they are unregenerate men and women, the fact that the Lord himself is asking these people to use their moral sensibilities to make a right judgment indicates that he believes they possess the capacity to do so. They were dead in trespasses and in sins; yet according to Christ himself they can make righteous judgments. They therefore were neither intellectually nor morally dead. They were moral beings, made in the image of God; capable of responding to the Lord's moral challenge and blameworthy if they did not. Clearly, some did respond. John tells us that there were those who had seen what Jesus had done, they had used their moral judgment on his signs and come to the conclusion that he was who he claimed to be, and so repented of their sins and believed in him. Others rejected him on the basis of spurious arguments about his origin, and some of them even tried to arrest him. Jerusalem was divided.

The end of the festival was approaching, and its last day was full of ceremony. Water would be collected from the pool of Siloam, to be poured out at the base of the altar in the temple court. The crowd would be singing some of the Psalms that spoke of redemption, with words that rang to heaven, "Save now, Lord, save now." At some stage there must have been a pause, a silence during which the attentive crowd heard a powerful voice ringing out:

> On the last and greatest day of the feast, Jesus stood and said in a loud voice, "If anyone is thirsty, let him come to me and drink. Whoever believes in me, as the Scripture has said, streams of living water will flow from within him."
>
> (John 7:37–38.)

"Is anyone still thirsty?" It must have had a dramatic shock effect on the religious leaders. Here they were, putting on the very best of religious ceremony, and this upstart teacher from Galilee has the cheek to suggest that it is not enough to satisfy everyone's thirst.

How dare he? He dared because he knew that many on that day were totally unsatisfied by the external religious ceremony, however expensive and impressive it was. They thirsted for an inner reality – the satisfaction that Christ had given earlier to the woman at the well by supplying her with the water of life as she came to trust him as Saviour and Lord.

Our Lord's appeal was dramatic. It was also genuine – offered to all and not just to some predetermined few. It was an offer made to those who did not yet know the Father. They could come to know him through trusting the Son; but they had to come, they had to drink. They could say yes or they could say no. Jesus' teaching made a powerful impact and divided the crowd. Some believed him and others didn't. Eventually they all went home, but not Jesus. He went to a favourite place on the Mount of Olives, presumably to be alone with his Father in the quiet of the garden.

John 8: Jesus forgives the woman taken in adultery

At dawn he appeared again in the temple courts, where all the people gathered round him, and he sat down to teach them. The teachers of the law and the Pharisees brought in a woman caught in adultery. They made her stand before the group and said to Jesus, "Teacher, this woman was caught in the act of adultery. In the Law Moses commanded us to stone such women. Now what do you say?" They were using this question as a trap, in order to have a basis for accusing him.

But Jesus bent down and started to write on the ground with his finger. When they kept on questioning him, he straightened up and said to them, "If any one of you is without sin, let him be the first to throw a stone at her." Again he stooped down and wrote on the ground.

At this, those who heard began to go away one at a time, the older ones first, until only Jesus was left, with the woman still standing there. Jesus straightened up and asked her,

"Woman, where are they? Has no-one condemned you?"
"No-one, sir," she said.
"Then neither do I condemn you," Jesus declared. "Go now and leave your life of sin."

(John 8:2–11.)

It was early the next day and Jesus was back in the temple. A crowd gathered and he began to teach them – following his strategy once more. John relates how his teaching was interrupted when the Pharisees dragged an adulterous woman before Jesus in the hope of forcing him to make a judgment as to what should be done with her. They cited Moses to the effect that she should be stoned. They were not doing this out of concern for keeping the law and judging the woman fairly; they simply wished to entrap Jesus by daring him to disagree with Moses. They were, so to speak, shining the light of Moses' law on her.

Jesus' response was to write on the ground, and when their questioning became insistent he asked for anyone who was without sin to throw the first stone. He then bent to write on the ground once more. We don't know what he wrote, but the idea of the finger of the Son of God writing on the ground recalls that the law given to Moses was "written with the finger of God". It is possible – and perhaps even plausible – that Jesus wrote those laws in the dust. However that may be, his writing had a dramatic effect. When the woman's accusers shone the law at her, they thought they were morally unblemished. Like people shining a powerful torch in front of them, they were themselves in the dark. And when the Light of the world began to shine, the light pierced their consciences and they left the scene – from the eldest to the youngest. Jesus had got them to use their moral judgment. This time not so much on his teaching as on themselves. Once again the point is made that, even as unregenerate people, they were capable of making moral judgments. Though spiritually dead, they were certainly not morally or intellectually dead.

Released now from her accusers, the remarkable thing is that the woman made no move to leave. Her own sins and those of her accusers had been exposed, but there was a quality about the Light

212

of the world that made her want to stay in his presence. Perhaps she felt safe and unthreatened. He asked her if anyone had condemned her. *No-one*, she said. *Then neither do I condemn you... Go now and leave your life of sin.* Christ did not condone her sin – she was to sin no more. He forgave her, and brought hope into her hitherto sad and unsatisfactory life.

Again Jesus spoke to the people:

> "I am the light of the world. Whoever follows me will never walk in darkness, but will have the light of life."
> The Pharisees challenged him, "Here you are, appearing as your own witness; your testimony is not valid."
> Jesus answered, "Even if I testify on my own behalf, my testimony is valid, for I know where I came from and where I am going. But you have no idea where I come from or where I am going. You judge by human standards; I pass judgment on no-one. But if I do judge, my decisions are right, because I am not alone. I stand with the Father, who sent me. In your own Law it is written that the testimony of two men is valid. I am one who testifies for myself; my other witness is the Father, who sent me."
> Then they asked him, "Where is your father?"
> "You do not know me or my Father," Jesus replied. "If you knew me, you would know my Father also." He spoke these words while teaching in the temple area near the place where the offerings were put. Yet no-one seized him, because his time had not yet come.
>
> (John 8:12–20.)

In this section the Lord begins by engaging in a deep and complex argument with a group of Pharisees. Forgive me for stressing the point, but the very fact that he does so demonstrates once more that he did not regard them as intellectually dead and beyond argument. You only enter into discussion with people if you expect them to understand what you are saying. He was arguing with them as a witness to them, and he expected them to grasp the content of that witness. He was treating them as responsible human beings.

He tells them that he is the Light of the world. Perhaps they had some dim inkling of what that meant, since it was they who had brought the adulterous woman to Jesus and had seen his powerful exposure of the sin of her would-be judges. Perhaps some of them had personally felt its power and had crept back to hear more of what he had to say. That Light was available for them, he told them. But on one condition: they had to follow him. This Light was no random blazing source of illumination that picked out one and not another in an arbitrary or mysterious way. All could enjoy its healing rays, provided they were prepared to follow him, take on board his teaching, trust and obey him as Lord.

Some had an intellectual quibble, aimed at sidetracking him. They said he was testifying to himself, which was perfectly true. While they had the forensic right to argue about witnesses, their claim that his testimony was actually false did not follow logically at all. For if Jesus was who he claimed to be, he was utterly unique and simply had to bear witness to himself.

On a much lower level, if an explorer reaches a remote destination on his own, then on his return he has to bear witness for himself. This does not mean his testimony is false. Whether we accept that testimony or not cannot depend on corroborating evidence, since there is none. No one else has seen what he has seen! Our response must depend on what we know of the man – his reliability, trustworthiness, and the like. Jesus claims that he knows where he has come from and where he is going. They had no knowledge of that, so the only information they could possibly get must come from accepting Jesus' testimony.

There was another angle to it, however. There was, in a sense, one other witness – the Father. This puzzled them, as it was intended to, and they responded with: *Where is your father?* Jesus replied that they did not know him or the Father. If they had known him they would have known the Father. It was enigmatic, but with hindsight we can understand what is going on. In the final movement of this section Jesus would make the supreme claim that he and the Father were one (John 10:30). So at this stage, in chapter 9, when they asked him where the Father was, the answer was that, in Christ, he was right in front of them. Step by step Jesus is narrowing the perceived distance between him and God. Remember that, to his questioners, any claim to be God was utter blasphemy, and at this stage it was inconceivable that it might be true.

John reminds us that the Lord was still teaching in the temple precincts – this time in the treasury (8:20). He was continuing to follow the strategy of witnessing to the world by letting the light shine through the words of his teaching. These were very tense moments, yet no attempt was made to arrest him. The God-ordained time for that had not yet come.

So he spoke to them again:

> *"I am going away, and you will look for me, and you will die in your sin. Where I go, you cannot come."*
>
> *This made the Jews ask, "Will he kill himself? Is that why he says, 'Where I go, you cannot come'?"*
>
> *But he continued, "You are from below; I am from above. You are of this world; I am not of this world. I told you that you would die in your sins; if you do not believe that I am he, you will indeed die in your sins."*
>
> *"Who are you?" they asked.*
>
> *"Just what I have been claiming all along," Jesus replied. "I have much to say in judgment of you. But he who sent me is reliable, and what I have heard from him I tell the world."*
>
> *They did not understand that he was telling them about his Father. So Jesus said, "When you have lifted up the Son of Man, then you will know that I am he and that I do nothing on my own but speak just what the Father has taught me. The one who sent me is with me; he has not left me alone, for I always do what pleases him." Even as he spoke, many put their faith in him.*
>
> (John 8:21–30.)

A little earlier Jesus had said, *I know where I came from and where I am going* (John 8:14). As directly relevant to the issue of defining his unique relationship of identity with the Father, he now expands on the topic of his origin and destiny. He was going away – this is a clear reference to his death. They would seek him – and one can imagine the frantic and vain efforts made by the Jewish leadership to find his body after the resurrection. They would die in their sin – the rejection of Jesus as Son of God and Messiah was *the* sin. It meant that they would never enter the Father's presence, which was an absolute tragedy for those who were at that very moment listening to the Father witnessing through the Son. He was indeed going away into death, but that death would be the gateway for his return to the Father.

They were mystified. Did he mean that he was going to commit suicide, when he said where he was going they couldn't come? No; it had to do with the difference in their origins. They were from below; he was from above. They belonged to this world, the world of which he testified that their deeds were evil; whereas his origin was with the Father in heaven. And because they belonged to this world they were in danger of dying "in their sins" – that is, dying unforgiven. Yet that did not mean there was no hope for them. The situation could be completely altered if they were prepared to believe that *I am he* (verse 24 margin).

Once again these words, if untrue, were blasphemous, hinting as they did at the name of God, I Am (see Exodus 3:14). They represented a further claim to deity. This immediately provoked the question, "Who are you?" They were finding it hard to accept the obvious conclusion; yet, as Jesus now points out, it is what he has been telling them consistently from the start. He has been saying things about them; he has more to say, and all that he says is what he has heard from the Father. Once more he stresses his closeness to the Father.

John pauses to comment that they did not understand that he was speaking of the Father, so Jesus further explains that they will understand who he is, and what his relationship is to the Father, when they have lifted him up. It is the cross that ultimately will reveal exactly who Jesus is. Not of course, immediately. Many who became believers on the Day of Pentecost trusted Christ because they realised then that the cross was the final revelation of the love of

God and the means by which salvation could be offered to those who were prepared to repent and believe. The cross would also reveal the nature of Christ's authority:

> *... you will know that I am he, and that I do nothing on my own but speak just what the Father has taught me.*
>
> (John 8:28.)

On the day of Pentecost Peter's audience was presented with the cross, the resurrection, and the ascension, as evidence that Jesus was exalted as Lord at the right hand of God in heaven. There was no doubt then that his authority was identical with that of the Father.

Right then, however, the cross had yet to happen. Even so, as he announced it, Jesus told the crowd once more that at that precise moment he was not alone, the Father was with him, for he always did what pleased him. His words had power and his teaching reached many hearts. Even though they did not understand everything he said, and his words had not yet been fulfilled, nevertheless he had given them enough evidence, and they believed in him. Yes, he had told them earlier that they knew neither him nor his Father, that they were from beneath, and of this world; but it was now clear that Jesus had not implied that they could never get to know him. Many did, right there and then.

Or did they? Were they genuine? This is a question that has been raised more than once in John's Gospel. In 2:23–25 there were people who appeared to put their faith in Jesus, having seen the signs he did, but it did not go deep enough. Hence the Lord was concerned here to make clear to the crowd the difference between superficial commitment and genuine faith.

> *To the Jews who had believed him, Jesus said, "If you hold to my teaching, you are really my disciples. Then you will know the truth, and the truth will set you free."*
>
> *They answered him, "We are Abraham's descendants and have never been slaves of anyone. How can you say that we shall be set free?"*

Jesus replied, "I tell you the truth, everyone who sins is a slave to sin. Now a slave has no permanent place in the family, but a son belongs to it for ever. So if the Son sets you free, you will be free indeed. I know you are Abraham's descendants. Yet you are ready to kill me, because you have no room for my word. I am telling you what I have seen in the Father's presence, and you do what you have heard from your father."

"Abraham is our father," they answered.

"If you were Abraham's children," said Jesus, "then you would do the things Abraham did. As it is, you are determined to kill me, a man who has told you the truth that I heard from God. Abraham did not do such things. You are doing the things your own father does."

"We are not illegitimate children," they protested. "The only Father we have is God himself."

Jesus said to them, "If God were your Father, you would love me, for I came from God and now am here. I have not come on my own, but he sent me. Why is my language not clear to you? Because you are unable to hear what I say. You belong to your father, the devil, and you want to carry out your father's desire. He was a murderer from the beginning, not holding to the truth, for there is no truth in him. When he lies, he speaks his native language, for he is a liar and the father of lies. Yet because I tell the truth, you do not believe me! Can any of you prove me guilty of sin? If I am telling the truth, why don't you believe me? He who belongs to God hears what God says. The reason you do not hear is that you do not belong to God."

(John 8:31–47.)

Real faith in Christ shows itself by its fruit in the lives of those who profess it. It is not a superficial thing. One of its evidences is a deepening commitment to the word of Christ. A disciple is a learner. The hallmark of a true disciple is a readiness to learn more and more of the truth, thereby discovering that knowledge of truth leads to freedom. Genuine faith perseveres.

At the mention of freedom some in the crowd protested strongly. They were descendants of Abraham. They were free men and women; they had never been in bondage to anyone. But the freedom of which Jesus spoke was freedom from sin. Remember that many of his listeners had witnessed the scene with the adulterous woman, and had taken note of the way Jesus had exposed the sin of those who were eager to stone her to death. So Jesus was now making sure that those who had responded to his teaching had really understood that salvation was nothing if it was not salvation from sin. If they had never really repented, and continual sinning marked their lives, then they were slaves of sin. Only the Son – Jesus, the Son of God – could set them free, and if he did they would enjoy real freedom.

Jesus then admitted their claim to be the offspring of Abraham. He wanted the whole crowd to understand the issues, but some wouldn't receive his word and would try to kill him. The reason for that, he said, was that they had different fathers. This stung them into repeating their claim to be children of Abraham. But if that were the case, Jesus retorted, you would be doing the works of Abraham. Abraham would never have attempted to murder a person who told the truth from God. You are showing no evidence of moral and spiritual kinship with Abraham. The fact is that you are doing the works your father did.

They did not quite get what he was implying, but that was soon to change. They pressed their claim to have only one father, with a not-so-subtle accusation, *We are not illegitimate children* (verse 41), the implication being that Jesus may well have been in that category. Very few people would have known anything about his true parentage, and one can imagine the rumours following him through life, that Joseph was not his real father. No, they were not like that: their father was God! If that were the case, Jesus replied, they would love him, for he came from God. But they could not bear to even hear his word, let alone abide in it. And so the Light of the world now exposed them as those who could not take his word at any price, which meant that their true father was the devil.

This was very strong language. Jesus pointed out that Scripture told them that the devil was a murderer and a liar from the beginning;

and by refusing the truth in the teaching of Jesus these people were showing their real parentage. Jesus challenged them to prove him guilty of a single sin – which, of course, they were unable to do. No other man could make that challenge and be taken seriously, yet in the case of Jesus it has stood for over twenty centuries. To expose their sin, all he had to do earlier was to write on the ground. If he was telling the truth, why did they not believe him? Since people who are of God hear the words of God, the only possible answer is that they were not of God. No matter what they professed to be, they were not (all) genuine believers.

> The Jews answered him, "Aren't we right in saying that you are a Samaritan and demon-possessed?"
>
> "I am not possessed by a demon," said Jesus, "but I honour my Father and you dishonour me. I am not seeking glory for myself; but there is one who seeks it, and he is the judge. I tell you the truth, if anyone keeps my word, he will never see death."
>
> At this the Jews exclaimed, "Now we know that you are demon-possessed! Abraham died and so did the prophets, yet you say that if anyone keeps your word, he will never taste death. Are you greater than our father Abraham? He died, and so did the prophets. Who do you think you are?"
>
> Jesus replied, "If I glorify myself, my glory means nothing. My Father, whom you claim as your God, is the one who glorifies me. Though you do not know him, I know him. If I said I did not, I would be a liar like you, but I do know him and keep his word. Your father Abraham rejoiced at the thought of seeing my day; he saw it and was glad."
>
> "You are not yet fifty years old," the Jews said to him, "and you have seen Abraham!"
>
> "I tell you the truth," Jesus answered, "before Abraham was born, I am!" At this, they picked up stones to stone him, but Jesus hid himself, slipping away from the temple grounds.
>
> (John 8:48–59.)

Some of them were making wild accusations that Jesus was no Jew but a demon-possessed Samaritan. What is amazing is that he continued the conversation, in spite of such blatant and foolish provocation. The reason was that he loved these people and still wished to appeal to them. Far from having a demon, he replied, he was honouring God; and yet they were dishonouring him. Not that he was seeking his own glory and honour – God sought that and in the last analysis he would be the judge. Ignoring their spite, he wound up his teaching for the day by making his final appeal to them: *if anyone keeps my word, he will never see death* (verse 51).

Throughout the day's teaching Jesus had constantly been emphasizing the importance of his word. Again and again he stressed that what he was saying was from the Father; it was his word that could bring forgiveness and freedom. Now, as the Light of the world, he threw his ineffable light on death itself and uttered the immortal words, *if anyone keeps my word he will never see death*. Blinded with rage his listeners used the claim to renew their accusation of demonic possession. Everybody dies – even the greatest. Abraham died, and so did the prophets. Did Jesus think he was greater than Abraham?

Once more the focus is on his identity, yet Jesus is not going to glorify himself. His glory comes from the Father – the very God they claim to be theirs. Their claim is bogus: they do not know God, they have never known him. Jesus does know him, so for him to deny it would be to align himself with them and prove to be a liar. Jesus both knows God and keeps his word, but they do neither.

Is he claiming to be greater than Abraham? Yes he is! In fact Abraham rejoiced to see Jesus' time – he saw it and was glad.

The crowd was amazed. The man who stood before them saying that he had seen Abraham wasn't even fifty years old. *Before Abraham was born, I am*, said Christ. The implications were stunning. Jesus was even more clearly using the ancient name of God, Yahweh – *I am*. He was using it to claim, not merely that he had seen Abraham, but that he had pre-existed Abraham eternally.

Such words had never been heard before. They reverberated around Jerusalem's temple, a building designed to be in a sense the residence of God on earth. It was God who spoke to them that day, and some of those thronging the teacher in the temple courts became tragically unaware that they had just had a lengthy audience with the Creator himself. But not all. John ends his narrative here with people bending to the ground to find stones to stone Jesus for blasphemy. At the beginning of the day they had been preparing stones for the woman they accused of adultery. Now they turn against Jesus. Rage against God is an ugly thing.

John 9: Jesus heals the man born blind

The theme of the Light of the world is continued now in chapter 9 – obviously so, since it is concerned with the healing of a blind man. It will help therefore if we begin by thinking about light at the physical level, and recall what is involved in being able to see.

First, there must be a light source that illuminates; secondly, there must be something to be seen; and thirdly, we must possess the faculty of sight. All three of these ingredients must be present simultaneously. The same is true at the moral and spiritual level: if no light had ever come into the world, if there was nothing to be seen, and if people were incapable of seeing in the first place, it would surely be unjust if they were condemned for loving darkness instead of light. But the light did come, there was something to be seen, and they were capable of seeing it. They did see it and then rejected it. Therefore they are culpable and God's judgment of them is just.

These ingredients are all found in John's Gospel. *The true light, which enlightens everyone, was coming into the world* (John 1:9 ESV). God's initiative was to send light into the world. There is a light source and we should note its universality: *enlightens everyone*.

If people are ever going to be able to see, it is not enough that there is a light, they must also have the faculty of sight. When Jesus came across this man in Jerusalem his disciples asked him: *Rabbi, who sinned, this man or his parents, that he was born blind?* (John 9:2). Jesus replied that neither the man nor his parents were guilty. It was not the man's fault that he couldn't see.

As we discussed in connection with John 3 in the last chapter, this lays down the principle that God does not hold a man guilty for not seeing what he cannot see.

Jesus then did an extraordinary thing. He spat on the ground and made mud with the saliva, used it to anoint the man's eyes, and then instructed him to go and wash in the Pool of Siloam. When he did that, the man instantly received the faculty of sight. This led to a fascinating run-in with the Pharisees, who refused to believe that he was blind. The man did not know who had healed him. He simply said that whereas once he was blind, now he could see. The Pharisees continued to insist that *this man* (Jesus) was *a sinner* (verse 24); but the man who had been blind brilliantly argued that God does not listen to sinners: *If this man were not from God, he could do nothing* (verse 33). At this point they threw him out.

Jesus then applies what has happened at the deeper moral and spiritual level:

> Jesus heard that they had thrown him out, and when he found him, he said, "Do you believe in the Son of Man?"
>
> "Who is he, sir?" the man asked. "Tell me so that I may believe in him."
>
> Jesus said, "You have now seen him; in fact, he is the one speaking with you."
>
> Then the man said, "Lord, I believe," and he worshipped him.
>
> Jesus said, "For judgment I have come into this world, so that the blind will see and those who see will become blind."
>
> Some Pharisees who were with him heard him say this and asked, "What? Are we blind too?"
>
> Jesus said, "If you were blind, you would not be guilty of sin; but now that you claim you can see, your guilt remains.
>
> (John 9:35–41.)

It is clear from this final statement of Jesus that not only physical blindness but also moral and spiritual blindness are at stake here. He tells the Pharisees that if they were blind they would have no guilt. He is laying down the principle at the spiritual level that he had already referred to at the moral level. If a person cannot see something then he cannot be blamed for not seeing it – there is no guilt attached. However, the Pharisees claimed that they could see. They said that they knew about Jesus – that he was a sinner, for instance. Since they had made that judgment, the Lord held them guilty, and he told them so (verse 41).

Furthermore, there was something to be seen. In his upper-room discourse Jesus said to the disciples:

> *If I had not come and spoken to them, they would not be*
> *guilty of sin. Now, however, they have no excuse for their sin.*
> *He who hates me hates my Father as well. If I had not done*
> *among them what no-one else did, they would not be guilty of*
> *sin. But now they have seen these miracles, and yet they have*
> *hated both me and my Father.*
>
> (John 15:22–24.)

Jesus was God's message. If there had been no message, no one could have been held guilty for not believing it. Just as you cannot blame people for failing to see what they cannot see, you cannot blame people for not believing a message they have never heard. But the message had come; they had heard it, and it was backed up by powerful evidence. They had seen it, yet they had rejected it. They therefore had no excuse and God's judgment of them was righteous.

It is important at this point to mention the obvious. The statements that we have just discussed are not deductions by theologians or philosophers; they come from the Lord himself. If Jesus the Son of God lays down the principle that people cannot be held guilty for not seeing what they cannot see, and not believing what they have never heard, then we need to accept it – whatever Calminius or anyone else has taught!

John 10: Jesus as the Shepherd at the Feast of Dedication

"Truly, truly, I say to you, he who does not enter the sheepfold by the door but climbs in by another way, that man is a thief and a robber. But he who enters by the door is the shepherd of the sheep. To him the gatekeeper opens. The sheep hear his voice, and he calls his own sheep by name and leads them out. When he has brought out all his own, he goes before them, and the sheep follow him, for they know his voice. A stranger they will not follow, but they will flee from him, for they do not know the voice of strangers." This figure of speech Jesus used with them, but they did not understand what he was saying to them.

So Jesus again said to them, "Truly, truly, I say to you, I am the door of the sheep. All who came before me are thieves and robbers, but the sheep did not listen to them. I am the door. If anyone enters by me, he will be saved and will go in and out and find pasture. The thief comes only to steal and kill and destroy. I came that they may have life and have it abundantly.

I am the good shepherd. The good shepherd lays down his life for the sheep. He who is a hired hand and not a shepherd, who does not own the sheep, sees the wolf coming and leaves the sheep and flees, and the wolf snatches them and scatters them. He flees because he is a hired hand and cares nothing for the sheep. I am the good shepherd. I know my own and my own know me, just as the Father knows me and I know the Father; and I lay down my life for the sheep. And I have other sheep that are not of this fold. I must bring them also, and they will listen to my voice. So there will be one flock, one shepherd. For this reason the Father loves me, because I lay down my life that I may take it up again. No-one takes it from me, but I lay it down of my own accord. I have authority to lay it down, and I have authority to take it up again. This charge I have received from my Father."

> *There was again a division among the Jews because of
> these words. Many of them said, "He has a demon, and is
> insane; why listen to him?" Others said, "These are not the
> words of one who is oppressed by a demon. Can a demon open
> the eyes of the blind?"*
>
> (John 10:1–21 ESV.)

John's Gospel is written with the objective of supplying evidence
that Jesus is the Messiah, the Son of God, and encouraging people
to receive eternal life by trusting him as Lord and Saviour (see John
20:31). In chapter 10 he relates a parable with its wonderful and
much loved imagery of a shepherd and his sheep, designed to help us
to see how the genuine, true, and good shepherd may be recognised
among all the other voices demanding our attention and allegiance.

The first obvious thing is the shepherd's approach. The genuine
shepherd enters the sheepfold by the gate, opened to him by the
gatekeeper who knows him. Once inside the fold, all he has to do
is to call the sheep and they recognise his voice. They will avoid all
others and flee from them. At first the disciples did not understand
what Jesus meant, but fairly rapidly they must have realised that he
was talking about his approach to the nation.

The identity of the gatekeeper is referred to at the end of the
chapter:

> *Then Jesus went back across the Jordan to the place where John
> had been baptising in the early days. Here he stayed and many
> people came to him. They said, "Though John never performed
> a miraculous sign, all that John said about this man was true."
> And in that place many believed in Jesus.*
>
> (John 10:40–42.)

In a pointed move, Jesus went to the very place where John *the
gatekeeper* had proclaimed him as *the Lamb that takes away the sins
of the world* (1:29). The people who came to him across the Jordan
River could see that everything John said about Jesus was true. John
had fulfilled his work of gate-keeping, and the people responded by

putting their trust in Jesus as Lord. The role of John the Baptist is very important historically, though we cannot pursue it here. It is corroborative of Jesus' claim to be the True Shepherd-Messiah.

By way of explanation Jesus changes the metaphor slightly, and says that he is the door of the sheep. Many have claimed to be the gateway or door to a deeper experience of God, but the majority of them are charlatans and exploiters who don't care about the sheep. What they care about is how much they can make out of them, even if it leads to their destruction. Because they are not the genuine shepherds the sheep don't recognise them.

Now Jesus brings the metaphor face to face with reality:

> I am the door. If anyone enters by me, he will be saved and will go in and out and find pasture.
>
> (John 10:9 ESV.)

He lays down the condition for salvation – he is the door and if anyone enters by him he will be saved. He does not suggest hidden extra preconditions that hint at determinism – if anyone whom God has sovereignly and unconditionally pre-chosen enters... No! Salvation is open to anyone who enters – but they have to enter. If they do they will be led by the Good Shepherd and enjoy the wide blessings of salvation. It is clear, therefore, that "entering" is a further metaphor for trusting the Lord Jesus as Saviour.

Jesus recognises that there are unscrupulous false shepherds who do not really care for the sheep and will abandon them if a wolf turns up. The Good Shepherd is to be distinguished from them, in that he alone is prepared to pay the ultimate price and lay down his life for the sheep. He knows his sheep intimately and they know him, just as he knows the Father and the Father knows him.

Jesus then mentions other sheep that are not of this fold. Presumably the first fold with John the Baptist as its gatekeeper represents Israel, to whom Jesus first came. The other fold represents the Gentiles, who would supply many sheep in days to come. There would then be one flock under one shepherd. The book of Acts tells us how that developed.

Five times over in this short paragraph our Lord refers to the laying down of his life. He describes it as a voluntary act and the reason the Father loves him. This is the heart of the gospel. The Good Shepherd is to be recognised supremely as such by his death on the cross for the sheep.

Earlier, in the temple, Jesus had told the Pharisees the effect that his death on the cross would have:

> When you have lifted up the Son of Man, then you will know that I am he, and that I do nothing on my own but speak just what the Father has taught me.
>
> (John 8:28.)

The cross would tell the world who Jesus is. It is the supreme act that draws people to the Father through Jesus:

> And I, when I am lifted up from the earth, will draw all people to myself.
>
> (John 12:32 ESV.)

We note here the universality of the appeal of the cross. It will not draw just a certain predetermined group; it is there for all people without exception.

But the cross had not happened yet, and the crowd was divided once more. Some thought he was mad, driven insane by a demon. Recalling his recent miracle of healing the man born blind, others used their moral judgment and concluded that madness was out of the question. Many just couldn't make up their minds as to who he was. The result was, by the time the Feast of Dedication came round, speculation was rife in Jerusalem.

> It was winter, and Jesus was in the temple area walking in the Solomon's Colonnade. The Jews gathered round him, saying, "How long will you keep us in suspense? If you are the Christ, tell us plainly."
>
> Jesus answered, "I did tell you, but you do not believe.

> *The miracles I do in my Father's name speak for me, but you*
> *do not believe because you are not my sheep. My sheep listen*
> *to my voice; I know them, and they follow me. I give them*
> *eternal life, and they shall never perish; no-one can snatch*
> *them out of my hand. My Father, who has given them to me,*
> *is greater than all; no-one can snatch them out of my Father's*
> *hand. I and the Father are one."*
>
> (John 10:22–30.)

We started this section with Jesus in the temple teaching the people who had crowded round him. Now he is back in the same place, and the Jews crowd round him again. They accuse him of keeping them in suspense, and ask him to tell them straight if he is the Messiah. He points out that he has told them – on many occasions in fact. Their problem is that they don't believe. By doing many signs in his Father's name, he has been giving them plenty of evidence. But they don't believe. They don't believe because they are not his sheep.

Theistic determinists today say this shows conclusively that in eternity past God did not choose these people to be his sheep, so they will be eternally condemned by God's sovereign, unconditional will. However, this argument is deeply flawed, as we shall see if we follow the rest of the conversation between the Lord and the Jews.

Christ stresses to them why it is obvious that they are not his sheep. They don't listen to his voice and they don't follow him. They have not received eternal life. It must have been wonderful for those in the crowd that had believed in him to hear his words about them:

> *I give them eternal life, and they shall never perish; no-one*
> *can snatch them out of my hand. My Father, who has given*
> *them to me, is greater than all; no-one can snatch them out of*
> *my Father's hand. I and the Father are one.*
>
> (John 10:28–30.)

This is a very strong statement regarding the certainty of eternal life and eternal protection. No one could snatch them out of his hand. Indeed, no one could snatch them out of his Father's hand. In fact, the two pairs of hands are the same: *I and the Father are one!* It hit the crowd with explosive force. They had asked him if he was the Messiah – now he was telling them that he was one with God the Father. It was just too much. To many there this was the height of blasphemy and deserved execution by stoning. Once more, then, these men reached down to the ground for the stones. But Jesus restrained them.

> *The Jews picked up stones again to stone him. Jesus answered them, "I have shown you many good works from the Father; for which of them are you going to stone me?" The Jews answered him, "It is not for a good work that we are going to stone you but for blasphemy, because you, being a man, make yourself God." Jesus answered them, "Is it not written in your Law, 'I said, you are gods'? If he called them gods to whom the word of God came – and Scripture cannot be broken – do you say of him whom the Father consecrated and sent into the world, 'You are blaspheming', because I said, 'I am the Son of God'? If I am not doing the works of my Father, then do not believe me; but if I do them, even though you do not believe me, believe the works, that you may know and understand that the Father is in me and I am in the Father." Again they sought to arrest him, but he escaped from their hands.*
>
> (John 10:31–39 ESV.)

Jesus referred once more to the many works he had done in the name and authority of the Father. But they retorted that they were stoning him, not for a good work, but for blasphemy. Their objection was theological. It was not substantial. Our Lord pointed out to them that in the Psalms God is recorded as having said to certain people: *You are "gods"* (Psalm 82:6). Now if God can in some sense address humans who have received his word as "gods", why should it be thought blasphemous if he claimed this? He is the Son of God, the one who had been consecrated and sent into the world by God the Father. This is an *a fortiori* argument – if it applies to the one case, how much more does it apply to the other!

Christ will not let himself be sidetracked by their apparent difficulty. Nor does he turn away from them by saying that they are not his sheep and, since their fate has been fixed from all eternity, it is no use carrying on the discussion. Not at all. Jesus comes back to the question of his works, saying in effect, "Look, if I am not doing the works of my Father, then just don't believe me. But if I am doing them, even if you don't believe what I say, start by believing the works, so you can see that the Father is in me and I am in the Father."

Christ had said earlier that these same people were not his sheep. Nowhere had he suggested that they could never become his sheep. This is the fundamental flaw in the deterministic argument. They were not his sheep yet, but if they did what he told them, and started by considering his works, they would come to understand who he was and could then become his sheep. Christ had said earlier that they were not his sheep. If this meant that there was no hope for them eternally, he would never have continued to offer them a way of coming to believe in him, effectively mocking them. When Saul of Tarsus was assenting to the stoning of Stephen (note the similar situation) he was certainly not one of Christ's sheep; but he became one on the Damascus road.

We must consider the position of these men who were standing before Jesus. As a result of a lifetime's theological training, they found his words shocking in the extreme. Never having heard anything like it before, they were probably terrified. Jesus was claiming that his voice was that of a Good Shepherd; but they heard it as the voice of a dangerous apostate.

That is another reason why he pointed them first to his works, to the things he had done. They were far less controversial than his claims; but Jesus hoped they would see that his works were consistent with them. They should start therefore with his works.

This was what had happened to the man born blind, as described in John 9. He did not know a lot of theology, and he was confused when the religious leaders started to talk to him about where the Messiah came from. But he did know one thing: it was unheard of that a man born blind should receive his sight. He started with the works of Jesus; the Lord gave him space to do so before he found him again; he ended up believing that Jesus was the divine Son of man, and worshipped him as God.

It is not easy even in the natural realm to get sheep to trust you. They are very sensitive and easily scared. Each one of them has the potential to get to know a shepherd; but trust takes time. Throwing a bunch of juicy green grass on the ground in front of a sheep is a start. Doing it again and again while reducing the distance may eventually lead to them eating out of your hand. They have reason now to trust you.

Jesus was gentle and compassionate with these men. He gave them an easier way to come to terms with his claims, yet sadly they brushed his words aside and moved in to arrest him. They were now wilfully blind.

In the passage we quoted earlier, we see that Jesus escaped:

> *Then Jesus went back across the Jordan to the place where John had been baptising in the early days. Here he stayed and many people came to him. They said, "Though John never performed a miraculous sign, all that John said about this man was true." And in that place many believed in Jesus.*

(John 10:40–42.)

Thus the section closes with a summary statement that exemplifies the fulfilment of the stated purpose of John's Gospel: *many believed in Jesus.* A further crowd of people had just become his sheep.

PART 4

ISRAEL AND DETERMINISM

CHAPTER 12

Israel and the Gentiles

Some of the strongest assertions of theistic determinism are based on Romans 9, where Paul gives examples of God's sovereignty in history. He speaks, for instance, of Jacob and Esau:

> *Yet, before the twins were born or had done anything good or bad – in order that God's purpose in election might stand: not by works but by him who calls – she was told, "The older will serve the younger." Just as it is written: "Jacob I loved, but Esau I hated."*

(Romans 9:11–13.)

Paul then refers to Pharaoh:

> *For the Scripture says to Pharaoh: "I raised you up for this very purpose, that I might display my power in you and that my name might be proclaimed in all the earth." Therefore God has mercy on whom he wants to have mercy, and he hardens whom he wants to harden.*

(Romans 9:17–18.)

From these statements and others that follow, the conclusion is drawn that God has selected some individuals for salvation and all others for reprobation (condemnation), without any reference to those individuals or their attitudes, foreseen or otherwise. This is called unconditional election.

Before we examine the validity of these arguments, let us step back a bit and recall once more that there is an unwavering emphasis on the sovereign initiative of God throughout the Bible. God is the

Creator – there would not be a universe or human beings without him. God is the sovereign upholder of the universe – none of its history is outside his control. Christ is the Saviour and Redeemer – apart from him there would be no salvation.

Furthermore, we have seen that God's initiative is expressed in Scripture in terms like election, foreknowledge, predestination, and calling, all of which occur together at the climax of one of the major sections of the letter to the Romans in chapter 8. By this stage Paul has already argued universal human guilt and the consequent need of salvation. He has explained that salvation is by faith in Christ and not of works. He has developed the theme of human responsibility to live a holy life in the power of God's Holy Spirit. He has described the inner battle against our human nature (the flesh) that we all experience as we seek to walk after the Spirit.

The inner battle is not the only battle, however. Paul himself was no stranger to suffering – he had lived with persecution for many years. And so in Romans 8 Paul addresses suffering directly. He describes the provision that God has made for him and his fellow believers to remain firm in their faith when the winds of adversity blow. Here is the wonderful passage in full:

> I consider that our present sufferings are not worth comparing with the glory that will be revealed in us. The creation waits in eager expectation for the sons of God to be revealed. For the creation was subjected to frustration, not by its own choice, but by the will of the one who subjected it, in hope that the creation itself will be liberated from its bondage to decay and brought into the glorious freedom of the children of God.
>
> We know that the whole creation has been groaning as in the pains of childbirth right up to the present time. Not only so, but we ourselves, who have the firstfruits of the Spirit, groan inwardly as we wait eagerly for our adoption as sons, the redemption of our bodies. For in this hope we were saved. But hope that is seen is no hope at all. Who hopes for what he already has? But if we hope for what we do not yet have, we wait for it patiently.

In the same way, the Spirit helps us in our weakness. We do not know what we ought to pray for, but the Spirit himself intercedes for us with groans that words cannot express. And he who searches our hearts knows the mind of the Spirit, because the Spirit intercedes for the saints in accordance with God's will.

And we know that in all things God works for the good of those who love him, who have been called according to his purpose. For those God foreknew he also predestined to be conformed to the likeness of his Son, that he might be the firstborn among many brothers. And those he predestined, he also called; those he called, he also justified; those he justified, he also glorified.

What, then, shall we say in response to this? If God is for us, who can be against us? He who did not spare his own Son, but gave him up for us all – how will he not also, along with him, graciously give us all things? Who will bring any charge against those whom God has chosen? It is God who justifies. Who is he that condemns? Christ Jesus, who died – more than that, who was raised to life – is at the right hand of God and is also interceding for us. Who shall separate us from the love of Christ? Shall trouble or hardship or persecution or famine or nakedness or danger or sword? As it is written:

"For your sake we face death all day long;
        we are considered as sheep to be slaughtered."

No, in all these things we are more than conquerors through him who loved us. For I am convinced that neither death nor life, neither angels nor demons, neither the present nor the future, nor any powers, neither height nor depth, nor anything else in all creation, will be able to separate us from the love of God that is in Christ Jesus our Lord.

(Romans 8:18–39.)

In all of Scripture this is one of the most magnificent statements of the love of God in taking the initiative to provide salvation in all of its aspects, so that nothing whatsoever can separate us from his love for us in Christ Jesus – not even death itself. I have emphasised the passage that is relevant to our discussion. In the context of suffering, weakness, and uncertainty, we are to know that God is working in all things for the good of those who love him. Paul describes them as those who have been called according to his purpose. What that grand purpose is, he is about to explain. But not before he gives another description of believers as those whom God foreknew, which (as we have seen) does not imply that God caused or forced them to do anything in advance. It is a great encouragement to believers under pressure to know that they have experienced the call of God; God has known them, and knows all about them – and he has a purpose for them. What is that purpose? He has predestined them to be conformed to the image of his Son.

Under the pressure of an assumed paradigm it is all too easy to read into this that Paul is saying that God has predestined them to be believers, and then using this statement to buttress theistic determinism. However, Paul is saying something completely different: that God has predestined those who are believers to be conformed to the image of his Son. That is, he plans to confer unimaginable dignity upon believers. As creatures of God they were made in the image of God. But now that they have put their faith in Christ and received his salvation, a destiny of almost indescribable glory awaits them. In his love for them God has determined that they should be like his Son. The sheer wonder of this purpose now defines the illimitable nature of God's grace and glory. In one sense, God could have predestined us to anything glorious that he willed, but he has chosen this ultimate accolade. The objective is that the Lord Jesus should be the firstborn (first to be glorified and also first in rank) among many brothers.

This is God's staggeringly gracious goal. Achieving it involves all of God's provision in the gospel that Paul has been expounding up to this point – calling, justification by faith, and glorification. It is the sheer glory of the achievement that calls forth Paul's triumphant and confident conclusion – *If God is for us, who can be against us?*

Arising directly from these glorious thoughts, however, there comes a question that deeply disturbs and concerns the apostle. In light of such a magnificent and gracious message, how is it that his fellow Israelites, Paul's own kith and kin, mainly reject such a wonderfully gracious message and deny that Jesus is the Messiah, the Son of God? Paul's pain is palpable as he explains:

> *I speak the truth in Christ – I am not lying, my conscience confirms it in the Holy Spirit – I have great sorrow and unceasing anguish in my heart. For I could wish that I myself were cursed and cut off from Christ for the sake of my brothers, those of my own race, the people of Israel. Theirs is the adoption as sons; theirs the divine glory, the covenants, the receiving of the law, the temple worship and the promises. Theirs are the patriarchs, and from them is traced the human ancestry of Christ, who is God over all, for ever praised! Amen.*
>
> (Romans 9:1–5.)

Paul faces an apparent contradiction. His nation of Israel by and large rejected Christ, who was also their own flesh and blood, even though as a nation they were uniquely privileged. God had adopted them as his people – as his sons, even, those who inherit the family assets; he had visited them in his glory at Sinai, and in the tabernacle, given them the covenants, the law, and the worship programme of the temple; he had lavished his promises on them. Not only that, it was God who had given them the patriarchs, from whom the ancestry of the Messiah would be traced – the Messiah who is none less than God himself. And they don't believe in him!

This was no new issue for Paul. He faced it many times as he sought to persuade men and women of the truth of the Christian message. For instance, he held lectures in the synagogue at Thessalonica on three sabbath days:

> *As his custom was, Paul went in to the synagogue, and on three Sabbath days he reasoned with them from the Scriptures, explaining and proving that the Christ had to suffer and rise*

from the dead. "This Jesus I am proclaiming to you is the
Christ," he said.

(Acts 17:2–3.)

One can easily imagine some intelligent Jew saying, "That was a very interesting talk, Paul, and I find it impressive that a rabbi with your undoubtedly high qualifications, having studied under Gamaliel, is prepared to argue in this way. However, what bothers me is that you seem to be on your own in this. Or am I mistaken? Can you tell me of any other senior rabbis who believe that your interpretations are correct?"

And Paul might reply, "Well there's Nicodemus, and Joseph of Arimathea, both on the Sanhedrin Council in Jerusalem."

"Is that all? If what you say is true – and I admit I was moved by it – surely one might expect the majority of the Jewish thinkers to accept it? After all, on the basis of our Scriptures you are claiming that Jesus is the Messiah expected by our nation, yet the experts in the interpretation of those Scriptures don't agree with you. Surely you can see why I am puzzled!"

Paul could see it, and it affected him deeply. He got the same question from Gentiles as well. "If something is really authentically Jewish, the Jews should be the first to accept it. And yet most of them reject it. How can that be?"

Paul was heartbroken about the situation and desperately wanted to do something about it. It threatened to become a serious stumbling block in the way of people taking the gospel seriously. As he writes in chapter 8, how can he believe that nothing shall separate us from the love of God, when it appears to many that something has separated Israel from God? How can Israel have lost her way so dramatically?

So Paul writes Romans 9–11 in order to show that, far from being an objection to the Christian message, what has happened historically with Israel, in their rejection of the Lord Jesus, in fact confirms the truth of it.

At this point some interpreters of Scripture argue that the ultimate answer to this question is given by Paul in his letter to the Galatians. There he abolishes all distinctions between Jews and non-Jews in his famous statement, that in Christ *there is neither Jew nor Greek...* (Galatians 3:28). Surely this means (it is argued) that all the promises given to Israel in the Old Testament are now to be understood as fulfilled in the church. Hence God has not cast off his people, since "his people" now equates to "the church" which is alive and thriving.

However, Paul's statement in Galatians is not relevant to his problem in Romans. In Galatians 3:21–29 Paul is discussing the basis of salvation, and he stresses that it is the same for everyone, whatever their ethnicity, social status, or gender – Jew, Greek, slave, free, man, woman. That common basis is faith in Christ alone. Paul is not talking there about the question of roles in history or in the world, which for obvious reasons might well be different for each of these groups. To deduce from these verses that, now that Christ has come, there is absolutely no difference between the roles of Jews and Gentiles, would be as absurd as saying that, since Christ has come, there is absolutely no difference between the roles of slave and free or between the roles of male and female. Their roles can remain the same without prejudice to their status in Christ.

By contrast Paul's concern in Romans 9–11 is not the basis of the gospel but why it is that the very nation that was privileged by God to be the vehicle of his revelation to the world now mainly rejects the gospel of the Messiah. That is the problem he has to address, and it is so complex that he takes three chapters to do it.

The first main argument is based on the fact that not all ethnic Israelites are the genuine people of God. His discussion involves considering the sovereignty of God in history regarding the role of different individuals and the nations descended from them.

The second main argument is that Israel's unbelief is culpable. God has made every provision for them. Paul goes through every excuse that might be raised to let Israel off the hook and concludes in each case that they are responsible for their unbelief.

The third main argument concentrates on the fact that there are some Israelites, like Paul, who do believe in Jesus. Indeed, all through history there has been a "remnant" of true believers within

Israel, whose number has at times been underestimated. Paul then discusses the historical roles that Israel and then the Gentiles have had in witnessing for God in the world, and concludes with the glorious hope for his nation that one day "all Israel will be saved". Paul is in no doubt that there remains a role for his nation in the future, but not until they come to faith in Jesus as Messiah.

CHAPTER 13

Why Doesn't Israel Believe?

But it is not as though the word of God has failed. For not all who are descended from Israel belong to Israel, and not all are children of Abraham because they are his offspring, but "Through Isaac shall your offspring be named." This means that it is not the children of the flesh who are the children of God, but the children of the promise are counted as offspring. For this is what the promise said: "About this time next year I will return, and Sarah shall have a son."

(Romans 9:6–9 ESV.)

We pause to re-emphasise that Paul's concern is for his fellow nationals, those of his own race. It is the ethnic race – not some spiritual group within it – to whom were entrusted the privileges and exalted role that Paul has spelt out in the earlier verses. Paul's concern, then, is for his contemporaries, those fellow Jews who despite their great privilege have nonetheless rejected salvation through Christ. He calls them his brothers; they are Israelites (note the present tense) yet they are unregenerate. God had chosen Israel for a special role in history, but that role did not amount to salvation. We should also note that God's choice of Israel as his people does not mean that everyone else was written off for condemnation. Indeed, one of the major reasons for choosing them was to be a "light to the Gentiles" – Joseph, Daniel, and Jonah, for example.

Furthermore, Paul's expression of sorrow for Israel would be very strange if he believed that these people were the "non-elect" whom God had chosen for eternal reprobation – which, in the opinion of some, would demonstrate God's glory.

What, then, is the significance of Israel's rejection of Jesus as the Messiah? Does it mean – a possibility Paul directly voices – that *the word of God had failed* (verse 6)? Paul says no, for *not all who are descended from Israel belong to Israel*. We must read this in the light of what he has just said about his fellow nationals who reject Christ – they are his brothers, they are Israel (present tense). However, they were not all what we might call genuine, spiritual Israelites. Early in John's Gospel Nathanael was amazed when Jesus addressed him as *a true Israelite, in whom there is nothing false* (John 1:47).

At the time of Jesus there were many people, including his disciples, who were true, spiritual Israelites and who welcomed him as the Messiah. The group swelled to thousands at the day of Pentecost in Jerusalem. It has continued through the centuries, and there have always been true Israelites who believe that Jesus is the Messiah, the Son of God. Romans 9 will end where it began, by stressing the fact that, as Isaiah predicted, the number of genuine believing Israelites will be much less than the population as a whole: *Though the number of the Israelites be like the sand by the sea, only the remnant will be saved* (verse 27, quoting Isaiah 10:22). Thus, far from implying that the word of God has failed, the current rejection of the Messiah by Israel as a whole will in fact establish that word.

Paul now makes a parallel point about Abraham, to whom all Israel traced their ancestry:

> *For not all who are descended from Israel belong to Israel, and not all are children of Abraham because they are his offspring, but "Through Isaac shall your offspring be named." This means that it is not the children of the flesh who are the children of God, but the children of the promise are counted as offspring.*
> (Romans 9:6–8 ESV.)

Abraham had two sons, Ishmael and Isaac. God blessed both of them, yet their status was not the same, and neither were their roles in history. Ishmael and his descendants were not entrusted with the promises that God gave to Isaac and his descendants. Paul's audience would readily have accepted that.

The term "offspring" translates the Greek word "seed", which plays a prominent role in Paul's vocabulary. The most important role given to Abraham – and carried on through Isaac, Jacob, and his descendants through Judah, David, and many others – was to carry the seed-line of the Messiah in the physical sense. In Galatians 3 Paul interprets the seed indicated in God's promise to Abraham in a very narrow and specific sense:

> *The promises were spoken to Abraham and to his seed. The Scripture does not say "and to seeds", meaning many people, but "and to your seed", meaning one person, who is Christ.*
> (Galatians 3:16.)

In Romans 9 his objective is much broader. It is to establish the principle that not all the natural descendants of Abraham are to be counted as his children – only the children of promise. Paul uses the term "children of the flesh" and opposes it to the terms "children of God" and "children of promise". Of course, in the physical sense, both sets of children were children of the flesh, which makes it clear that Paul is alluding to something deeper.

Paul refers briefly to the terms in which the promise was made, quoting Genesis:

> *Then the Lord said, "I will surely return to you about this time next year, and Sarah your wife will have a son."*
> (Genesis 18:10.)

This is enough of a hint for us to grasp why Paul uses the term "flesh". According to Genesis, God had promised Abraham earlier that he would have his own children. However, Sarah was barren, and as time went on she despaired of having her own child and encouraged Abraham to have a child by Hagar, her Egyptian maid. She seems to have thought that this was a satisfactory way of seeing that God's promise was fulfilled. Her attitude was a classic example of the idea that "God helps those who help themselves". She put her trust "in the flesh", as Paul would say. Paul knew all about this human tendency to trust human ability and achievement, rather than trusting God. That is precisely what he had done as a younger man when he was one of those Israelites who denied that Jesus was the Messiah. It was when he abandoned his trust in the flesh that he became "an Israelite indeed".

God was not dependent on Sarah's stratagem. It is absurd to think that God's project of bringing Messiah into the world as the Seed of Abraham (I call it the Seed Project) would be allowed to depend on Sarah's attempt to use her own resources. In the historical situation God was teaching Abraham and Sarah (not Isaac) what it meant to trust him rather than their own ability or resources. The child to be born would be a real gift, unmerited and undeserved, a child of promise and not of the flesh.

We should notice that this text has nothing to do with the personal salvation of Isaac, as many theistic determinists hold. The statement that Isaac was a child of promise is not made in connection with his personal, spiritual birth through faith in God, but his physical birth through the faith of Abraham and Sarah. God's selection of Isaac as the seed through whom he would fulfil his promise to bless the world was a sovereign choice. Ishmael was not given this role, again by God's sovereign choice. Contrary to the view of some theistic determinists again, however, far from abandoning Ishmael and condemning him, God promises to bless him. Listen to Abraham interceding with God for Ishmael:

And Abraham said to God, "If only Ishmael might live under your blessing!"

Then God said, "Yes, but your wife Sarah will bear you a son, and you will call him Isaac. I will establish my covenant with him as an everlasting covenant for his descendants after him. And as for Ishmael, I have heard you: I will surely bless him; I will make him fruitful and will greatly increase his numbers. He will be the father of twelve rulers, and I will make him into a great nation."

(Genesis 17:18–20.)

Abraham's request is that Ishmael may live under God's blessing, and God grants it to him. Isaac will have a special role, but Ishmael will be blessed also. In light of this, the use of this text to promote "double predestination" seems completely wrong.

Furthermore, the lesson taught to Abraham and Sarah, regarding how they became physical parents of a child and a nation, must not be confused with another spiritual lesson from the story in the New Testament:

> Now you, brothers, like Isaac, are children of promise. But just as at that time he who was born according to the flesh persecuted him who was born according to the Spirit, so also it is now. But what does the Scripture say? "Cast out the slave woman and her son, for the son of the slave woman shall not inherit with the son of the free woman." So, brothers, we are not children of the slave but of the free woman.
>
> (Galatians 4:28–31 ESV.)

The context here is an appeal to the believers in Galatia, who were under pressure to turn back to keeping the law for salvation. Paul tells them (and us) to put personal faith, all confidence for salvation, in God's promise and not human merit. That will make them (and us) spiritual children of Abraham and Sarah.[131]

But we must get back to Romans 9. Having established the principle that not all of Abraham's descendants are counted as his children, in the special sense of being the seed through whom the Messiah will be born, Paul turns to the generation after Abraham – that of his son Isaac. This second example differs from the first in that the children involved not only have the same father but the same mother. Even more than that, they were twins. This deflects any possible comeback on the first example, that the significant differences resided in the fact that Isaac and Ishmael had different mothers.

---

131 For a detailed exposition of this section of Galatians, see D. Gooding, *The Riches of Divine Wisdom*, Coleraine, Myrtlefield Trust, 2013, chapter 15.

Here, then, is the record of the births of the twin boys, Jacob and Esau:

Not only that, but Rebekah's children had one and the same time father, our father Isaac. Yet, before the twins were born or had done anything good or bad – in order that God's purpose in election might stand: not by works but by him who calls – she was told, "The older will serve the younger." Just as it is written: "Jacob I loved, but Esau I hated."

(Romans 9:10–13.)

This passage is one of the principal texts quoted to defend the idea that God has chosen some for salvation and the rest for reprobation, without any reference to the individuals involved. Theistic determinists point to the use of the word "election" in this passage, and claim that these verses refer to the individual salvation or condemnation of Jacob and Esau. However, we need to ask: chosen for what? What was the goal of the election? The answer is given: *the older will serve the younger.*

The Genesis account of Rebekah's pregnancy runs as follows:

Isaac prayed to the Lord on behalf of his wife, because she was barren. The Lord answered his prayer, and his wife Rebekah became pregnant. The babies jostled each other within her, and she said, "Why is this happening to me?" So she went to enquire of the Lord. The Lord said to her, "Two nations are in your womb, and two peoples from within you will be separated; one people will be stronger than the other, and the older will serve the younger."

(Genesis 25:21–23.)

The text has nothing to do with salvation or reprobation but with God's sovereign choice for different roles in history; and not even the roles of the individuals involved but of the nations to which they gave rise. As an individual, Esau never did serve Jacob, and Rebekah was told explicitly that it was nations and not individuals in view: *Two nations are in your womb, and two peoples from within you will be separated*. Later in the history of Israel, when David had become king, the Edomites (descended from Esau) came and paid homage to him and served him. It is easy to forget that Isaac blessed Esau, and in the later history God told Israel: *Do not abhor an Edomite, for he is your brother* (Deuteronomy 23:7).

The second quotation in Romans 9, *Jacob I loved, but Esau I hated*, comes from the prophet Malachi (1:2–3). It was written centuries after the events recorded in Genesis, and in its context it clearly refers once more to the nations and not to individuals. The passage of time had shown that Edom was a nation deserving God's judgment. Paul may well be hinting here that his fellow Israelites were exhibiting the same features as the Edomites.

Malachi also warned Judah that, in spite of God's love for them in giving them a unique role in history, they would be devastated by God's judgment if they did not repent of the evil that they allowed to run rampant among them. There were some that responded to Malachi's warning and repented:

> *Then those who feared the Lord talked with each other, and the Lord listened and heard. A scroll of remembrance was written in his presence concerning those who feared the Lord and honoured his name.*
>
> *"They will be mine," says the Lord Almighty, "in the day when I make up my treasured possession. I will spare them, just as in compassion a man spares his son who serves him. And you will again see the distinction between the righteous and the wicked, between those who serve God and those who do not."*
>
> (Malachi 3:16–18.)

Those who feared the Lord were the true people of God. The whole nation was descended from Jacob, and God loved them, but in his love he would discipline them and in the end remove the wicked, who neither loved nor honoured him. Once more we see that mere membership of the nation that God loved did not guarantee personal salvation. If Edom was not spared for certain behaviour, neither would Israel be spared for the same behaviour.

To sum up so far. These verses do not discuss individual election to salvation but corporate election to service and role. God chose (elected) the different roles these nations were to play. It was a sovereign choice. Neither of the children, Jacob or Esau, had done good or evil at this stage – they weren't even born. God's choice of privileged role was completely independent of them or their merits. The promise to Rebekah is an assignment of role and not an assignment of eternal destiny.

Consequently I find it difficult to take seriously statements like the following by theologians Ernst Käsemann and Geoffrey Bromiley:

> *The presence of a strong concept of predestination cannot be denied although only here does Paul present double-predestination. Not until this is admitted without reserve can one see its necessary delimitations and ask about its significance within the framework of the apostle's theology... Since the theme is Israel, the issue is soteriology. From v. 12a it follows even more precisely that the doctrine of the justification of the ungodly is anchored in the sovereign freedom of the Creator... God's word comes on the scene as a stigmatizing address with which salvation or perdition takes place for human beings.*[132]

But verse 12 says, *The older will serve the younger!* The issue is not soteriology. It has absolutely nothing to do with justification or salvation or perdition. Nor has it to do with individuals, except in so far as Jacob was chosen to father the race and Esau was not. God's elective purpose here has to do with service or role, and is about nations. The above statement, therefore, is fatally flawed.

Contrast the wise words of Griffith Thomas:

> *The primary thought of the apostle in these chapters is not individual salvation, but the philosophy of history... Israel's*

---

132 E. Käsemann and G. W. Bromiley, *Commentary on Romans*, Grand Rapids, Eerdmans, 1980, pp. 265–66.

election had for its object the service of his fellow men. St.
Paul is concerned not so much with individuals, as with
nations and masses of people. He speaks of God's choice of
Israel, not to eternal life as such, but to privileges and duty.[133]

Similarly, N. T. Wright holds that this passage does not concern itself directly with the predestination of individuals for soteriological concerns, but instead concerns itself with the question of God's faithfulness to the people of Israel. He writes:

Chapter 9 has long been seen as the central New Testament
passage on "predestination," though as we shall see the
theological tradition from Augustine to Calvin (and beyond)
did not grasp what Paul was actually talking about here.[134]

This principle outlined in these verses of Romans 9 is of fundamental importance, and it applies elsewhere in a way that can help us to understand it better. Every believer is a member of the body of Christ, but not every believer has the same role. Our different roles are assigned by a sovereign God: *But in fact God has arranged the parts in the body, every one of them, just as he wanted them to be* (1 Corinthians 12:18). Once again, the sovereign activity of God described here has nothing to do with salvation, nor does it violate the principle of human free will – it is rather a question of what God chooses to do with those that are saved.

Something that strikes me as very odd is that some leading theologians who maintain that these texts have to do with personal salvation freely admit that this is not the original meaning of the Old Testament passages. For instance, Douglas Moo says,

---

133 W. H. Griffith Thomas, *Commentary on Romans*, Grand Rapids, Kregel, 1974, pp. 115–16, 156–57, 222.

134 N. T. Wright, "The Letter to the Romans: Introduction, Commentary, and Reflections" in L. E. Keck (Sr. ed.), *The New Interpreter's Bible: A Commentary in Twelve Volumes*, vol. X., Nashville, Abingdon Press, 2002, p. 620.

*If Paul applies Old Testament texts according to their original
intent, the Calvinists' appeal to Romans 9 is undercut and
perhaps excluded altogether. Calvinist interpreters have then
made the mistake of reading election to salvation into a text
that is not about that at all.*[135]

Interestingly, Gerald Bray points out that four centuries of church
history had run their course before Augustine introduced a
deterministic interpretation of Romans 9:

*Only Augustine, and then only in his later writings,
was prepared to accept the full implications of divine
predestination.*[136]

Moo, who says that he is "generally (but not consistently) Calvinistic
in his soteriology", comes to the conclusion that "Paul does not always
apply his Old Testament quotations in accordance with their original
intent". It is certainly true that Paul often finds a deeper significance
in Old Testament texts in the light of the gospel of Christ that goes
beyond the original. However, in this particular case the context in
the Old Testament is the genesis of the people of God, Israel; and the
texts in their context are entirely germane to the question that Paul
is addressing, which rather validates Moo's comment regarding the
mistake of reading election to salvation into a text that is not about
that topic at all.

Harry Ironside wrote:

*There is no question here of predestination to heaven or
reprobation to hell; in fact eternal issues do no really come in
throughout this chapter, although, of course, they naturally
follow as the result of the use or abuse of God-given privileges.*

---

135 D. J. Moo, *The Epistle to the Romans*, Grand Rapids, Eerdmans, 1996,
p. 303.
136 G. L. Bray (ed.), *Romans*, Downer's Grove, IVP, 1998,
p. 244.

> *But we are not told here, nor anywhere else, that before
> children are born it is God's purpose to send one to heaven and
> another to hell… The passage has entirely to do with privilege
> here on earth.*[137]

We now proceed to the next part of the text:

> *What then shall we say? Is God unjust? Not at all! For he says
> to Moses, "I will have mercy on whom I have mercy, and I will
> have compassion on whom I have compassion." It does not,
> therefore, depend on man's desire or effort, but on God's mercy.
> For the Scripture says to Pharaoh: "I raised you up for this
> very purpose, that I might display my power in you and that
> my name might be proclaimed in all the earth." Therefore God
> has mercy on whom he wants to have mercy, and he hardens
> whom he wants to harden.*
>
> (Romans 9:14–18.)

Paul, as he does from time to time in Romans, now brings in an
imaginary objector, to raise a moral question – one that must have
been put to him often. Is God unjust; how can this all be fair? The
more one thinks about it this question of fairness is difficult, even
in connection with the accounts of Abraham's immediate family.
Consider, for instance, Sarah's treatment of Hagar and Ishmael in
sending them away in despair. God sends Hagar back the first time,
but when Isaac is born she is permanently dismissed. And what
about Jacob's deceit of Isaac, and his theft of the blessing from Esau?
This is the complex stuff of life, and the more complex it is the more
there tends to be a background feeling of unfairness.

In order to answer the question, Paul turns to two Old Testament
passages from the book of Exodus. They both concern seminal events
in the historical development of the nation of Israel. The first one is
the giving of the law at Sinai through Moses; and the second (though

137 H. A. Ironside, *Lectures on the Epistle to the Romans*, New Jersey,
       Neptune, 1928.

earlier in time) is the exodus, when Moses took Israel out of Egypt to form an independent nation, against the protests of Pharaoh. These quotations take us into two sides of God's activity in history: his mercy to Israel; and his hardening of Pharaoh's heart.

Let us look at the first. When God was giving the law to Moses, the nation was rebelling against God and demanding that Aaron should make them a god to go before them (see Exodus 32:1). Aaron fashioned a golden calf and Israel worshipped it. It was a very low point in the nation's history.

God's reaction was to tell Moses that he would destroy the people because of their blasphemy, but he would make a great nation from Moses' descendants. Moses pleads with God to turn from his fierce anger against the nation. His appeal is on the basis of God's promises:

> *Remember your servants Abraham, Isaac and Israel, to whom*
> *you swore by your own self: "I will make your descendants*
> *as numerous as the stars in the sky and I will give your*
> *descendants all this land I promised them, and it will be their*
> *inheritance for ever." Then the Lord relented and did not bring*
> *on his people the disaster he had threatened.*
>
> (Exodus 32:13–14.)

In response God relents and spares his people. He tells Moses to continue to lead them, and promises that he will send an angel to protect and defend them. Moses then pleads with God a second time that God should go with them, and there follows an awesome encounter between Moses and God:

> *Moses said to the Lord, "You have been telling me, 'Lead these*
> *people,' but you have not let me know whom you will send*
> *with me. You have said, 'I know you by name and you have*
> *found favour with me.' If you are pleased with me, teach me*
> *your ways so I may know you and continue to find favour*
> *with you. Remember that this nation is your people."*
>
> *The Lord replied, "My Presence will go with you, and I*
> *will give you rest."*

> Then Moses said to him, "If your Presence does not go with us, do not send us up from here. How will anyone know that you are pleased with me and with your people unless you go with us? What else will distinguish me and your people from all the other people on the face of the earth?"
>
> And the Lord said to Moses, "I will do the very thing you have asked, because I am pleased with you and I know you by name."
>
> Then Moses said, "Now show me your glory."
>
> And the Lord said, "I will cause all my goodness to pass in front of you, and I will proclaim my name, the Lord, in your presence. I will have mercy on whom I will have mercy, and I will have compassion on whom I will have compassion."
>
> (Exodus 33:12–19.)

It is the very last statement that is quoted in Romans 9. Its historical context is a demonstration of utterly undeserved mercy towards Israel on an occasion when God could justly have wiped them out. This makes Paul's choice of quotation highly relevant to his purpose. His readers would know that he was talking about an infamous incident in the desert when almost all of the nation of Israel was rejecting Moses their leader, whom God had raised up to deliver them. As a nation they were God's chosen people, but at that time very few of them had hearts that beat for God. Paul's anguish at his fellow Israelites' rejection of Messiah resonated powerfully with Moses' anguish at the people's rejection of God.

What is more, even if God had wiped the nation out, as he threatened to do, and started again with Moses, none of his promises would have been invalidated since they were to the nation as a whole, not to individuals within the nation.

And yet God did not destroy them; he pardoned them. It was an act of sheer mercy. One might say that God's dealing with Israel witnesses to his longsuffering, in light of his desire that no one should perish but all come to repentance:

*The Lord is not slow in keeping his promise, as some
understand slowness. He is patient with you, not wanting
anyone to perish, but everyone to come to repentance.*

(2 Peter 3:9.)

Moses then asked to see God's glory and was rewarded with a vision
of "all God's goodness":

*"But," he said, "you cannot see my face, for no-one may see me
and live." Then the Lord said, "There is a place near me where
you may stand on a rock. When my glory passes by, I will put
you in a cleft in the rock and cover you with my hand until I
have passed by. Then I will remove my hand, and you will see
my back; but my face must not be seen.*

(Exodus 33:20–23.)

It is in this context that we read the revelation of God's character, *I
will have mercy on whom I will have mercy*. Mercy, by definition, is
undeserved. Because of Israel's sin at this juncture of history, God
would have been justified in destroying them. They did not deserve
pardon, but in his mercy and compassion God gave it to them.

With regard to theistic determinism, we must now ask if this will
of God is arbitrary and independent of the objects of mercy. Surely
not. The incident we have just remembered involves Moses pleading
and the people mourning and showing evidence of repentance. We
should also note that the mercy of God on this occasion saved the
nation physically, but it did not necessarily save them spiritually.
Many of those who were spared would later rebel and fall in the
wilderness. Indeed, the vast majority of the generation that left Egypt
with Moses eventually failed to get into the promised land. The letter
to the Hebrews makes it clear why they didn't enter:

*For we also have had the gospel preached to us, just as they
did; but the message they heard was of no value to them,
because those who heard did not combine it with faith. Now
we who have believed enter that rest, just as God has said, "So*

I declared on oath in my anger, 'They shall never enter my rest.'" And yet his work has been finished since the creation of the world.

(Hebrews 4:2–3.)

This is clear evidence that, in the end, the behaviour of many people in the desert demonstrated that they had never believed the message that Moses preached to them. They were unbelievers. Nonetheless Paul's magnificent statement of God's grace and the freedom of his mercy here give a hint of the climax of his argument in this section of Romans:

For God has bound all men over to disobedience so that he may have mercy on them all. Oh, the depth of the riches of the wisdom and knowledge of God! How unsearchable his judgments, and his paths beyond tracing out!

(Romans 11:32–33.)

This is the measure of God's mercy and compassion: it is available for all and not just for a select few.

CHAPTER 14

The Hardening of Pharaoh's Heart

The description of God's mercy to Israel in Romans 9 raises an obvious question. Does God always show mercy? If not, does that not bring us straight back to the question of fairness in history and experience? Paul now addresses this question by going back in history to the time of the Exodus from Egypt.

> *For the Scripture says to Pharaoh, "I raised you up for this very purpose, that I might display my power in you and that my name might be proclaimed in all the earth." Therefore God has mercy on whom he wants to have mercy, and he hardens whom he wants to harden.*
>
> (Romans 9:17–18.)

This time Paul considers God's dealings not with a nation but with an individual who does not belong to Israel – the Egyptian Pharaoh. The central issue for us is the hardening of Pharaoh's heart.

What does this mean? Is it, as some theistic determinists, hold that God decreed in the remote eternal past that there would be a nation called Israel on which he would confer his blessing, and to which he would show mercy? Did he also determine that there would be another nation called Egypt, headed up by Pharaoh, made for no other purpose than showing his glory by destroying them and condemning them to eternal perdition? Is the major lesson to be learned here that God's will is both unconditional and irresistible?

I am aware that this kind of view has considerable support. For instance, Martin Luther wrote:

This mightily offends our rational nature, that God should of his mere unbiased will leave some men to themselves, harden them and condemn them; but he gives abundant demonstration, and does continually, that this is the case; namely, that the sole cause why some are saved, and others perish, proceeds from His willing the salvation of the former, and the perdition of the latter, according to that of St. Paul, "He hath mercy on whom he will, and whom he will he hardeneth."

(Romans 9:17–18.)[138]

Nevertheless – with due and real respect for Luther's immense, indeed unique, contribution to the spread of the gospel – we must examine the possibility that the reason his view on this issue "mightily offends our rational nature" is that it is not correct, as John Wesley maintained – also no mean contributor to the spread of the gospel. In fact, it is not so much that it offends our rational minds and that God's thoughts are beyond and above our thoughts, but that it offends our moral judgment. And, as we saw much earlier from John's Gospel, our Lord constantly invites us to use our moral judgment, both on his life and teaching and on ourselves.

Paul prefaces this section by referring to the moral dimension, and states categorically that there is no injustice with God. So it did not offend Paul's rational thinking. Once again he brings in an imaginary objector to raise this very point:

You will say to me then, "Why does he still find fault? For who can resist his will?"

(Romans 9:19 ESV.)

The objector raises the moral problem: if God's will is irresistible, there is no reason for God to judge that anything is wrong.

---

138 Cited by Jerome Zanchius (1516–90) in his book *Absolute Predestination*, republished by Sovereign Grace Publishers, Lafayette Indiana, 2001, p. 19. Original available in Martin Luther, *Vom Unfreien Willen*, in Kurt Aland (ed.), *Die Werke des Reformators in neuer Auswahl für die Gegenwart*, vol. 3, Stuttgart, Göttingen 1961ff., S. 151–334.

There are only two possible logical responses to this. Either the premise (God's will is irresistible) is correct, and the deduction (God has no right to find fault) is false; or the premise is incorrect and so the argument collapses. Scripture gives adequate support for the latter. Our Lord once wept over Jerusalem:

> *O Jerusalem, Jerusalem, you who kill the prophets and stone those sent to you, how often I have longed to gather your children together, as a hen gathers her chicks under her wings, but you were not willing.*
>
> (Matthew 23:37.)

Here it is the will of the Lord to gather the people under his protection, but they resisted his will, and the resistance was not broken by an arbitrary display of power.

The climax of Stephen's speech to the Sanhedrin at Jerusalem demonstrates that resistance to God has been a sad characteristic of the people of Israel throughout their history:

> *"You stiff-necked people, with uncircumcised hearts and ears! You are just like your fathers: You always resist the Holy Spirit! Was there ever a prophet your fathers did not persecute? They even killed those who predicted the coming of the Righteous One. And now you have betrayed and murdered him – you who have received the law that was put into effect through angels but have not obeyed it." When they heard this, they were furious and gnashed their teeth at him.*
>
> (Acts 7:51–54.)

Once again, their resistance was not overcome by irresistible force. It was allowed to stand, and Stephen was murdered.

Therefore we must read the story of Pharaoh in such a way as to challenge the objector's deduction that God's will is irresistible. Exodus tells us that God instructed Moses to go to Pharaoh and ask him to let his enslaved people go. The sequence in brief is as follows. Moses makes his request; Pharaoh refuses, and makes the burden on Israel heavier. God appears to Moses and promises to bring the nation to the promised land. He tells Moses that he will harden Pharaoh's heart (Exodus 7:3).

There is no doubt that God foresees and foreknows everything but, as we saw earlier, that does not mean he causes what subsequently happens. Moses goes to Pharaoh again, with Aaron as his spokesman. They do a miracle, which is reproduced by Pharaoh's magicians. Pharaoh's heart was hardened (Exodus 7:13), and there then follows a lengthy series of plagues:

1. **Blood**. Moses and Aaron turn the water of the Nile to blood. The magicians appear (to Pharaoh at least) to be able to do the same, so *Pharaoh's heart became hard* (7:22).

2. **Frogs**. Again the magicians imitate this, although they cannot get rid of the frogs. Pharaoh pleads for the frogs to be removed, and Moses prays that God would do so. When Pharaoh sees the respite, *he hardened his heart and would not listen to Moses and Aaron, just as the Lord had said* (8:15).

3. **Gnats**. The magicians cannot follow through and tell Pharaoh that it is *the finger of God. But Pharaoh's heart was hard and he would not listen, just as the Lord had said* (8:19).

4. **Flies**. This time Pharaoh agrees to let the people go. Moses prays for a cessation of the plague, and again *Pharaoh hardened his heart* (8:32).

5. **Livestock disease**. But *his heart was unyielding* (9:7).

6. **Boils**. But *the Lord hardened Pharaoh's heart and he would not listen to Moses and Aaron, just as the Lord had said to Moses* (9:12). This is the first time the Lord's name is mentioned in connection with Pharaoh's heart being hardened.

7. **Hail**. Pharaoh calls Moses, confesses his sin, and asks Moses to plead with the Lord for respite. He says that he will then let the people go. Moses agrees to do so but tells Pharaoh, *I know that you and your officials still do not fear the Lord God*

(9:30). Some of the Egyptians, however, have begun to fear the Lord, and they organise shelter for their slaves and cattle. The message still does not get through to Pharaoh. *When Pharaoh saw that the rain and hail and thunder had stopped, he sinned again: He and his officials hardened their hearts. So Pharaoh's heart was hard and he would not let the Israelites go...* (9:34–35).

8. **Locusts.** Moses announces the plague, and Pharaoh's servants appeal to him to let the people go, in light of the fact that *Egypt is ruined* (10:7). Pharaoh brings Moses and Aaron back into his court and says that he will let the men go, but not the women and children. He accuses them of having some evil purpose in mind and drives them out. The plague ensues and Pharaoh confesses his sin both against God and Moses, and asks for forgiveness and respite. *But the Lord hardened Pharaoh's heart, and he would not let the Israelites go* (10:20).

9. **Darkness.** There is darkness in Egypt, although not where the Israelites live. Pharaoh calls Moses and tells him to go but to leave their flocks behind. Moses says, *Our livestock too must go with us; not a hoof is to be left behind We have to use some of them in worshipping the Lord our God... But the Lord hardened Pharaoh's heart, and he was not willing to let them go. Pharaoh said to Moses, "Get out of my sight! Make sure you do not appear before me again!"* (10:26–28).

10. **Death of the firstborn.** God tells Moses that there is to be one more plague, after which Pharaoh will let the people go. At midnight all firstborn will die, unless they are in a house protected by the blood of a lamb. Instructions for Passover are given, and each Israelite household smears the blood of the Passover lamb on their doorposts and lintel. At midnight the firstborn in the unprotected houses die. Pharaoh tells Moses and Aaron to go and serve the Lord – and asks for their blessing (12:29–32).

The sequel: Moses leads the Israelites out of Egypt until they reach the coast, where they encamp. God then tells Moses:

> *Pharaoh will think, "The Israelites are wandering around the land in confusion, hemmed in by the desert." And I will harden Pharaoh's heart, and he will pursue them. But I will gain glory for myself through Pharaoh and all his army, and the Egyptians will know that I am the Lord.*
>
> (Exodus 14:3–4.)

Pharaoh's reaction:

> *When the king of Egypt was told that the people had fled, Pharaoh and his officials changed their minds about them and said, "What have we done? We have let the Israelites go and have lost their services!" So he had his chariot made ready and took his army with him. He took six hundred of the best chariots, along with all the other chariots of Egypt, with officers over all of them. The Lord hardened the heart of Pharaoh king of Egypt, so that he pursued the Israelites, who were marching out boldly.*
>
> (Exodus 14:5–8.)

Finally, God instructs Moses:

> *Raise your staff and stretch out your hand over the sea to divide the water so that the Israelites can go through the sea on dry ground. I will harden the hearts of the Egyptians so that they will go in after them. And I will gain glory through Pharaoh and all his army, through his chariots and his horsemen. The Egyptians will know that I am the Lord when I gain glory through Pharaoh, his chariots and his horsemen.*
>
> (Exodus 14:16–18.)

The very length and detail of this story is an indicator of its importance. What is immediately striking is the frequent repetition of the concept of the hardening of Pharaoh's heart. That hardening is described to us in various ways: Pharaoh hardens his heart, Pharaoh's heart is hardened, and God hardens Pharaoh's heart. Over the course of events there seems to be a swing between Pharaoh's own actions and God's, which might well indicate that this story illustrates both human responsibility and God's sovereignty.

The fact that the hardening of Pharaoh's heart occurs not once but many times implies that he was softer and more responsive at times: God did not harden Pharaoh's heart once and for all, such that it was hard from then on. Far from it; we read of Pharaoh repeatedly asking Moses and Aaron to pray for him, and on several occasions he confesses his sin. Moses does pray for him, God shows mercy, the prayer is granted, and respite comes.

The next question is: what does the hardening of the heart mean in this context? The deterministic answer is that it has to do with Pharaoh's eternal destiny. The immediate impression given by the text, however, is that it has to do with the stiffening of Pharaoh's resolve not to lose the vast Hebrew slave labour force on which his economy was dependent. It is true that his resistance was against God; and when he had gone beyond the point of no return there may well have been additional eternal implications. To read them into the story at its beginning, however, would seem to contradict the righteousness of God.

The pressure on Pharaoh gradually increased in intensity. His earlier excuses for not letting the people go were based on his magicians being able (to a certain extent) to reproduce the plagues. These excuses fade in the third plague when they recognise *the finger of God*. Pharaoh can fight it no longer, and he eventually has to let the people go. He quickly regrets it, God hardens his heart, and he perishes in the sea.

Now we have to ask ourselves what we make of all of this. Many people are tempted to read it deterministically. On the one side of the equation God enables Moses to perform miracles; on the other he seems to treat Pharaoh as a helpless puppet on a string. If this is the case, how can we regard the prayers for mercy, and indeed the whole process, as anything but disingenuous?

Let us look more closely, then, at what is involved in the hardening of Pharaoh's heart. According to the text God does not take action until the sixth plague, immediately after which there is a confrontation between Moses and Pharaoh, and we reach the crucial point where God explains his reasoning to Pharaoh:

> But the Lord hardened Pharaoh's heart and he would not listen to Moses and Aaron, just as the Lord had said to Moses.
>
> Then the Lord said to Moses, "Get up early in the morning, confront Pharaoh and say to him, 'This is what the Lord, the God of the Hebrews, says: Let my people go, so that they may worship me, or this time I will send the full force of my plagues against you and against your officials and your people, so you may know that there is no-one like me in all the earth. For by now I could have stretched out my hand and struck you and your people with a plague that would have wiped you off the earth. But I have raised you up for this very purpose, that I might show you my power and that my name might be proclaimed in all the earth. You still set yourself against my people and will not let them go. Therefore, at this time tomorrow I will send the worst hailstorm that has ever fallen on Egypt, from the day it was founded till now. Give an order now to bring your livestock and everything you have in the field to a place of shelter, because the hail will fall on every man and animal that has not been brought in and is still out in the field, and they will die.' "
>
> Those officials of Pharaoh who feared the word of the Lord hurried to bring their slaves and their livestock inside. But those who ignored the word of the Lord left their slaves and livestock in the field.
>
> (Exodus 9:12–21.)

The statement I have emphasised is crucial for our understanding of this text. God tells Pharaoh that a stage has now been reached where he could have struck Pharaoh down and killed him. What is the force of the words *could have* here? Obviously God had the power to destroy Pharaoh all along, so the issue is not power. Rather it is an issue of morality. It had now come to the point that God could justifiably act and judge Pharaoh. God then announces that it is his intention to keep Pharaoh alive, in order both to demonstrate his power to Pharaoh and also to witness to God's name in all the earth through what was about to happen. Pharaoh had consistently resisted (as God predicted he would) and shown himself to be of a certain character. He repeatedly pleads for mercy, and when by the grace of God he is granted it, he reneges on his promises and hardens his attitude. He experiences God's mercy and longsuffering again and again, until his resistance reaches a point of no return. To use a phrase that we shall soon discuss in Romans 9, he had *prepared* himself *for destruction* (Romans 9:22). Now that he had demonstrated that he deserved judgment, God chose to exercise his right to do so in a particular way that would sound out a powerful message to the world. There is a point of no return and, in any case, it is evident that death ends the opportunity for repentance and faith for everyone: *it is appointed for man to die once, and after that comes judgment* (Hebrews 9:27 ESV).

In speaking of Pharaoh, Paul is surely expecting his fellow nationals to apply the lesson to themselves. After all, Jesus had warned those Jewish religious leaders who opposed him that, by attributing his works to the devil, they were in danger of blasphemy against the Holy Spirit. The warning was stark:

> *And so I tell you, every sin and blasphemy will be forgiven men, but the blasphemy against the Spirit will not be forgiven. Anyone who speaks a word against the Son of Man will be forgiven, but anyone who speaks against the Holy Spirit will not be forgiven, either in this age or in the age to come.*
>
> (Matthew 12:31–32.)

Clearly a point can be reached where forgiveness is no longer possible – not because God is not merciful, but because no other "gospel" is energised by the power of the Holy Spirit. If a person rejects that message, there is no alternative means of salvation. This applies not only to Pharaoh but also to Israel, as we shall see in Romans 11.

We have already seen that the issue of the righteousness of God's judgments is of central importance to the discussion. For instance, the fact that God will one day judge people for not believing implies that they must possess a God-given capacity to repent and believe. Similarly here, the fact that God states that he is in a position to execute judgment on Pharaoh implies that Pharaoh did have the capacity to respond to God's offer of grace before God eventually stepped in. It is for this reason that Paul confidently rejects the claim that God is unjust. There is no contradiction between God's mercy and his hardening, since neither is arbitrary.

Let us recall for a moment that this is Paul's answer to the question, Is God unjust? Put this way, it assumes that the answer is going to be in the negative – God is not unjust. And as I have tried to explain, that is in fact the case. However, one objection that is sometimes made to this kind of explanation is that, if this is what Paul had meant, no one would have suggested that God is unfair. The argument could not easily be misunderstood in that way. In other words, there must be a strong deterministic element here, otherwise there would be no objection. The hardening of Pharaoh's heart must have been an arbitrary act of God – which does seem unfair.

I find this unsatisfactory, for reasons I shall give below. I think, however, that the accusation of unfairness is an almost instinctive reaction to any kind of differentiation of roles in history and even in the church. God in his sovereignty has chosen that Jacob and Israel have one role, Esau and his nation another; you are a gifted evangelist, and someone else is a back room helper. Why are we all different?

If God's will is irresistible and human behaviour determined, then, logically, any apparent resistance cannot be real since that too is predetermined. If it is impossible to resist his will, then it is pointless to ask questions such as: is God unjust? But the expected answer to this question is no. God's will can be resisted, as we have already pointed out in connection with Christ's weeping over Jerusalem.

With this as background we can now return to Paul's analysis in Romans 9.

> *You will say to me then, "Why does he still find fault? For who can resist his will?" But who are you, O man, to answer back to God? Will what is moulded say to its moulder, "Why have you made me like this?" Has the potter no right over the clay, to make out of the same lump one vessel for honourable use and another for dishonourable use? What if God, desiring to show his wrath and to make known his power, has endured with much patience vessels of wrath prepared for destruction, in order to make known the riches of his glory for vessels of mercy, which he has prepared beforehand for glory – even us whom he has called, not from the Jews only but also from the Gentiles?*
>
> (Romans 9:19–24 ESV.)

Paul's reply might seem to be sharp – even beside the point: *Who are you, O man, to answer back to God?* But this interpretation does not do justice to the character of the God of mercy and love that Paul has been describing throughout the whole of this letter. Paul is not referring to some almighty despot who dare not be questioned by a puny human. He is reminding us that, when it comes to speaking of God, we should humbly remember that we are his creatures – moulded from clay and created in his image. Not only that, we are recipients of his mercy and patience.

The imagery of a potter and the clay is a familiar one in Scripture and in wisdom literature generally:

> *The Lord says: "These people come near to me with their mouth and honour me with their lips, but their hearts are far from me. Their worship of me is made up only of rules taught by men. Therefore once more I will astound these people with wonder upon wonder; the wisdom of the wise will perish, the intelligence of the intelligent will vanish." Woe to those who go to great depths to hide their plans from the Lord, who do their*

work in darkness and think, "Who sees us? Who will know?"
You turn things upside down, as if the potter were thought to
be like the clay! Shall what is formed say to him who formed
it, "He did not make me"? Can the pot say of the potter, "He
knows nothing"?

(Isaiah 29:13–16.)

Isaiah's use of this imagery is in the context of his indictment of Israel's religion as being purely formal and heartless. Our Lord quotes these words to expose the culpable hypocrisy of the Pharisees and scribes of his day, who were using their tradition as a cloak to cover their breaking of the commandments. They were acting as if God did not see them – a very foolish thing for creatures made by God to do. It would be like a pot thinking that the potter who made it had no insight or understanding. As Paul's questioner was in danger of doing, they too had forgotten the nature of their created status. God would deal with religious hypocrites according to their behaviour. He is no arbitrary, deterministic potter.

Paul centres his imagery on the very essence of the craft of pottery. A potter can take a lump of clay and make of it what he wills. He can make a beautiful vase to decorate a palace, or he can make humble jars and plates for everyday use in the humblest of homes. The application is to both Israel and Pharaoh. They were of the same lump in that they both rebelled against God and sinned grievously. God could righteously have condemned them. Neither had a right to mercy. By definition, mercy cannot be merited. Moses interceded for Israel, they repented and God showed mercy and restored them to their role. Pharaoh sinned repeatedly and Moses interceded for him also, but in the end he hardened his heart and passed the point of no return.

Cranfield comments:

The conclusion to be drawn is that God must be acknowledged
to be free – as God, as the One who has ultimate authority –
to appoint men to various functions in the on-going course of
salvation-history for the sake of the fulfilment of his overall

purpose. And it cannot be emphasised too strongly that
there is naturally not the slightest suggestion that the potter's
freedom is the freedom of caprice, and that it is, therefore,
perverse to suppose that what Paul wanted to assert was a
freedom of the Creator to deal with His creatures according to
some indeterminate, capricious, absolute will.[139]

God is sovereign, and that is a glorious thing. He acts according to his will, and his activity is right because he never acts contrary to his own character. It is not the sovereignty of a despotic power. He does what he wills but his will is consistent with his utterly holy and righteous character.

The prophet Jeremiah's use of the potter imagery confirms this:

This is the word that came to Jeremiah from the Lord: "Go
down to the potter's house, and there I will give you my
message." So I went down to the potter's house, and I saw him
working at the wheel. But the pot he was shaping from the clay
was marred in his hands; so the potter formed it into another
pot, shaping it as seemed best to him.

Then the word of the Lord came to me: "O house of
Israel, can I not do with you as this potter does?" declares
the Lord. "Like clay in the hand of the potter, so are you
in my hand, O house of Israel. If at any time I announce
that a nation or kingdom is to be uprooted, torn down and
destroyed, and if that nation I warned repents of its evil, then I
will relent and not inflict on it the disaster I had planned. And
if at another time I announce that a nation or kingdom is to
be built up and planted, and if it does evil in my sight and does
not obey me, then I will reconsider the good I had intended to
do for it.

"Now therefore say to the people of Judah and those
living in Jerusalem, 'This is what the Lord says: Look! I am
preparing a disaster for you and devising a plan against you.

---

139 C. E. B. Cranfield, *Romans 1–8*, vol. 1, Edinburgh, T & T Clark, p. 492.

*So turn from your evil ways, each one of you, and reform your
ways and your actions.'"*

(Jeremiah 18:1–11.)

The action of the potter is not capricious – the clay is living and what
the potter does with it is in part dependent on its response to him. As
the divine potter, God wishes to show his abundant mercy to those
who return to him (to return here means to repent).

 N. T. Wright says:

> *The image of potter and clay was not designed to speak in
> general terms about human beings as lifeless lumps of clay,
> over against God as the only living, thinking being; it was
> designed to speak very specifically about God's purpose in
> choosing and calling Israel and about what would happen
> if Israel, like a lump of clay, failed to respond to the gentle
> moulding of his hands.*[140]

Paul now presses the application to what he calls *vessels of wrath* and
vessels of mercy:

> *What if God, desiring to show his wrath and to make known
> his power, has endured with much patience vessels of wrath
> prepared for destruction, in order to make known the riches
> of his glory for vessels of mercy, which he has prepared
> beforehand for glory – even us whom he has called, not from
> the Jews only but also from the Gentiles?*

(Romans 9:22–24 ESV.)

What do the terms *vessels of wrath* and *vessels of mercy* mean? From
the context Pharaoh is an obvious example of the first category and
Moses of the second. N. T. Wright again: "… the idea of a 'vessel of
mercy' doesn't mean so much a vessel which receives mercy but a

---

140 Tom Wright, *Paul for Everyone: Romans Part 2: Chapters 9–16*, London,
 SPCK, 2004: see section on Romans 9:14–24.

vessel through which God brings mercy to others".[141] That is, these were not simply people on whom God's wrath fell, or to whom God's mercy was shown; they were people who became examples or advertisements to the wider world of the nature of God's dealings. For instance, once Pharaoh had hardened his attitude, God told him that he was going to use him as a warning to show his power to the world. It has been very effective. The story of what happened to precipitate the exodus from Egypt has captured the imagination of millions. Who can calculate the number of people who have come to faith in God and Christ as a result of hearing the Passover story explained in terms of its ultimate fulfilment in Jesus the Passover Lamb?

The Old Testament also tells of God's mercy to Rahab, who sided with the people of God when she, with the rest of her tribe, heard of what God had done in Egypt. To the Israelite spies she said:

> I know that the Lord has given this land to you and that a
> great fear of you has fallen on us, so that all who live in this
> country are melting in fear because of you. We have heard
> how the Lord dried up the water of the Red Sea for you when
> you came out of Egypt... When we heard of it, our hearts sank
> and everyone's courage failed because of you, for the Lord your
> God is God in heaven above and on the earth below.
>
> (Joshua 2:9–11.)

Pharaoh was a vessel of wrath, and Rahab's response in trusting God made her a vessel of mercy. Many have heard her story and have been converted through it.

Another major example of a vessel of mercy is Paul himself:

> I thank Christ Jesus our Lord, who has given me strength, that he
> considered me faithful, appointing me to his service. Even though
> I was once a blasphemer and a persecutor and a violent man, I
> was shown mercy because I acted in ignorance and unbelief. The

---

141 *Ibid*.

grace of our Lord was poured out on me abundantly, along with the faith and love that are in Christ Jesus.

Here is a trustworthy saying that deserves full acceptance: Christ Jesus came into the world to save sinners – of whom I am the worst. But for that very reason I was shown mercy so that in me, the worst of sinners, Christ Jesus might display his immense patience as an example for those who would believe on him and receive eternal life.

(1 Timothy 1:12–16.)

To millions throughout history Paul has become a vessel of mercy, as God *considered* him *faithful*, discerning that he had *acted in ignorance and unbelief*. Many have come to trust Christ by thinking that, if God could be merciful and save a man like Paul, then surely there is real hope for them, if they too now prove themselves *faithful*.

There are some who take these texts to mean that in eternity God mysteriously or even arbitrarily chose who was to be a vessel of wrath and who was to be a vessel of mercy; and that choice permanently and unconditionally fixes their destinies. There is a fundamental flaw in this reasoning, even apart from the fact that it makes no moral sense. The flaw is to assume that, if someone is a vessel of wrath, they can never become a vessel of mercy. But that is false, as Jeremiah's use of the potter analogy indicates. Paul was a vessel of wrath who became a vessel of mercy. Also, in Ephesians, Paul describes the believers as having once been children of wrath, but because they had repented and trusted Christ as Saviour and Lord they had become vessels of mercy (see Ephesians 2:3–4).

Moreover we should not forget Paul's initial arguments in Romans when he demonstrates conclusively that all of us are guilty and therefore deserving of the wrath of God. The whole thrust of the gospel is to bring forgiveness and justification to children of wrath – which means all human beings. In that sense, we are all of the same "lump". Some will respond positively and become believers, and even vessels of mercy; whereas others will respond negatively and remain children of wrath. Then God may sometimes righteously use them as vessels of wrath, as he did Pharaoh.

THE HARDENING OF PHARAOH'S HEART

There is a striking passage earlier in Romans that relates to chapter 9:

> *So when you, a mere man, pass judgment on them and yet do the same things, do you think you will escape God's judgment? Or do you show contempt for the riches of his kindness, tolerance and patience, not realising that God's kindness leads you to repentance? But because of your stubbornness and your unrepentant heart, you are storing up wrath against yourself for the day of God's wrath, when his righteous judgment will be revealed.*
>
> (Romans 2:3–5.)

Our text in Romans 9 invokes many of these concepts – patience, wrath, kindness, and hardness of heart. The people Paul had in mind in Romans 2 were at that time storing up wrath and so being prepared for righteous judgment – that is, judgment that was deserved and not arbitrary. But that did not mean that those people could not repent. Indeed, Paul is appealing to them to understand that God's very patience with them was designed to lead them to repentance. Vessels of wrath can become vessels of mercy, if they have not yet reached the point of no return.

Paul then tells us that the vessels of mercy are those whom God has called, not from the Jews only but also from the Gentiles (9:24). What happened in history with Paul's nation has led to the gospel being taken to the Gentiles. Yet the fact that the Hebrew prophets foretold that God would reach out to the Gentiles does not mean that the word of God has come to nothing as far as Israel is concerned.

This again shows that a deterministic reading of these chapters is implausible. For instance, since God's choice of Jacob and Esau had nothing to do with the question of eternal destiny, there would be descendants of Jacob who would not believe and descendants of Esau who would. Similarly for Isaac and Ishmael. God's intention is to show mercy, and so he makes his gracious offer to all.

As he says in Hosea: "I will call them 'my people' who are not my people; and I will call her 'my loved one' who is not my loved one," and, "It will happen that in the very place where it was said to them, 'You are not my people,' they will be called 'sons of the living God'."

Isaiah cries out concerning Israel: "Though the number of the Israelites be like the sand by the sea, only the remnant will be saved. For the Lord will carry out his sentence on earth with speed and finality." It is just as Isaiah said previously: "Unless the Lord Almighty had left us descendants, we would have become like Sodom, we would have been like Gomorrah."

(Romans 9:25–29.)

Hosea was talking about Israel at a time when they had reached such a low point in rejecting God that he referred to them as *not my people*. Paul takes the promise to restore them as an indicator that God would also reach out to the Gentiles (verse 24).

Paul was deeply concerned that the majority of his nation Israel was opposed to the gospel. He now points out that God had told Isaiah that, although ethnic Israel might be very large numerically, only a relatively small number would be saved (verse 27). The Old Testament forewarned that a time would come when Israel would oppose the message of salvation, and Paul lived in such a time. Yet God had promised to leave them a remnant, of which Paul was a member. Rather sadly he continues to quote Isaiah, that, if God had not left them that remnant, they would have ended up like Sodom and Gomorrah – those infamous vessels of wrath. However, Paul will have happier things to say about Israel's future in Romans 11. The vessels of wrath will become vessels of mercy.

CHAPTER 15

Is Israel Responsible?

We move now to Paul's second main argument, where the emphasis lies squarely on Israel's responsibility for the situation in which they now find themselves. The apostle pauses for breath in this long and detailed explanation. And we should take a breather too as we consider one of his characteristic questions: what shall we say, then? What is to be our reaction to what he has said so far?

I hope one thing is obvious by now. This chapter does not teach or support a doctrine of unconditional deterministic election for salvation or reprobation. If, however, that is not obvious to some by this stage, it should be put beyond all doubt by Paul's now pushing the argument forward into its next phase, where he concentrates on Israel's responsibility, indeed culpability, for the state they are in. This may be one reason why some theistic determinists concentrate on Romans 9 without paying similar attention to Romans 10 and 11.

Paul proceeds to examine more closely the reasons for Israel's unbelief, and he concludes that they are culpable – it is their fault. For God had made every provision for them and pleaded with them to trust him: *All day long I have held out my hands* to them (Romans 10:21). In this section Paul shows that the arguments that might be raised to let Israel off the hook are groundless – the nation is without excuse. However, we should balance that fact with Paul's anticipation that Israel will eventually be provoked to jealousy by the fact that so many Gentiles have come to believe in Christ (see Romans 11:11–12).

Paul has been speaking of the gospel message being taken up by the Gentiles. He now analyses the difference between them and the Jews regarding their attitude to the key matter – the main subject of Romans – justification by faith. The irony of the situation is that, in

Paul's day, Gentiles grasped justification by faith, whereas Israel did not. Is the reason for that unconditional deterministic election – because God had not chosen them to be vessels of mercy? Far from it! The fault is entirely theirs. Israel made the mistake of trying to achieve God's righteousness by their own meritorious work rather than being prepared to trust God. Paul explains:

> *What, then, shall we say? That the Gentiles, who did not pursue righteousness, have obtained it, a righteousness that is by faith; but Israel, who pursued a law of righteousness, has not attained it. Why not? Because they pursued it not by faith but as if it were by works. They stumbled over the "stumbling-stone". As it is written: "See, I lay in Zion a stone that causes men to stumble and a rock that makes them fall, and the one who trusts in him will never be put to shame."*
>
> (Romans 9:30–33.)

There is very strong emphasis here on human responsibility – with the terms *pursue*, *faith*, and *trust* being used. We should note that Paul is not suggesting that no Gentiles were interested in moral righteousness – that would be absurd. Paul is using the term "righteousness" here with the meaning – as he now explains – of righteous status before God. That righteous status before God can only be received as a result of putting faith in "the stumbling stone".

Some interpreters – those who hold that Romans 9:6–29 has to do with the sovereignty of God in individual election to salvation – do indeed affirm that Paul turns at the end of the chapter to human responsibility, but some of these come to a highly asymmetrical conclusion, sometimes called, single predestination. For instance Martyn Lloyd-Jones writes:

> *In verses 6 to 29, [Paul] explains why anybody is saved – it is the sovereign election of God. In these verses he is showing us why anybody is lost, and the explanation of that is their own responsibility... It is God's action alone that saves a man. So why is anybody lost? Is it because they are not elected? No.*

What accounts for the lost is their rejection of the gospel... We are responsible for our rejection of the gospel, but we are not responsible for our acceptance of it.[142]

With all due respect to Lloyd-Jones, from whom I have learned a great deal, this makes no sense whatsoever. Moral logic and common sense demand that, if no one is responsible for accepting the gospel, then no one is responsible for rejecting it. Furthermore, we have repeatedly seen that there is no asymmetry in the biblical presentation of the gospel – a person will be saved or lost according to whether they believe or reject, and the responsibility is equal in both cases, since the person has the ability to accept or reject. The major defect in Lloyd-Jones' argument is his taking the earlier part of Romans 9 as having to do with election to salvation.

Another attempt to preserve the asymmetry alluded to above is made by D. James Kennedy by appealing to an illustration.

Here are five people who are planning to hold up a bank. They are friends of mine. I find out about it and I plead with them. I beg them not to do it. Finally they push me out of the way and they start out. I tackle one of the men and wrestle him to the ground. The others go ahead, rob the bank, a guard is killed, they are captured, convicted, sentenced... The one man who was not involved in the robbery goes free. Now I ask you this question: whose fault was it that the other men died?... Now this other man who is walking around free – can he say: "Because my heart is so good, I am a free man?"

The only reason he is free is because of me; because I restrained him. So those who go to hell have no one to blame but themselves. Those who go to heaven have no one to praise but Jesus Christ. Thus we see that salvation is all of grace from its beginning to its end.[143]

---

142 D. M. Lloyd-Jones, *Romans Chapter 9*, Edinburgh, Banner of Truth, 1991, p. 285.

143 D. J. Kennedy, *Truths That Transform*, Grand Rapids, Revell, 1974, pp. 39–40.

It is hard to imagine an illustration less appropriate to describe the grace of God in the gospel of the Lord Jesus Christ. When people in the villages of Galilee saw the wonderful works of the Lord and asked him to leave, he left. He did not invade their personal space with violence. Wrestling someone to the ground seems a grotesque way to illustrate the loving appeal of Christ. Moreover, in the illustration there is not the slightest trace of repentance on the part of the man who ended up "free".

Additionally, I find it rather inconsistent that Tim Keller cites this illustration with approval in a book where he describes election as God freely choosing those who freely come. The man in the illustration did not "freely come". Keller mentions this in his explanation of Romans 9 in connection with a question that seems to lurk behind many expressions of theological determinism:

> For the biggest question is: If God could save everyone, why doesn't he? And here Paul seems to say that God's chosen course (to save some and leave others) will in the end be more fit to show forth God's glory than any other scheme we can imagine. This may seem strange to us, but that is the point – we are not God, and cannot know everything or decide what is best.[144]

Yes, we are not God and cannot know everything, and there are many issues that we must leave at that; but this is not one of them. For, as we have seen, Scripture tells us repeatedly and explicitly that the criterion for judgment is whether or not a person believes – a position that upholds human moral responsibility and does make sense. There is nothing strange about it. Is it not, therefore, possible that in this case Keller's sense of strangeness (meaning, I presume, unfairness) is an instinctive and justifiable reaction to actual unfairness? Surely, the answer to Keller's question is that God has provided a salvation that is available to all, and whether a person is saved or not depends on two factors: on God's part, on the provision

---

144 T. Keller, *Romans 8–16 For You*, Epsom, Good Book Company, 2015.

of that salvation; and on our side, on our faith not on our merit – on whether or not we avail ourselves of that salvation with the capacity for exercising trust that God has given us. Otherwise, there is a major problem with theodicy, as it is but a small step to deducing that God is directly responsible for evil.

How different from Kennedy's illustration of salvation is that given by our Lord in John 3 – the placing by Moses of a brass serpent on a pole, with the injunction that if those bitten by the venomous snakes looked at the serpent they would live. They were all poisoned people, they could not save themselves, far less could they merit salvation; yet they could look at the serpent graciously provided by God and live. If they were not prepared to look, they would die.

In coming to terms with Israel's unbelief, Paul now returns to some of the lessons that he taught in detail in the earlier part of the letter, where he uses Abraham in particular as an example of what faith is – the very opposite of works. The problem with unbelieving Israel is that, though physically descended from Abraham, they had not understood the prime lesson that his life was meant to teach them – what it means to trust God. Paul defines that more precisely for his own day: Israel had stumbled over the stumbling stone – Christ. We have looked at this in detail in earlier chapters and seen how the Jews of Paul's time repeatedly stumbled over Christ's message of forgiveness and eternal life through repentance and faith. They would *work* for God, but they would not *trust* his Son the Messiah for salvation. They refused to believe when they could have believed, and so became culpable.

It was actually worse than that. In the context of telling a parable against the religious authorities in Jerusalem who were seeking to kill him, Christ identifies himself as the stone of stumbling:

> He went on to tell the people this parable: "A man planted
> a vineyard, rented it to some farmers and went away for a
> long time. At harvest time he sent a servant to the tenants
> so they would give him some of the fruit of the vineyard. But
> the tenants beat him and sent him away empty-handed. He
> sent another servant, but that one also they beat and treated

shamefully and sent away empty-handed. He sent still a third, and they wounded him and threw him out.

"Then the owner of the vineyard said, 'What shall I do? I will send my son, whom I love; perhaps they will respect him.'

"But when the tenants saw him, they talked the matter over. 'This is the heir,' they said. 'Let's kill him, and the inheritance will be ours.' So they threw him out of the vineyard and killed him.

"What then will the owner of the vineyard do to them? He will come and kill those tenants and give the vineyard to others."

When the people heard this, they said, "May this never be!"

Jesus looked directly at them and asked, "Then what is the meaning of that which is written: 'The stone the builders rejected has become the capstone'? Everyone who falls on that stone will be broken to pieces; but he on whom it falls will be crushed."

The teachers of the law and the chief priests looked for a way to arrest him immediately, because they knew he had spoken this parable against them. But they were afraid of the people.

(Luke 20:9–19.)

This parable expresses very well how the religious leaders were preparing themselves to be vessels of wrath by their constant rejection of the vineyard owner's servants and, finally, even his beloved son. They were not doing this because they were helpless puppets on a string, which is why God's judgment upon them for their actions was deserved and righteous. We should not forget that Saul of Tarsus was part of the persecuting crowd. He was a vessel of wrath who became a vessel of mercy.

At the start of Romans 10 Paul repeats the strong sentiments expressed at the beginning of chapter 9, revealing once more his heart for his people:

Brothers, my heart's desire and prayer to God for the Israelites is that they may be saved. For I can testify about them that they are zealous for God, but their zeal is not based on knowledge. Since they did not know the righteousness that comes from God and sought to establish their own, they did not submit to God's righteousness. Christ is the end of the law so that there may be righteousness for everyone who believes.

(Romans 10:1–4.)

Far from abandoning his people as vessels of wrath, Paul prays for their salvation. The fact that he prayed meant that he did not think there was now no hope for them, that they constituted the "non-elect" whose doom was determined and final. He recognises that the people of Israel are zealous for God but that their zeal lacks knowledge. That was a tragedy for Paul, since this zeal was very real. Indeed, when we consider the zeal that many of our Jewish friends and acquaintances show for God, it should make us question the level of our own zeal for him as Christians. At one level they can put us to shame.

The saddest thing for Paul was that his fellow Jews did not understand the great message that Abraham had grasped when he *believed God, and it was credited to him as righteousness* (Romans 4:3). Using again the account of Abraham's faith, Paul argues in Galatians that Israel did not understand that *the law was put in charge to lead us to Christ that we might be justified by faith* (Galatians 3:24). Paul understood their stumbling very well. He himself had been mightily zealous for God in pursuing the law in a zeal that expressed itself in violent persecution of the church. He not only stumbled at the stone – God himself accused him of kicking it. His determination to establish his own righteousness by zealous performance of the law had blinded Paul completely to the righteousness that God offered through faith in Christ. He had not seen that the goal of the law was to bring him to Christ. In his misplaced zeal for the law he thought that he was fulfilling the law by fighting Christ – just like the tenants in the parable. In the end, by the mercy of God, his eyes were opened. Here is his rueful statement:

*... though I myself have reasons for such confidence. If anyone
else thinks he has reasons to put confidence in the flesh, I have
more: circumcised on the eighth day, of the people of Israel,
of the tribe of Benjamin, a Hebrew of Hebrews; in regard to
the law, a Pharisee; as for zeal, persecuting the church; as for
legalistic righteousness, faultless.*

*But whatever was to my profit I now consider loss for
the sake of Christ. What is more, I consider everything a loss
compared to the surpassing greatness of knowing Christ Jesus
my Lord, for whose sake I have lost all things. I consider them
rubbish, that I may gain Christ and be found in him, not
having a righteousness of my own that comes from the law,
but that which is through faith in Christ – the righteousness
that comes from God and is by faith.*

(Philippians 3:4–9.)

Many Christians, even though they are not of Jewish ethnicity,
understand that stumbling block all too well. It seems to be endemic
in the human psyche to imagine that, if there is a God, the only way
to earn his favour and acceptance is the religious way – by our own
meritorious attempts to keep his law. By nature we find it difficult
to humble ourselves, to recognise our sinfulness and admit that we
cannot establish our own righteousness but must accept it as a free
gift from God through Christ. We find it hard to give all the glory
to God.

For Jews, however, this is a massive stumbling block, which is
why Paul again and again grounds the gospel in the Old Testament
scriptures. The verses that follow explain how Christ is the goal of
the law for righteousness for everyone who believes, whether they
are Jew or Greek:

Moses describes in this way the righteousness that is by the law: "The man who does these things will live by them." But the righteousness that is by faith says: "Do not say in your heart, 'Who will ascend into heaven?'" (that is, to bring Christ down) "or 'Who will descend into the deep?'" (that is, to bring Christ up from the dead). But what does it say? "The word is near you; it is in your mouth and in your heart," that is, the word of faith we are proclaiming: That if you confess with your mouth, "Jesus is Lord," and believe in your heart that God raised him from the dead, you will be saved. For it is with your heart that you believe and are justified, and it is with your mouth that you confess and are saved. As the Scripture says, "Anyone who trusts in him will never be put to shame." For there is no difference between Jew and Gentile – the same Lord is Lord of all and richly blesses all who call on him, for, "Everyone who calls on the name of the Lord will be saved."

(Romans 10:5–13.)

At the beginning of this passage Paul cites Leviticus 18:5 regarding the nature of a law-based righteous status. Earlier in Romans he has shown that the problem is not the law: it is that no one can keep the law. Indeed the function of law is to act as a kind of spiritual thermometer: *For by works of the law no human being will be justified in his sight, since through the law comes knowledge of sin* (Romans 3:20).

It is worth comparing this with Galatians 3, where Paul also cites Leviticus 18:5 (*the man who obeys them will live by them*):

Clearly no-one is justified before God by the law, because, "The righteous will live by faith." The law is not based on faith; on the contrary, "The man who does these things shall live by them."... What, then, was the purpose of the law? It was added because of transgressions until the Seed to whom the promise referred had come... Is the law, therefore, opposed to the promises of God? Absolutely not! For if a law had been given that could impart life, then righteousness would certainly have come by the law. But the Scripture declares that the whole world is a prisoner of sin, so that what was promised, being given through faith in Jesus Christ, might be given to those who believe. Before this faith came, we were held prisoners by the law, locked up until faith should be revealed. So the law was put in charge to lead us to Christ that we might be justified by faith. Now that faith has come, we are no longer under the supervision of the law. You are all sons of God through faith in Christ Jesus...

(Galatians 3:11–12, 19, 21–26.)

So the proper function of the law is to give people an awareness of their sin, so that they will trust Christ and not their own merit in order to be justified. Christ is the goal of the law, the only one who has fulfilled the law in its entirety, and it is he who offers us righteousness if we will trust him.

Paul explains further:

But the righteousness that is by faith says: "Do not say in your heart, 'Who will ascend into heaven?'" (that is, to bring Christ down) "or 'Who will descend into the deep?'" (that is, to bring Christ up from the dead).

(Romans 10:6–7.)

The phrase *Do not say in your heart* is taken from Deuteronomy:

Beware lest you say in your heart, "My power and the might of my hand have gained me this wealth."... Do not say in your heart, after the Lord your God has thrust them out before you, "It is because of my righteousness that the Lord has brought me in to possess this land..."

(Deuteronomy 8:17; 9:4 ESV.)

These were warnings to Israel not to boast in their own merit – sentiments apposite to the topic of law-righteousness, which would have been recognised by Paul's readers. However, Paul does not quote the body of these statements but rather uses the phrase to remind his readers of a later passage in Deuteronomy:

> *Now what I am commanding you today is not too difficult*
> *for you or beyond your reach. It is not up in heaven, so that*
> *you have to ask, "Who will ascend into heaven to get it and*
> *proclaim it to us so that we may obey it?" Nor is it beyond the*
> *sea, so that you have to ask, "Who will cross the sea to get it*
> *and proclaim it to us so that we may obey it?" No, the word is*
> *very near you; it is in your mouth and in your heart so that*
> *you may obey it.*
>
> (Deuteronomy 30:11–14.)

There was no excuse for anyone to think that the message was too distant or too difficult. God had revealed it to Moses, and he had shared it with the people. All they had to do was to take ownership of it.

Paul applies this now to the message of the gospel in his own day, when God's fullest revelation had come through the incarnation and resurrection of Jesus. Sadly it was precisely the kind of misplaced pride that is described in Deuteronomy 8 and 9 that resulted in the Jews of Paul's day rejecting both the incarnation and resurrection. Ascending to heaven to bring the Messiah down, and going to the abyss to bring him up from the dead, are cynical attitudes about Christ on the part of those who do not take him seriously.

Cynicism is good at manufacturing excuses, and Paul will not let them get away with it. He is making the point that they have no excuse whatsoever, since the good news about Jesus is neither distant nor difficult. It had been brought as near as it could possibly be:

> *"The word is near you; it is in your mouth and in your heart,"*
> *that is, the word of faith we are proclaiming: That if you*
> *confess with your mouth, "Jesus is Lord," and believe in your*
> *heart that God raised him from the dead, you will be saved.*
> *For it is with your heart that you believe and are justified, and*
> *it is with your mouth that you confess and are saved. As the*

Scripture says, "Anyone who trusts in him will never be put to shame." For there is no difference between Jew and Gentile – the same Lord is Lord of all and richly blesses all who call on him, for, "Everyone who calls on the name of the Lord will be saved."

(Romans 10:8–13.)

Now that the incarnation, death, and resurrection of Jesus have occurred, a basis for salvation has been established for all who call upon the name of the Lord. There is no hint that the reason for Jewish cynicism is due to an arbitrary decision of a deterministic God. They can be saved if only they will do two things.

The first is to confess with their mouths Jesus as Lord (a very early Christian confessional formula), to make public that they believe he is the Son of God. This would affirm their belief in the incarnation.

The second thing is to believe in their hearts in the resurrection of Jesus.

Note that the order of these responses is expressed both ways round: the first reflecting the order in Deuteronomy, the second the natural order – belief in the heart first, and then public confession. Paul would seem to regard them as inseparable

Your mouth and your heart belong to you! Speech and trust are something of which you are capable. God has implanted both of these capacities in you as part of his image. Paul once more picks up his earlier phrase in connection with the stone of stumbling: *Anyone who trusts in him will never be put to shame* (verse 11). This is for everyone – Jews and Gentiles. There is now no distinction between them, as far as the basis for salvation goes; although, as we shall see in Romans 11, there are still distinctions regarding their respective roles in the fulfilment of God's purposes in history.

God's rich salvation is available, then, to all who are prepared to *call on the name of the Lord*, in accordance with the prophecy of Joel: *And everyone who calls on the name of the Lord will be saved* (Joel 2:32). It was with these words that the apostle Peter launched Christianity onto the world stage on the day of Pentecost (Acts 2:21).

He told the crowd that Joel's prophecy of the outpouring of God's Spirit had just been fulfilled, as a consequence of the resurrection of Jesus from the dead. The climax of his sermon was:

> "*Therefore let all Israel be assured of this: God has made this Jesus, whom you crucified, both Lord and Christ.*"
>
> *When the people heard this, they were cut to the heart and said to Peter and the other apostles, "Brothers, what shall we do?"*
>
> *Peter replied, "Repent and be baptised, every one of you, in the name of Jesus Christ for the forgiveness of your sins. And you will receive the gift of the Holy Spirit. The promise is for you and your children and for all who are far off – for all whom the Lord our God will call."*
>
> (Acts 2:36–39.)

Many in the listening crowd of Jews were devastated as they discovered that they had murdered their Messiah. *What shall we do?* they cried. Peter told them what to do, for they were capable of doing it. God was calling them through the gospel – all of them, near and far. He had come so near that his Spirit was in their midst. He had provided salvation for them in Jesus. All they had to do was repent and call on his name; and because they had publicly crucified him they were to stand clear of the rejecting crowd and publicly be baptised in his name.

Returning to Romans 10 we find that Paul is now concerned to leave no stone unturned in his desire to place the responsibility for rejecting the Messiah fairly and squarely on his fellow nationals, not on any inscrutable or deterministic election of God. If that had been the case, he would only have had to state that they were non-elect, and that would have been an end to it.

Can the grace of God be resisted?

In TULIP the logical corollary of "U" (unconditional election) is "I" (irresistible grace). In the next paragraphs Paul shows conclusively that the Jews had every opportunity to call on the name of the Lord. They could have believed, but they didn't, and so they are culpable. They are guilty of resisting God's grace. Hence God's grace is resistible, showing once more that theological determinism is false.

Paul now considers four possible excuses for Israel's unbelief:

How, then, can they call on the one they have not believed in?

And how can they believe in the one of whom they have not heard?

And how can they hear without someone preaching to them?

And how can they preach unless they are sent? As it is written: "How beautiful are the feet of those who bring good news!"

He goes on:

But not all the Israelites accepted the good news. For Isaiah says, "Lord, who has believed our message?" Consequently, faith comes from hearing the message, and the message is heard through the word of Christ. But I ask: Did they not hear? Of course they did: "Their voice has gone out into all the earth, their words to the ends of the world." Again I ask: Did Israel not understand? First, Moses says, "I will make you envious by those who are not a nation; I will make you angry by a nation that has no understanding." And Isaiah boldly says, "I was found by those who did not seek me; I revealed myself to those who did not ask for me." But concerning Israel he says, "All day long I have held out my hands to a disobedient and obstinate people."

(Romans 10:14–21.)

Paul's logic is hard to resist. You cannot call on someone if you don't believe in him; you can't believe if you haven't heard; you can't hear unless the message has been brought to you; and the message can't be preached unless someone has been commissioned by God to do so – it is not enough for them simply to mouth words.

We must, however, attend to a matter of translation here. The Greek text does not say: "how shall they believe in him *of* whom they have never heard?"; rather the much stronger, *how can they believe in the one of whom they have not heard?* This is not hearing in some superficial sense, like half-listening to someone while you are reading a book. This is listening with deep concentration. If you are going to believe in Christ you must not simply hear about him, you must hear him. You must hear his voice, and not simply the voice of the messenger. Recall, *My sheep listen to my voice* (John 10:27); God speaks through his Word (Jesus) and he authenticates himself. That is the basis of believing.

As ever with the gospel, the initiative lies with God. He has commissioned and sent out preachers and teachers – notably Paul himself, although Paul does not mention that fact here. The message has been preached, and through it the people have heard God's voice. Had they not heard, they would have had an excuse for not believing it. But they have heard, and so they have no excuse whatsoever for their unbelief.

It needs to be stressed that God is saying through this scripture that they did hear. This again refutes the idea that they didn't hear because they couldn't hear, that they were unregenerate and dead in trespasses and in sins. They were unregenerate, but like Adam they were perfectly capable of hearing the voice of God.

Paul backs up his argument from Old Testament Scripture: *Lord, who has believed our message?* This quotation from Isaiah 52:7 should be put alongside our Lord's use of the same prophetic text in John's Gospel:

While you have the light, believe in the light, that you may become sons of light. When Jesus had said these things, he departed and hid himself from them. Though he had done so many signs before them, they still did not believe in him, so that the word spoken by the prophet Isaiah might be fulfilled: "Lord, who has believed what he heard from us, and to whom

*has the arm of the Lord been revealed?" Therefore they could
not believe. For again Isaiah said, "He has blinded their eyes
and hardened their heart, lest they see with their eyes, and
understand with their heart, and turn, and I would heal
them."*

(John 12:36–40 ESV.)

Isaiah saw a day coming when, as in his own day, the people would
not believe the message preached to them. His prophecy was fulfilled
when the people refused to believe the Lord Jesus, in spite of the
many signs he did and in spite of his constant appeal to them to
believe. Accordingly, there came a point where, as Isaiah predicted,
the Lord hardened them. Their behaviour was like that of Pharaoh.

They had heard. Indeed, Paul points out that the message has
gone out all over the Gentile world, as predicted in Psalm 19:4. The
world, as Paul explains in Romans 1:20, had a general awareness of
God's existence and power through creation, but as Paul points out
in Romans 9:4 the Jews had a far greater knowledge through the
revelation God gave them in the Old Testament period in terms of
covenant, ritual, and prophecy.

Paul now introduces a possible new excuse: perhaps they had
heard the message and didn't understand? Hasn't he already said
in this chapter that Israel were ignorant? It is true that they were
ignorant in the sense that they did not understand the difference
between righteousness based on the law and the righteousness
that comes through faith; but they were not ignorant of Scripture.
Moses had pointed that out to them in Deuteronomy 32:21. If the
Gentiles, who had minimal knowledge compared to Israel, have
come to call on the name of the Lord, then you cannot seriously
think that Israel did not know. Paul calls on Isaiah to emphasise
this point:

*And Isaiah boldly says, "I was found by those who did not seek
me; I revealed myself to those who did not ask for me."*

(Romans 10:20.)

Israel must have known, since even the Gentiles have found the Lord.

We should make another observation here. Paul's purpose in citing the Old Testament is not simply to establish that Scripture points out that Israel would have a negative reaction to the gospel. He is demonstrating again and again that the Old Testament teaches that one day the message would be taken to the Gentile nations. That would have been a very reassuring fact for the *apostle of the Gentiles* (Romans 11:13), to say nothing of the Gentile believers.

Paul ends the chapter with a very moving and heartfelt statement. He quotes God's appeal to Israel in Isaiah 65:2:

> But concerning Israel he says, "All day long I have held out my hands to a disobedient and obstinate people."
>
> (Romans 10:21.)

The holding out of hands is a universal symbol of invitation, entreaty, and welcome. This is God's openhearted gesture to Israel, even as they rebel. His will is expressed by his outstretched hands – he wanted Israel to come back, but they would not have him. If we accept theistic determinism it is hard to see that this is anything more than disingenuous play-acting. It suggests that God has a "public will of disposition" whereby he is willing to save anyone, while there is also a "secret" or "decretive will" that has long since decided that certain people should perish eternally. Their only chance of responding to God is if he gives them the faith to do so, but he has chosen not to. That, surely, is what outstretched hands do not express.

A statement that is often cited in this context is that of Moses:

> The secret things belong to the Lord our God, but the things revealed belong to us and to our children for ever, that we may follow all the words of this law.
>
> (Deuteronomy 29:29.)

This tells us that God has not revealed everything to us. However, that is a very different matter to claiming that the secret things include an unrevealed will of God that contradicts the things that have been revealed – for instance, this piece of revelation:

> *The Lord is not slow in keeping his promise, as some understand slowness. He is patient with you, not wanting anyone to perish, but everyone to come to repentance.*
>
> (2 Peter 3:9.)

It would be theologically very dangerous to suggest that God's will and desire – revealed here – that none should perish and all reach repentance is contradicted by some secret will that says the opposite. We are not dealing with paradox here but straight contradiction. A paradox has two sides each of which we believe to be true even though we cannot (yet) see how to reconcile them. A contradiction has two sides where we can see that they cannot be reconciled. God does not deal in contradictions.

Another theological danger that arises when recourse is made to God having some *secret* will and agenda is the central claim of the New Testament that the Lord Jesus Christ *reveals* God in all his glory to us. Jesus is, according to Hebrews 1:3, *the radiance of God's glory and the exact representation of his being.* This is a very strong and clear statement to the effect that the character of Jesus *is* the character of God. If, therefore, we wish to know exactly what God is like, we need to look at Jesus.

When we do that in our present context we find the open-handed attitude of the Lord's appeal to Israel in Romans 10 to be exactly the same deeply moving sentiment expressed by Jesus when he saw the unbelief of Jerusalem:

> *O Jerusalem, Jerusalem, you who kill the prophets and stone those sent to you, how often I have longed to gather your children together, as a hen gathers her chicks under her wings, but you were not willing. Look, your house is left to you desolate. For I tell you, you will not see me again until you say, "Blessed is he who comes in the name of the Lord."*
>
> (Matthew 23:37–39.)

One would have thought that this gracious appeal by Jesus the Son of God himself would have been irresistible. He wished to show them mercy and enfold them in his arms. It was an utterly genuine offer. There was no secret and disingenuous agenda behind it – no hint that God could have saved them if he had given them the faith to believe but chose not to. No attitude of Jesus would contradict the attitude of God. We must not impugn the character of God in that way. God's offer was completely genuine, made with the same heart of love that led him to give his Son. However, God is not a cosmic dictator and could not or would not force them to respond. They had the choice, and they resisted his grace and rejected him. The judgment of God eventually fell on Israel, although Paul will soon give indication of a coming change of heart.

CHAPTER 16

Has Israel a Future?

Paul is now two-thirds through his long and complex argument. Even if we are principally interested in its bearing on the matter of theistic determinism, it is important to follow it right to the end, as he has yet to discuss the hardening that has happened to Israel.

First of all he traced God's sovereign dealings in history to show that, in spite of the disobedience of Israel, the word of God regarding Israel has not come to nothing. He then showed that Israel's disobedience is their own fault: in rejecting the Messiah they are entirely responsible for the sad state they have reached. It is emphatically not God's fault; he has taken the initiative and in his sovereign care provided everything necessary for them to respond and be saved.

Now, finally, Paul tackles the question of the future. Are we to conclude from Chapters 9 and 10 that God has rejected his people? We should emphasise once more that Paul is still speaking of the nation of Israel, as he has been all along. He does not say, "Of course God has not rejected his people, since his people are now the church and all the promises made to Israel in the Old Testament have been and will ultimately be fulfilled in the church." If that had been the case, Paul would only have needed to point this out and finish the argument at that point in a single sentence.

But that is not the case. His evidence that God has not rejected his people Israel is that there are still people of that nation, ethnic Jews, who do believe in Jesus as Messiah. As the first example Paul mentions himself, pointing out that he is an Israelite in the sense of being a physical descendant of Abraham:

HAS ISRAEL A FUTURE?

I ask then: Did God reject his people? By no means! I am an Israelite myself, a descendant of Abraham, from the tribe of Benjamin.

(Romans 11:1.)

We notice that Paul does not say, "I was a descendant of Abraham and now I am a Christian." Paul was a Christian, but he did not cease to be a Jew, a member of Israel. His very existence is evidence that God has not rejected his people Israel.

God did not reject his people, whom he foreknew. Don't you know what the Scripture says in the passage about Elijah – how he appealed to God against Israel: "Lord, they have killed your prophets and torn down your altars; I am the only one left, and they are trying to kill me"? And what was God's answer to him? "I have reserved for myself seven thousand who have not bowed the knee to Baal." So too, at the present time there is a remnant chosen by grace. And if by grace, then it is no longer by works; if it were, grace would no longer be grace.

(Romans 11:2–6.)

For centuries God has known his people and has had dealings with them. Note that since the first verse Paul has been speaking of the whole nation, so that this concept of foreknowledge applies to the whole nation. God has not cast them off, even though there have been times when the number in Israel who followed the Lord was very small. But often that group of genuine believers was larger than people thought. For instance, Elijah in his depression began to feel he was the only one left, but God reassured him that there were over seven thousand who had not capitulated to the worship of false gods. When we are feeling down it is very easy for any of us to get things out of proportion. We cease to be objective, and our self-pity can easily make us feel that we are alone in trying to maintain the truth.

So, says Paul, there is a remnant even now that is chosen by grace. Again he stresses that the grace of God is not merited, nor that

God decides upon them irrespective of their response. That would be to contradict all that he has been saying in Romans 10. God comes with his arms open wide, and those that respond are chosen by grace. Quite a number have done just that.

> *What then? What Israel sought so earnestly it did not obtain, but the elect did. The others were hardened, as it is written: "God gave them a spirit of stupor, eyes so that they could not see and ears so that they could not hear, to this very day." And David says: "May their table become a snare and a trap, a stumbling-block and a retribution for them. May their eyes be darkened so they cannot see, and their backs be bent for ever."*
> (Romans 11:7–10.)

Paul posed a similar question in Romans 9:30. There the answer he gave was that they *did not seek it by faith*. He is not contradicting that now by saying that the "elect", in the sense of some arbitrarily chosen group within Israel, obtained it, while the rest were "hardened" by the same arbitrary decree. Paul explains (see Romans 11:7–10) by using a quotation from the Old Testament that takes us back to Deuteronomy and Isaiah. Let us look at them in their wider contexts.

> *These are the terms of the covenant the Lord commanded Moses to make with the Israelites in Moab, in addition to the covenant he had made with them at Horeb.*
> *Moses summoned all the Israelites and said to them: "Your eyes have seen all that the Lord did in Egypt to Pharaoh, to all his officials and to all his land. With your own eyes you saw those great trials, those miraculous signs and great wonders. But to this day the Lord has not given you a mind that understands or eyes that see or ears that hear. During the forty years that I led you through the desert, your clothes did not wear out, nor did the sandals on your feet. You ate no bread and drank no wine or other fermented drink. I did this so that you might know that I am the Lord your God.*

> *When you reached this place, Sihon king of Heshbon*
> *and Og king of Bashan came out to fight against us, but*
> *we defeated them. We took their land and gave it as an*
> *inheritance to the Reubenites, the Gadites and the half-tribe of*
> *Manasseh.*
> *Carefully follow the terms of this covenant, so that you*
> *may prosper in everything you do."*
>
> (Deuteronomy 29:1–9.)

God here demonstrates his grace at the end of their desert journey by renewing his covenant with Israel. He has just set before them a long list of blessings and curses, and made it clear that their experience of these will depend on whether they obey or disobey his word. They have had ample evidence of God's presence and goodness over many years. And even now God is prepared to be gracious to them and promise them a future. Clearly the lack of understanding and blindness are not permanent.

Paul then makes two references to the prophet Isaiah. The first is in the account of Isaiah's calling and commissioning to speak God's word to Israel:

> *Then I heard the voice of the Lord saying, "Whom shall I*
> *send? And who will go for us?" And I said, "Here am I. Send*
> *me!" He said, "Go and tell this people: 'Be ever hearing, but*
> *never understanding; be ever seeing, but never perceiving.'*
> *Make the heart of this people calloused; make their ears dull*
> *and close their eyes. Otherwise they might see with their*
> *eyes, hear with their ears, understand with their hearts, and*
> *turn and be healed."*
>
> (Isaiah 6:8–10.)

The second is this:

> *The Lord has brought over you a deep sleep: he has sealed*
> *your eyes (the prophets); he has covered your heads (the*
> *seers). For you this whole vision is nothing but words sealed*

in a scroll. And if you give the scroll to someone who can read, and say to him, "Read this, please," he will answer, "I can't; it is sealed." Or if you give the scroll to someone who cannot read, and say, "Read this, please," they will answer, "I don't know how to read."

The Lord says: "These people come near to me with their mouth and honour me with their lips, but their hearts are far from me. Their worship of me is made up only of rules taught by men. Therefore once more I will astound these people with wonder upon wonder; the wisdom of the wise will perish, the intelligence of the intelligent will vanish." Woe to those who go to great depths to hide their plans from the Lord, who do their work in darkness and think, "Who sees us? Who will know?" You turn things upside down, as if the potter were thought to be like the clay! Shall what is formed say to him who formed it, "He did not make me"? Can the pot say of the potter, "You know nothing"? In a very short time, will not Lebanon be turned into a fertile field and the fertile field seem like a forest? In that day the deaf will hear the words of the scroll, and out of gloom and darkness the eyes of the blind will see.

(Isaiah 29:10–18.)

I have given the broader context here to show that Isaiah 29 uses the imagery of potter and clay mentioned in Romans 9; and it is also the source of our Lord's words to the hypocritical religious leaders in Matthew that we discussed earlier.

The message is consistent with Romans 9. There is no arbitrary hardening of Israel. God only takes action after long patience with their disobedient behaviour. He gives them evidence after evidence of his presence and care, before he executes his completely righteous prerogative to blind them so that they cannot see the evidence any more. Even then, as we have seen in Isaiah 29:18–19, God holds out future hope for the nation – a hope to which Paul will soon turn in Romans 11.

Paul backs up his analysis with a further quote, this time from the Psalms:

You know how I am scorned, disgraced and shamed; all my enemies are before you. Scorn has broken my heart and has left me helpless; I looked for sympathy, but there was none, for comforters, but I found none. They put gall in my food and gave me vinegar for my thirst. May the table set before them become a snare; may it become retribution and a trap. May their eyes be darkened so that they cannot see...

(Psalm 69:19–23.)

Paul is remembering a time when King David was surrounded by pitiless and violent enemies. As David surveyed them he was broken-hearted and asked God to step in and stay their hand.

In all these quotations the blindness is judicial: not an arbitrary act but a divine response to unbelief and anti-God behaviour. The punishment fits the crime. The main point here is that such reactions were anticipated in the Old Testament.

It is instructive to compare these examples of God's blinding of obdurate people with the occasion in Acts 13:6–12, when Paul exercised his God-given authority and Elymas, the magician who was withstanding Paul, was temporarily struck blind. God also struck Paul blind on the Damascus road, and he was only able to see again after he had allowed a Christian, Ananias, to lay hands on him, calling him *brother Saul* (Acts 9:17–18). It was a moment of huge transition, with implications for the whole of subsequent history, as Saul the persecutor, vessel of wrath, became Paul the vessel of mercy.

One can easily imagine that Paul's own experience gave him deep insight into his understanding of his nation's unbelief and its consequences.

So I ask, did they stumble in order that they might fall? By no means! Rather through their trespass salvation has come to the Gentiles, so as to make Israel jealous. Now if their trespass means riches for the world, and if their failure means riches for the Gentiles, how much more will their full inclusion mean!

(Romans 11:11–12 ESV.)

Picking up on the imagery used in 9:32, Paul now describes what has happened as a form of stumbling. He asks what this stumbling amounts to. Does it mean that they have fallen – in the sense of irrevocably fallen – with no hope of getting up again? The answer is a resounding no. In light of Israel's trespass (literally, false step) salvation has come to the Gentiles. The hope is that this will now have the effect of making the Jews jealous and eventually lead to their repentance and conversion to Christ. If the failure and sin of Israel means rich blessing for the Gentiles, can you imagine what their *full inclusion* will mean? It will signify untold blessing for the entire world, whether Jew or Gentile! What has happened to the Jews through their unbelief is not permanent.

We should recall that the church in Rome at that time was mixed ethnically; there were groups both of Jews and Gentiles, although we have no idea of their relative sizes. We can imagine that up to this point each group followed Paul's argument with increasing interest. The Jews among them would share Paul's pain at Israel's unbelief and wonder how he resolved it; the Gentiles would wish to know the implications of Israel's unbelief for the credibility of Christianity.

> *I am talking to you Gentiles. Inasmuch as I am the apostle to the Gentiles, I make much of my ministry in the hope that I may somehow arouse my own people to envy and save some of them. For if their rejection is the reconciliation of the world, what will their acceptance be but life from the dead?*
>
> (Romans 11:13–15.)

Paul's next move is to address his Gentile readers and remind them that he is the apostle to the Gentiles. He is proud of that fact (in the right sense, of course) but he wishes to make it clear that he is not forgetting his fellow Jews. On the contrary, he hopes that his ministry to the Gentile world will provoke some of his fellow Jews to the kind of jealousy that might well lead them to salvation. Over the centuries sheer jealous curiosity has led many Jews to re-examine the claims of Jesus. In doing so they have found what they were missing and have come to salvation by trusting him as Lord. Millions of people all over the world believe that the God of the universe is the God of Abraham, Isaac, and Jacob. It is through Jesus, himself a Jew, that they have come to believe it. Surely that should make anyone think – and I have used it many times to provoke such thoughts.

Paul next repeats the point he made in verse 12: if the rejection of Israel has led historically to a vast number of Gentiles being saved (and you can imagine Paul's heart pulsating with joy at the thought), if Israel is accepted again, the effect will be like life from the dead. However, jealousy can have the effect of provoking arrogance in the opposite direction, and Paul will be swift to deal with it. He now uses two metaphors to expand these ideas:

> If the part of the dough offered as firstfruits is holy, then the whole batch is holy; if the root is holy, so are the branches. If some of the branches have been broken off, and you, though a wild olive shoot, have been grafted in among the others and now share in the nourishing sap from the olive root, do not boast over those branches. If you do, consider this: You do not support the root, but the root supports you. You will say then, "Branches were broken off so that I could be grafted in." Granted. But they were broken off because of unbelief, and you stand by faith. Do not be arrogant, but be afraid. For if God did not spare the natural branches, he will not spare you either.
>
> Consider therefore the kindness and sternness of God: sternness to those who fell, but kindness to you, provided that you continue in his kindness. Otherwise, you also will be cut off. And if they do not persist in unbelief, they will be grafted in, for God is able to graft them in again. After all, if you were cut out of an olive tree that is wild by nature, and contrary to nature were grafted into a cultivated olive tree, how much more readily will these, the natural branches, be grafted into their own olive tree!
>
> (Romans 11:16–24.)

The main metaphor here is that of an olive tree with its roots and branches. Paul is speaking to his Gentile readers and compares them to a wild olive shoot that is grafted into the olive tree in place of branches that have been broken off. We deduce therefore that the *cultivated* tree with *natural* branches represents Israel, its roots being the patriarchs. The olive tree is used in the Old Testament as a metaphor for Israel (e.g. Jeremiah 11:16); Hosea says:

> *I will heal their waywardness and love them freely, for my anger has turned away from them. I will be like the dew to Israel; he will blossom like a lily. Like a cedar of Lebanon he will send down his roots; his young shoots will grow. His splendour will be like an olive tree, his fragrance like a cedar of Lebanon. Men will dwell again in his shade. He will flourish like the corn. He will blossom like a vine, and his fame will be like the wine from Lebanon.*

> (Hosea 14:1, 4–7.)

The relevance of this to Romans 11 is obvious. Hosea refers to Israel's stumbling and pleads with them to return to the Lord, and promises that they will flourish again.

Olive trees are used as metaphors for God's two witnesses in Zechariah 4. These witnesses are literally "sons of oil" since the olive tree was the source of oil for the lamps in the temple; it was also used to fuel the lamps on the lampstand in the tabernacle (see Exodus 27:20). Thus the olive tree is an appropriate metaphor for witness.

This fits perfectly into the context in Romans 11, where we can reasonably take the olive to represent God in the world, starting with Abraham and the patriarchs (the root) and continuing throughout history with Israel. For many centuries Israel carried the main weight of witness to God in the world. That does not mean that no Gentiles became believers – far from it, as we have seen – but the main burden of testimony was borne by Israel. However, they were disobedient, so the natural olive branches were broken off and a wild olive grafted in. God disciplined Israel and granted to the Gentiles the privilege of bearing the main testimony to him in the world. This has been the case for centuries, ever since Paul was appointed apostle to the Gentiles. However, as Paul carefully explained, it does not mean that no Jews became believers. Paul is not talking about individual Jews being broken off and being lost eternally. He is talking about the witness of the nation as a whole.

Paul then warns the Gentiles that they should not become arrogant and think that they are superior because God has shifted the privilege of witness away from Israel to them. They are never to forget that the natural branches still support them, and not the other way round. Christian witness has its roots in the Old Testament. It rests on the witness of Abraham and the patriarchs, Moses and the prophets, and it is fundamentally dependent on the natural olive tree for the physical line of descent that resulted in the Messiah coming into the world.

It is perfectly true that the natural branches were broken off. But why?

> ... they were broken off because of unbelief, and you stand
> by faith. Do not be arrogant, but be afraid. For if God did
> not spare the natural branches, he will not spare you either.
> Consider therefore the kindness and sternness of God: sternness
> to those who fell, but kindness to you, provided that you
> continue in his kindness. Otherwise, you also will be cut off.
> (Romans 11:20–22.)

The warning is very straight. It was Israel's unbelief that led to them losing their privilege and status. Now the Gentiles are standing fast because of their faith, but they need to be careful not to allow unbelief to creep in, otherwise they too will lose the privilege.

It needs to be emphasised once more that Paul is not addressing individual Gentile believers here and threatening them with eternal damnation if they cease to believe. He is talking about the danger of the Gentile church losing its corporate privilege of being the main vehicle of God's witness to the world.

All are to take note that God's kindness and severity are not arbitrary or based on some principle hidden from our view; nor indeed are they irrevocable. This warning needs to be heeded. Israel and Judah lost their way by compromising with the idolatries and immoral practices of their age, with their leaders and teachers often caught up in the apostasy. The people lost their confidence in the authority of the word of God and were lulled into a false sense of security. They refused to listen to the prophets that God had sent to warn them of the consequences of their behaviour. The exile was the result, and the temple at the heart of their testimony was destroyed.

Sadly, it is all too easy to find parallels within the professing Gentile Christian church. Prominent church leaders deny the fundamentals of the gospel – particularly anything supernatural, like the incarnation and the resurrection of the Lord Jesus. An air of unreality has led droves of people to vote with their feet and abandon places of worship for the shopping mall and the sports field. Slowly but surely God has been squeezed out of the public square.

God will not always put up with this failure of maintaining a clear witness in the world, says Paul. Just as Israel lost its role, so might the Gentiles. If they wander from God's covenant they too could be cut off.

What about Israel then?

> And if they do not persist in unbelief, they will be grafted in, for God is able to graft them in again. After all, if you were cut out of an olive tree that is wild by nature, and contrary to nature were grafted into a cultivated olive tree, how much more readily will these, the natural branches, be grafted into their own olive tree!
>
> (Romans 11:23–24.)

Notice the condition – *if they do not persist in unbelief.* If there is a fundamental change in their attitude to God, then God will graft them in again, and believing Jews will once more have a major role of testifying to God in the world. No one should be surprised at this. If, *contrary to nature* (that is, without the law and the covenant), the Gentiles were grafted into the cultivated tree of Israel, then grafting Israel back is surely to be expected.

Up to this point Paul's comments have been essentially conditional: if this, then that. He now approaches the climax of his long argument and reveals to his readers that Israel will indeed be grafted in again.

> I do not want you to be ignorant of this mystery, brothers, so that you may not be conceited: Israel has experienced a hardening in part until the full number of the Gentiles has come in. And so all Israel will be saved, as it is written: "The deliverer will come from Zion; he will turn godlessness away from Jacob. And this is my covenant with them when I take away their sins."
>
> (Romans 11:25–27.)

Paul here discloses a mystery – a term he uses many times to describe something previously hidden but now revealed. He tells the Christians at Rome that Israel has been hardened but the hardening is temporary. It will end when the *full number of the Gentiles has come in.* I shall not go into the various interpretations that have been offered for this phrase – first because I find none of them satisfactory, and secondly because they are not germane to our objective. Up to this point we have been given strong indication that, just as Israel lost the right and privilege of being the main vehicle of testimony to God in the world, the Gentiles who have taken over that role run the risk of losing it as well, for similar reasons. It is not obvious how the idea of the fullness of the Gentiles fits in with this. However, we are also anticipating the termination of Israel's disobedience, and Paul promises, *all Israel will be saved.* This is more likely to mean the majority of the nation rather than every last member of it.

Paul cites Isaiah 59:20 to confirm this hope. Israel will be saved when a deliverer will come to deal with the sins of the nation. In other words, Israel will not experience salvation until they repent, recognise their Messiah and what he has done for them, and God renews his covenant with them.

I have already alluded to the fact that it is contentious to say that Israel as a nation has a future in the purposes of God – even a repentant Israel. Yet the hope of the restoration of Israel was very much alive at the time of Christ. As he was about to ascend to heaven he informed the eager disciples that it would happen, but not at that time – it would have to await his return from heaven (Acts 1:6–11 and compare Acts 3:21). For more detail regarding this, and why it is implausible to suggest here (and elsewhere in Romans 9–11) that Paul uses the term "Israel" to denote the church rather than the nation, please refer to my book on Daniel.[145]

The Deliverer spoken of by Isaiah is surely the Lord himself, and the text here in Romans resonates with the prediction made in Revelation:

> *Look, he is coming with the clouds, and every eye will see him, even those who pierced him; and all the peoples of the earth will mourn because of him. So shall it be! Amen.*
>
> (Revelation 1:7.)

Paul sums up the situation at his vantage point in history:

> *As far as the gospel is concerned, they are enemies on your account; but as far as election is concerned, they are loved on account of the patriarchs, for God's gifts and his call are irrevocable. Just as you who were at one time disobedient to God have now received mercy as a result of their disobedience, so they too have now become disobedient in order that they too may now receive mercy as a result of God's mercy to you. For God has bound all men over to disobedience so that he may have mercy on them all.*
>
> (Romans 11:28–32.)

In terms of the gospel going out to the world, at the time when Paul wrote Romans the bulk of Israel was opposed to it (just as Paul had been). Yet when we think of the role that God chose for them to play

---

145 See the author's *Against the Flow: The Inspiration of Daniel in an Age of Relativism*, Oxford, Lion Hudson, 2015, Appendix A.

in history, they are still beloved (I take it, by both God and Paul) because of the forefathers. In any case, God made the sovereign decision to give that role to Israel, and that is irrevocable. God is not going to change his mind about that. Both Israel and the Gentiles have known times of disobedience and both have experienced mercy. When we think of God's overarching sovereign strategy in history, we see that God's purpose is to have mercy on all – not just on some chosen subset of people, whose fate is determined without any reference to them, but mercy on all who are willing to respond to his offer.

These chapters are difficult; the whole topic is difficult. All sides would admit that. Yet, as we have considered the intricate way in which the sovereignty of God and his gift of human responsibility have intertwined in the affairs of nations and individuals, however small and inadequate our understanding may be, our hearts and minds should surely join Paul's in overflowing with a high note of praise arising from the incomparable mercies of God.

> Oh, the depth of the riches of the wisdom and knowledge of God! How unsearchable his judgments, and his paths beyond tracing out! "Who has known the mind of the Lord? Or who has been his counsellor?" "Who has ever given to God, that God should repay him?" For from him and through him and to him are all things. To him be the glory for ever! Amen.
>
> (Romans 11:33–36.)

PART 5

ASSURANCE AND DETERMINISM

CHAPTER 17

Christian Assurance

Paul's exposition in Romans of the complex interrelationship between the sovereignty of God and human responsibility is breathtaking in its sweep. It leaves us with a clear sense of wonder and a great deal that we do not understand. Yet it also exudes an unmistakable joy and certainty. We may not be able to answer every question, but we can know enough in order to trust God with the layers of mystery that remain. A question that frequently arises is: what level of assurance may a Christian legitimately enjoy?

The topics of assurance and security are important in more general contexts. The philosopher Immanuel Kant had a list of fundamental questions that he regarded as of central importance in orienting ourselves in this world. One of them is: "What can I know?"[146] The claim to know or to be sure of anything or anyone raises a whole array of (often difficult) questions that belong to the philosophical discipline of epistemology. My aim here is not to attempt to answer such questions at the philosophical level, so much as to try to understand what the Bible itself teaches on the matter.

Before we focus in on this, we should realise that many of us live in cultures where any kind of certainty is not only unfashionable but, especially where religion is concerned, may well be regarded as undesirable or even dangerous. The "certainties" of reward in paradise with which fundamentalist Islamist teachers motivate young people to engage in suicidal jihad are sadly all too well known. In the popular mind such certainty then becomes linked with arrogance and violence, and we can understand why. In reaction many people have bought into a postmodern relativism where *nothing* is certain. That is why, in

---

146 The others are: what can I hope for; what must I do?

our defence of Christianity to our contemporaries as true, we need to ensure that we make it very clear that our Lord repudiated violence to defend either him or his message.[147]

Now it is obvious from everyday life that some things are uncertain by their very nature (like the weather) and some things are universally certain (like death and taxes, as Benjamin Franklin put it). Many other things lie in between. I cannot be absolutely certain that the flight I am about to take will not crash, because some do. But I take the risk of flying since the probability of crashing is very low. I cannot be absolutely sure that I will survive a routine medical operation, but most do and so I take the risk. I cannot be absolutely sure that a friend will not let me down, but my confidence in him is high because of years of experience.

It is natural and normal for us as human beings to wish for secure relationships, employment, housing, food, medical care, and innumerable other things that we associate with "the good life". Also, much in commercial life depends on security. Indeed, we might say that central to the matter of security in all areas is trust – in other words, faith – which brings us straight back to the theme of this chapter.

When we turn to the question of assurance of salvation we can surely all agree on what the New Testament teaches: that those who believe in Christ as Lord, Saviour, and Son of God are secure. Jesus himself explicitly says so: *he who believes has everlasting life* (John 6:47). There can therefore be no doubt on this issue. Not only that, but the apostle John later teaches that God wishes believers to know that they possess eternal life:

And this is the testimony: God has given us eternal life, and this life is in his Son. He who has the Son has life; he who does not have the Son of God does not have life. I write these things to you who believe in the name of the Son of God so that you may know that you have eternal life.

(1 John 5:11–13.)

---

147 For more detail see the author's book *Gunning for God*, Oxford, Lion Hudson, 2011.

This implies that the first way in which we can know that we have eternal life is by ensuring that we *have the Son*, an expression that is explained in the next phrase as meaning *believing in the name of the Son of God*. This is the central message of John's Gospel, as we have already seen. In this matter of assurance of eternal life, the first thing to check out is: have I trusted Christ for my salvation?

For a great deal of assurance consists in understanding the precise nature of what salvation by faith means. Abraham is held out to us in the Bible as a paradigm of a man who believed God and who, like the rest of us, wished to be sure of the fulfilment of the promises that God had made to him. Paul cites this in the context of teaching believers where their assurance lies:

> It was not through the law that Abraham and his offspring received the promise that he would be heir of the world, but through the righteousness that comes by faith… Therefore, the promise comes by faith, so that it may be by grace and may be guaranteed to all Abraham's offspring…
>
> (Romans 4:13,16.)

The passage goes on to tell of Abraham's unwavering faith in the promise of God that he should have a son even though he and Sarah were very old:

> Yet he did not waver through unbelief regarding the promise of God, but was strengthened in his faith and gave glory to God, being fully persuaded that God had power to do what he had promised. This is why "it was credited to him as righteousness." The words "it was credited to him" were written not for him alone, but also for us, to whom God will credit righteousness – for us who believe in him who raised Jesus our Lord from the dead. He was delivered over to death for our sins and was raised to life for our justification.
>
> (Romans 4:20–25.)

At the risk of tiresome repetition it is to be noted that there is nothing here about unconditional election. Abraham's certainty rests on the reliability of the God in whom he trusts, not on Abraham's merit or works. Those who trust Christ can be sure, because their salvation is not of works but by faith, and that assurance rests on the character and trustworthiness of the One in whom that faith is placed.

A second way of knowing that we have eternal life is by observing the spiritual and moral outworking of our faith in our behaviour:

> We know that we have come to know him if we obey his commands. The man who says, "I know him," but does not do what he commands is a liar, and the truth is not in him.
>
> (1 John 2:3–4.)

> We know that we have passed from death to life, because we love our brothers. Anyone who does not love remains in death.
>
> (1 John 3:14.)

Jesus made a similar point when he said, *by their fruit you will recognise them* (Matthew 7:20). If there is no moral consistency between our lives and our professed belief in God, then our claim to know God will not be credible. It is in this context that Peter exhorts his readers to *make your calling and election sure* by our development of Christian character and moral virtues. The phrase "making sure" means "confirming". That is, the development of visible Christian moral virtues in a person's life confirms the genuineness of their claim to be believers. True faith in God will be evidenced by its moral consequences in the life of a believer.

A third way of knowing is by the inner witness of the Holy Spirit who indwells every believer and gives to them an intuitive sense of knowing God. The apostle Paul describes it in this way:

> For you did not receive a spirit that makes you a slave again to fear, but you received the Spirit of sonship. And by him we cry,

"Abba, Father." The Spirit himself testifies with our spirit that we are God's children.

(Romans 8:15–16.)

There is sometimes a danger of disparaging intuition. However, when it comes to knowing persons rather than facts, intuition plays an important role – especially intuition that is prompted by God's Spirit testifying with our spirit. It is of course wise to have our intuition backed up by other things, such as those we have just mentioned in connection with assurance of salvation, but this inner sense still has a part to play.

Some people will respond to this by saying: "Yes I can see that the *believer* is secure. After all, our Lord says so, as you have pointed out. My problem, though, is what happens if I stop believing? It will obviously be no comfort to me to speak of the eternal security of the believer if I no longer believe."

This raises the question: is it possible genuinely to believe the gospel and subsequently to cease believing it? Is it possible to lose the eternal life once possessed? And if it is, what does this do to my assurance of salvation?

Elusive assurance

At the theological level, opinions are divided on this issue. As we have seen, the P in the TULIP acronym stands for the perseverance, or preservation, of the saints. That doctrine is regarded as closely connected with the doctrine of unconditional election (U) for obvious reasons: if God predetermines and elects then, essentially by definition, the elect cannot become the un-elect. They will persevere.

However, it turns out in practice that it is one thing to believe that the elect will persevere, it is entirely another to be sure that one belongs to the ranks of the elect oneself. Indeed, it would appear (paradoxically) that the doctrine of the perseverance of the saints does not necessarily lead to a genuine and deep assurance of salvation.

If we ask those who hold this view how a man or woman might know whether her or she is one of the elect – chosen by God with no personal involvement on their part (certainly not of merit, but not even of their faith) – then we discover, paradoxically again, that their confidence does depend on their behaviour. So there is a real irony in the fact that those who believe in unconditional election have major personal problems with assurance. Whereas they accept more or less by definition that the elect are secure and will never be lost, how can they know that they are among the elect?

John Calvin himself struggled with this:

> For there is scarcely a mind in which the thought does not rise, Whence your salvation but from the election of God? But what proof have you of your election? When once this thought has taken possession of any individual, it keeps him perpetually miserable, subjects him to dire torment, or throws him into a state of complete stupor... Therefore, we dread shipwreck, we must avoid this rock, which is fatal to everyone who strikes upon it...[148]

The agonies of uncertainty of many Puritans are well known. For example, Edward Elliott, writing about Puritan groups in New England, says:

> ... in reaction to an early stress upon the assuring side of Puritan doctrines, the ministers sought to regain control by stressing uncertainty. They observed that in view of the absolute corruption that men inherited from Adam there were probably few that were predestined to heaven. They argued that, even if a man thinks he is saved, he is probably wrong. Candidates for church membership were urged to look within, to search out secret wickedness and proof of damnation. Upon such examination many began to find themselves unworthy of election. Such was the ominous message of the New England

---

148 J. Calvin, *Institutes of the Christian Religion*, III, xxiv, 4.

*ministers that those who arrived from England in the 1640's
and 1650's would hear when they sought church membership.*

Elliott goes on to say that

*... the ministers were careful to point out that even a
successful relation of the conversion experience could not
provide real assurance of election: one must always doubt
and search the heart. They warned that even the confusion
of a young man about his temporal calling could be
evidence that he was deceiving himself about his spiritual
life. Thus, instead of building self-esteem, the ministers even
transformed the idea of the calling into an effective tool
for creating doubt and, incidentally, lessening the spiritual
value of one's practical life.*

Elliott concludes:

*In all, the theological developments in New England in the
1640's and 1650's bred "uncertainty of outcome [which] could
lead and often did lead to an inner tension and agony of soul
disruptive in a new society". Indeed, nervous breakdowns
and suicides were not uncommon.*[149]

Much more recently R. C. Sproul is reported to have said:

*A while back I had one of those moments of acute self-
awareness... and suddenly the question hit me, "R.C., what
if you are not one of the redeemed? What if your destiny
is not heaven after all, but hell?" Let me tell you that I was
flooded in my body with a chill that went from my head to
the bottom of my spine. I was terrified... I began to take
stock of my life, and I looked at my performance... I could*

---

149 E. Elliott, *Power and the Pulpit in New England*, Princeton University
Press, 1975, pp. 40–41.

not be sure about my own heart and motivation. Then I remembered John 6:68. Jesus had been giving out hard teaching, and many of His former followers had left Him. When He asked Peter if he was also going to leave, Peter said, "Where else can I go? Only you have the words of eternal life." In other words, Peter was also uncomfortable, but he realised that being uncomfortable with Jesus was better than any other option.[150]

This is a very strange interpretation. There is no evidence that Peter was "uncomfortable". He was expressing his confident conviction that Jesus was unique in having words of eternal life, as is revealed in the very next verse. Sproul's statement shows once more that the deterministic belief that election is entirely due to a seemingly arbitrary act of God can lead to stress and doubt – here am I and I can do nothing about my salvation, yet in order to know whether I am saved or not I have to engage in deep introspection to see if there is any evidence of it. On that showing, election is entirely due to God, my knowledge of it is entirely up to me. This seems a sure-fire recipe for insecurity. New Testament scholar Howard Marshall quips:

Whoever said, "The Calvinist knows he cannot fall from salvation but does not know whether he has got it," had it summed up nicely.[151]

There is a sense in which this is not surprising. Real assurance lies in the fact that one has reached out with empty hands to trust and receive forgiveness from the Saviour who himself gives us these magnificent words of assurance:

150 Speaking at the Ligonier National Conference, June 2000, cited by R. N. Wilkin, Associate Editor of the Journal of the Grace Evangelical Society, at: https://faithalone.org/journal/1997ii/Wilkin.html
151 Cited in D. A. Carson, "Reflection on Christian Assurance," *Westminster Theological Journal*, 1992, 54:1, 24.

… whoever hears my word and believes him who sent me has eternal life and will not be condemned; he has crossed over from death to life.

(John 5:24.)

As Peter said to Jesus in the words recorded above, *we have believed, and have come to know…* (John 6:69 ESV). Assurance is bound up with faith in Christ, not so much in the sense of its quantity but of its object – Christ himself.

This can be illustrated by a common human experience. Here is a young man Jim who is sitting despondently in his room, wondering if he really does love Jane and whether or not he should ask her to marry him. His feelings are all over the place, and the more he tries to analyse them, the more uncertain he becomes. A friend, Tom, arrives and announces that he has just been talking to Jane in the park, and he remarks how fortunate Jim is to have such a wonderful girlfriend. As Jim listens to Tom's description of Jane, his depression and doubt vanish and are replaced by a sense of certainty. What has made the difference? His mind has been redirected to think about Jane rather than his feelings for her. And the more a Christian thinks about Christ, rather than their own feelings or faith, the more certain that faith will grow.

What happens if a person stops believing?

On the other hand, we should not forget that there are many Christians who hold that one implication of human freedom is that it must be possible for believers to opt out of their salvation and effectively lose it. They cite as evidence the famous "warning passages" in Hebrew 6 and 10, which we shall consider in Chapter 19. This is often held to be a characteristically "Arminian" view.

I shall argue, however, that neither this view nor that of theological determinism does justice to Scripture. I hold that Scripture teaches on the one hand that eternal life is precisely that – eternal – and so, almost by definition, it cannot be lost. Regeneration is irreversible. That is, I hold that God does "preserve the saints" in the sense that a genuine believer cannot be lost; but – and it is an important caveat – the reason is not to be found in the notion of unconditional election.

To set this question in context we turn to what Jesus himself taught. When he sent out his disciples to preach the gospel, he instructed them on what kinds of response to expect. He told them the famous parable of the sower which, as he himself observed (Mark 4:13), is foundational for the understanding of all the other parables.

> *While a large crowd was gathering and people were coming to Jesus from town after town, he told this parable: "A farmer went out to sow his seed. As he was scattering the seed, some fell along the path; it was trampled on, and the birds of the air ate it up. Some fell on rock, and when it came up, the plants withered because they had no moisture. Other seed fell among thorns, which grew up with it and choked the plants. Still other seed fell on good soil. It came up and yielded a crop, a hundred times more than was sown."*
>
> *When he said this, he called out, "He who has ears to hear, let him hear."*
>
> (Luke 8:4–8.)

The disciples were told that their preaching would evoke four kinds of reaction. What is striking is that only the fourth is of any value – the first three are of none. This may initially have surprised the disciples, who might well have assumed in light of their own response to Jesus that a majority of their hearers might come to accept him. But no. We must listen carefully to Jesus' own explanation of the parable:

> *The seed is the word of God. Those along the path are the ones who hear, and then the devil comes and takes away the word from their hearts, so that they may not believe and be saved. Those on the rock are the ones who receive the word with joy when they hear it, but they have no root. They believe for a while, but in the time of testing they fall away. The seed*

that fell among thorns stands for those who hear, but as they go on their way they are choked by life's worries, riches and pleasures, and they do not mature. But the seed on good soil stands for those with a noble and good heart, who hear the word, retain it, and by persevering produce a crop.

(Luke 8:11–15.)

The first group simply hear the word but the devil takes it away. The second group receive the word with joy and they believe *for a while*. When testing comes they fall away. If we ask what the problem with them is, we are told that they have no root and so, when pressure is put on them, they fall away. The third group would appear to be similar in the sense that the thorns represent the pressures that life puts on people. The fourth group by contrast brings forth fruit that lasts.

Jesus clearly teaches that it is possible for some people to believe for a little while and then fall away. We naturally ask what kind of people does he have in mind? Are these genuine believers who have repented and trusted the Lord for forgiveness and eternal life, and then through pressure of circumstance have loosened their grip on that salvation and eventually lost it altogether?

No, they are not. The key phrase is *they have no root*. That is, their response was superficial: it fell short of true repentance and belief. Observe that our Lord is not suggesting that they once had a root that later died. They never had a root and so there was nothing there to grow and lead to the fruit that evidences genuine salvation – as in the fourth kind of ground in the parable. They never had become children of God.

We have seen that the true nature of faith is one of the major themes of the Gospel of John, and it is therefore not surprising that it is John who gives us several examples of a faith that is inadequate and superficial, in order that we might understand the difference between this and genuine trust in Christ. Early on in his record John describes a visit Jesus made to the annual Passover festival in Jerusalem. He did a number of *signs* there – John's technical term for the supernatural acts that Jesus did, each of which carried a deeper meaning as it constituted a "sign" that pointed to his identity as the Son of God. There was a surge of enthusiastic response on the part of the many people. Here is John's description of what happened:

> ... *many believed in his name when they saw the signs that he was doing. But Jesus on his part did not entrust himself to them, because he knew all people and needed no one to bear witness about man, for he himself knew what was in man.*
>
> (John 2:23–24 ESV.)

They *believed*, says John, but their belief was merely a superficial enthusiasm for a miracle-worker and not a deep-seated commitment resulting from true repentance and faith in Jesus. This is clear from the fact that Jesus did not entrust himself to them. Genuine salvation involves coming into a new relationship with the Lord. It is characterised by love and trust on both sides. We deduce from this that these people did not experience real conversion, only to go on and lose it. They were never regenerate in the first place. They had no root.

Later on in his account John describes Jesus teaching in the temple about his unique relationship with the Father. John notes:

> *Even as he spoke, many put their faith in him. To the Jews who had believed him, Jesus said, "If you hold to my teaching, you are really my disciples. Then you will know the truth, and the truth will set you free."*
>
> (John 8:30–32.)

Their reaction was astonishing and very revealing. You would have expected them, as "believers" in Christ, to be eager to hear his teaching on how to grow in their faith and become mature disciples. Yet the moment he suggested that they needed to be set free – because there were certain things in their lives that were enslaving them – they reacted with undisguised anger. They insisted that they were children of Abraham and had never been enslaved to anyone. Their anger degenerated into unmasked hatred when Jesus said that sin enslaves people. He told them straight that, far from showing the characteristics of children of Abraham, they were behaving like children of the devil. Their hatred then filled with murderous intent, as they took up stones to kill him. Some believers! Their behaviour proved that they had never repented – indeed, that they were determined not to repent. They were not genuine believers and never had been. They had no root.

Each of these examples concerns people whose professed faith was found to be superficial and inadequate at a very early stage. But what about people who have professed faith for a considerable time and been involved in Christian work, even at the level of church leadership?

John gives us a sad example of what can happen even in this case. In 1 John he describes what occurred – possibly in the church at Ephesus – when certain of the leaders introduced serious doctrinal heresy into the church before eventually leaving. As leaders they would by definition have been taken to be genuine believers, and this fact leads to the question: surely if such people leave both the faith and the church, it shows that it is in the end possible for a true believer eventually to be lost?

Let us see what John has to say about them. So serious is their heresy that John calls them antichrists and says:

> *They went out from us, but they were not of us; for if they had been of us, they would have continued with us. But they went out, that it might become plain that they all are not of us.*
>
> (1 John 2:19 ESV.)

These people departed in two senses: theologically, they abandoned the true doctrines about Christ; and physically, they left the church community. What did that mean in terms of their spiritual state? John says that their action showed that *they were not of us*, that is, they never had been genuine believers. If they had been, he adds, they would have stayed; but they left, and that demonstrates that they were not genuine, even though to all appearances they had been. Recall the final part of the parable of the sower:

> *But the seed on good soil stands for those with a noble and good heart, who hear the word, retain it, and by persevering produce a crop.*
>
> (Luke 8:15.)

The heretical teachers didn't endure. They had no root. In the end they proved themselves to be unbelievers.

John backs this up later in his letter by saying:

> *No-one who lives in him keeps on sinning. No-one who continues to sin has either seen him or known him.*
>
> *Dear children, do not let anyone lead you astray. He who does what is right is righteous, just as he is righteous. He who does what is sinful is of the devil, because the devil has been sinning from the beginning. The reason the Son of God appeared was to destroy the devil's work. No-one who is born of God will continue to sin, because God's seed remains in him; he cannot go on sinning, because he has been born of God. This is how we know who the children of God are and who the children of the devil are: Anyone who does not do what is right is not a child of God; nor is anyone who does not love his brother.*
>
> (1 John 3:6–10.)

Observe the strong emphasis on the present continuous tense: *keeps on sinning.* John is not saying that genuine believers cannot sometime act inconsistently, or even give in to temptation. Early on in his letter he makes clear that this is possible and that God has made gracious and merciful provision for it.

> *My little children, I am writing these things to you so that you may not sin. But if anyone does sin, we have an advocate with the Father, Jesus Christ the righteous. He is the propitiation for our sins, and not for ours only but for the sins of the whole world.*
>
> (1 John 2:1–2 ESV.)

There is a way for the true child of God who trips up to be restored to the Lord by repentance and the work of Christ.

However, in 1 John 3, John is thinking of people who, far from occasionally tripping up, make a constant practice of doing wrong, are consistently unrighteous in their dealings with others, and even hate their brothers – they keep on sinning. And what kind of evidence is that? Does it demonstrate that once they were genuine children of God, and now they have ceased to be? No. John says that they have never seen (past tense) God. They never were children of God but rather exhibited the works of the devil.

The apostle Peter backs this up in his description of some people who had been overcome by erroneous teaching that involved distorting Christianity into a licence for permissive behaviour:

> If they have escaped the corruption of the world by knowing our Lord and Saviour Jesus Christ and are again entangled in it and overcome, they are worse off at the end than they were at the beginning. It would have been better for them not to have known the way of righteousness, than to have known it and then to turn their backs on the sacred command that was passed on to them. Of them the proverbs are true: "A dog returns to its vomit," and, "A sow that is washed goes back to her wallowing in the mud."

(2 Peter 2:20–22.)

At first sight, this passage looks as if it might support the idea that a true believer might finally succumb to the world and be lost. The people referred to by Peter are characterised by having at one stage escaped the defilements of the world, of having knowledge of the Lord and of the way of righteousness. Alas, they then get re-entangled in defilement and turn back from obeying God's moral commandments – a situation that Peter describes as being *worse off at the end than they were at the beginning.*

Now it could well be that Peter had in mind that phrase from the Lord himself. The context is given in the following passage:

When the unclean spirit has gone out of a person, it passes
through waterless places seeking rest, but finds none. Then it
says, "I will return to my house from which I came." And when
it comes, it finds the house empty, swept, and put in order.
Then it goes and brings with it seven other spirits more evil
than itself, and they enter and dwell there, and the last state of
that person is worse than the first. So also will it be with this
evil generation.

(Matthew 12:43–45 ESV.)

Jesus, like Peter, was talking about moral defilement. Christ spoke of a man who had experienced some kind of moral reformation. But there was something inadequate about this, in that it left his house empty. Presumably, given the context, the Lord meant by this that the man had never invited God through his Holy Spirit to come and dwell in his life. He had never taken the step of becoming a child of God and so had no resistance to even more evil influence than before. There was nothing of God's Spirit in his life to resist the onslaught of demonic evil.

Something very similar had happened to the people Peter describes, as is made clear by the vivid illustrations he gives, taken from ancient proverbs and fables. First he uses the terms "dogs" and "pigs" to describe them, terms that would have startled and even offended his Jewish readers. Dogs and pigs were unclean animals. The very choice of terms shows us that Peter is not speaking of genuine believers. The term for them, often used by Peter, was sheep.

However, Peter is not so much using these terms to offend as to point to a common characteristic of dogs and pigs. If a dog eats some unwholesome food and brings the whole thing up, it will often return and eat the stuff again. It is in its nature to do so. That is what has happened to these people, says Peter. They have experienced a revulsion against the moral mess in their lives, vomited the rotten stuff up, and obtained some temporary relief. But such moral reform is not the same as receiving new life and the divine nature that accompanies it (see 2 Peter 1:4). So after a time, like dogs, they went back to the old stuff again.

It is the same with pigs. Peter imagines a situation (possibly borrowed from a fable current at the time) where a pig had cleaned itself up in the public baths. However, being a pig, the moment it saw a muddy pool it leapt into it with abandon. That is what pigs do; it is their nature. Once more Peter makes the point that there had been no change of nature.

This second illustration might even be amusing, but it is making a very serious point, and Peter wishes us to remember it. Moral reformation is a good thing, but it is not the same as regeneration. It is ultimately only the power of a regenerate life that can resist the appeal of teaching that is subtly clothed in Christian garb but is actually geared to leading people back into a permissive lifestyle.

What this all goes to establish is that there are only two groups of people:

1.   genuine believers who prove their genuineness;

2.   people who never were believers.

There is no third group consisting of people who once were genuine believers but have lost their salvation.

Indeed, there is a real danger in postulating the existence of such a third group, as it can give the impression that the true situation is less serious than it really is. From time to time I have met atheists who seem to delight in telling me that they know all about what I believe since they were once "born again" but have come to see that there is nothing in it. But if the true picture is that they mistook temporary moral reformation for regeneration, and they never were born again, that is very sad indeed. For this would mean that they are claiming to have rejected a reality that they never actually experienced.

CHAPTER 18

Will Faith in God Endure?

We have argued that there is a strong connection between being a true and genuine believer in Christ and enduring – persisting in one's profession of faith and producing the fruit of character that is consistent with it. This enables us to make our question as to whether a true believer can be lost even more specific: if endurance is the key, what assurance is there that this will actually transpire? Furthermore, if you make a present condition (being a true believer) dependent on a future eventuality (enduring), then are you not saying that we cannot be sure, indeed it would be arrogant to be sure, before we have completely run life's course? Surely we cannot know what may lie ahead of us in terms of trials and even persecutions. Could our faith not be broken by all kinds of things – personal rejection, tragedy, pain, disease, disappointment… to say nothing of active persecution, prison, and even torture?

Not surprisingly Scripture has anticipated the question and given us not one but several different approaches to it. The first is due to the apostle Paul and occurs at the important point in his letter to the Romans where he has established that justification is by faith and not by merit.

> *Therefore, since we have been justified through faith, we have peace with God through our Lord Jesus Christ, through whom we have gained access by faith into this grace in which we now stand. And we rejoice in the hope of the glory of God. Not only so, but we also rejoice in our sufferings, because we know that suffering produces perseverance; perseverance, character; and character, hope. And hope does not disappoint us, because*

God has poured out his love into our hearts by the Holy Spirit, whom he has given us.

(Romans 5:1–5.)

Paul describes the standing into which justification by faith has brought the true believer in Christ. First, we have peace with God. This is no mere feeling of peace, although a sense of God's peace is important. The reason we can sense it is that it is objectively real. Elsewhere Paul talks of Christ *making peace through his blood, shed on the cross* (Colossians 1:20). We enter into the benefit of that reconciliation when we put our trust in him.

Secondly, we stand in grace. It is by grace – which by definition we did not and could not deserve – that we were saved in the first place, and it is in grace that we continue to stand. This is no temporary status that may be withdrawn according to our behaviour. It is God's permanent attitude to us in consequence of which we can rejoice in hope of obtaining his glory one day. The word here translated *rejoice* carries the idea of deep confidence rather than that of superficial feelings of happiness. We can look to the future, not with misgiving and uncertainty, but with assurance that one day we shall enter the wonderful glory of the presence of God.

At this point Paul addresses our question. How can such confidence be justified in the face of our ignorance of the future, and what might it bring in the way of trials and pressures that could disrupt our peace and faith? Paul's answer is striking: *Not only so, but we also rejoice in our sufferings...* (verse 3). How could Paul encourage believers to have confidence even in the face of suffering, if he knew that it had the potential to break a believer's faith such that they could be lost eternally? The answer is that he couldn't. He says that we can be confident even in the face of trials because we can know, not just wish or feel, *that suffering produces perseverance; perseverance, character; and character, hope. And hope does not disappoint us, because God has poured out his love into our hearts by the Holy Spirit, whom he has given us* (verses 3–5).

This statement is of central importance because it lays the basis for all that Paul subsequently has to say about the process of sanctification and the eventual realisation of the goal of salvation in glory.

Just as Jesus did in the parable of the sower, Paul explains that suffering produces endurance. This is the quality that characterises the fourth type of ground in that parable. Paul is talking about the genuine believer, the person in whom the seed of the word has taken root and who can therefore weather the storms and even grow through them. Paul is not playing the theoretical armchair philosopher here. In his life he experienced a great deal of trial, threat, and persecution involving physical aggression:

> Five times I received from the Jews the forty lashes minus one. Three times I was beaten with rods, once I was stoned, three times I was shipwrecked, I spent a night and a day in the open sea, I have been constantly on the move. I have been in danger from rivers, in danger from bandits, in danger from my own countrymen, in danger from Gentiles; in danger in the city, in danger in the country, in danger at sea; and in danger from false brothers. I have laboured and toiled and have often gone without sleep; I have known hunger and thirst and have often gone without food; I have been cold and naked. Besides everything else, I face daily the pressure of my concern for all the churches. Who is weak, and I do not feel weak? Who is led into sin, and I do not inwardly burn?
>
> If I must boast, I will boast of the things that show my weakness… But he said to me, "My grace is sufficient for you, for my power is made perfect in weakness." Therefore I will boast all the more gladly about my weaknesses, so that Christ's power may rest on me. That is why, for Christ's sake, I delight in weaknesses, in insults, in hardships, in persecutions, in difficulties. For when I am weak, then I am strong.
>
> (2 Corinthians 11:24–30; 12:9–10.)

Paul stood in grace and found that the grace of God was sufficient to enable him to endure far more than most men and women are called upon to face. He embodied the doctrine he taught. Furthermore, he is supported in this by the apostle James who says the same thing:

> *Consider it pure joy, my brothers, when you face trials of*
> *many kinds, because you know that the testing of your faith*
> *develops perseverance.*
>
> (James 1:2–3.)

We might also recall that both of these men, Paul and James, paid the ultimate price for their commitment to the Lord – martyrdom.

Thus far we have seen that our assurance rests in the magnificent promise of our Lord that he *should lose nothing* (John 6:39 ESV). John has more to say in his Gospel about how this works, but that will be best understood when illuminated by the teaching we find in the letter to the Hebrews, which is almost entirely devoted to explain one of the most glorious offices our ascended Lord now bears – that of high priest after the order of Melchizedek.

The letter is written to Jewish believers who were coming under increasing pressure to abandon their confession of faith in Christ. Time and again the writer urges his readers to hold on to that confession and not to give up:

> *Since then we have a great high priest who has passed through*
> *the heavens, Jesus, the Son of God, let us hold fast our*
> *confession.*
>
> (Hebrews 4:14 ESV.)

The main topic, then, is holding fast to confession of faith in Christ – that is, endurance – and so is directly relevant to our discussion.

The high priests in Israel were inadequate because, in the end, no matter how able and sympathetic they might have been, they were but mortal. They might well have been a great help to you spiritually but, inevitably, one day you discover they have died: they can no longer help you and you have to start again with somebody else.

The writer to the Hebrews points out that Jesus the Son of God is infinitely superior to merely mortal priests:

*Now there have been many of those priests, since death
prevented them from continuing in office; but because Jesus
lives for ever, he has a permanent priesthood. Therefore he is
able to save completely those who come to God through him,
because he always lives to intercede for them.*

(Hebrews 7:23–25.)

One of the main roles of the high priest in ancient Israel was to
intercede for the people, particularly on the Day of Atonement
(*Yom Kippur*) when he entered into the presence of God in the inner
compartment of the tabernacle, and later temple, where that symbolic
throne the ark of the covenant was placed. He appeared briefly
before God and sprinkled blood on the ark and on the floor before
it. He then left and went out to the people. It was a foreshadowing
of an infinitely greater reality – the ministry of the resurrected and
ascended Christ in heaven itself where, we are told, he intercedes
for us. His intercession applies to everyone who draws near to God
through him – that is, all believers. The humblest believer is as secure
as an apostle – indeed Peter says this explicitly when he addresses his
second letter:

*To those who have obtained a faith of equal standing with ours
by the righteousness of our God and Saviour Jesus Christ.*

(2 Peter 1:1 ESV.)

This is nothing short of awesome, and as we discuss it we sense
that we are on holy ground. Scripture everywhere instructs us to
pray to the Lord – a privilege of incalculable value. Yet it is surely
an altogether greater thing that the Lord himself prays for us. His
priesthood is based on an indissoluble life. It is permanent and
eternal. Consequently, he has the ability to save to the uttermost.
Those for whom he prays endure.

How our high priest *saves completely* is illustrated in the trials
and tribulations of the apostle Peter. Just before Jesus was put on trial
he told Peter that he would deny his Lord three times:

*"Simon, Simon, Satan has asked to sift you as wheat. But I
have prayed for you, Simon, that your faith may not fail. And
when you have turned back, strengthen your brothers."*

*But he replied, "Lord, I am ready to go with you to prison
and to death."*

*Jesus answered, "I tell you, Peter, before the cock crows
today, you will deny three times that you know me."*

(Luke 22:31–34.)

Peter clearly did not believe that he was capable of such disloyalty,
and yet that was exactly what happened soon afterwards when,
warming himself at a fire, he was deeply embarrassed by a young
servant woman:

*A servant girl saw him seated there in the firelight. She looked
closely at him and said, "This man was with him." But he
denied it. "Woman, I don't know him," he said.*

(Luke 22:56–57.)

Two similar incidents occurred in the next hour or so, and a cock
crowed, just as Jesus had said it would.

Imagine that you and I had been watching all this from the
shadows nearby and, when Peter was being most vehement in his
denials, I whispered to you, "Is that man a believer?" What would
you have said? You might well have said: "Well, he was once a
believer, but he has clearly lost it somewhere along the way." Now,
if that is the case, then Jesus' prayer for him failed – which is
unthinkable.

It is important to see that our Lord prayed for Peter's faith. He
wasn't praying for anything else – for his testimony or control of
his language, both of which did fail rather disastrously as he cursed
and swore that he was not associated with the Lord. Christ prayed
for that crucial link between Peter and his God – Peter's faith in
him. And his faith did not fail. When the cock crew and he realised
just what had happened, he went out and wept bitterly. Yet his was
not the weeping of a lost soul but of a genuine believer at heart,

who deep down loved the Lord but who now realised how much of a mess you can get into by failing to heed what the Lord says to you. Christ told Peter, *when* [not if] *you have turned back, strengthen your brothers* (Luke 22:32). There was no doubt in Christ's mind that Peter would turn again, that his faith would resurface and endure. And it did. In a telling sequence of human and divine co-operation, Christ interceded, Peter repented and waited in prayer, Christ sent the Holy Spirit at Pentecost, and Peter had the courage powerfully to confess Christ before a large crowd in Jerusalem.

Again we should notice that it is the Lord, and not Peter, who took the initiative and did the praying, but it is Peter's faith that is the object of his prayer. The Lord preserves the faith of a believer, but the believer has to exercise that faith first or it will not exist to be preserved. It may sound simplistic, but surely God would not have given Peter, or us, a high priest if we did not need one. We do need one, because the issue at stake is the preservation and continuance of our faith.

In his first letter Peter himself gives us more insight into his own experience of the Lord's preservation of his faith. He writes to encourage men and women who are experiencing increasing harassment, suffering, and persecution for their faith.

Blessed be the God and Father of our Lord Jesus Christ! According to his great mercy, he has caused us to be born again to a living hope through the resurrection of Jesus Christ from the dead, to an inheritance that is imperishable, undefiled, and unfading, kept in heaven for you, who by God's power are being guarded through faith for a salvation ready to be revealed in the last time. In this you rejoice, though now for a little while, if necessary, you have been grieved by various trials, so that the tested genuineness of your faith – more precious than gold that perishes though it is tested by fire – may be found to result in praise and glory and honour at the revelation of Jesus Christ. Though you have not seen him, you love him. Though you do not now see him, you believe in him and rejoice with joy that is

*inexpressible and filled with glory, obtaining the outcome of
your faith, the salvation of your souls.*

(1 Peter 1:3–9 ESV.)

We see straight away that Peter's argument follows the same pattern
as Paul's: it starts with hope and certainty of salvation; then comes
the facing of trials and testing; and finally joy in the certainty of glory.

Peter informs his readers that one implication of their
regeneration by the power of God is a confident expectation of an
inheritance in heaven that awaits them – indeed, it is being kept for
them. They are not there yet, and in the meantime on the journey
they are guarded by the power of God. Except we notice that this
is not quite what Peter says. He says that they are guarded by the
power of God *through faith.* This statement leads us straight back to
our question – what if their faith fails under pressure and suffering?
Would that not imperil their ever reaching the heavenly inheritance
and so destroy both their hope and their joy?

Peter's answer is the same as Paul's. He uses an analogy to help
us understand exactly what happened to him under pressure. He
likens the trials of faith to the process of refining gold. He talks about
the *tested genuineness* of faith as being more valuable than gold that
perishes, even though the gold is tested by fire. The word translated
tested genuineness refers to what is left at the end of the process –
the pure gold that comes through. The refining of gold involves
putting into a crucible a lump that is a mixture of gold and all kinds
of impurities. The heat of the fire causes the gold to melt, and the
impurities rise to the top where they can be skimmed off, leaving
pure gold in the crucible.

There are several important features here:

1. The process is geared, not to destroying or even losing
   any gold, but to refining it and hence making it even more
   valuable. So our Lord tells Peter he will come through: *When
   you have turned back...*

2. However, there is a point in the process of refining gold
   where an onlooker who had never seen it before might think

WILL FAITH IN GOD ENDURE?

the gold had been destroyed. That is the point where the heat melts the gold, which then sinks to the bottom of the crucible, so that only the scum of impurities is visible at the top. Something like that happened to Peter under the heat of questioning. When he was aggressively denying Christ, all sign of the gold deep in his heart disappeared, and we would then have seen only the impurities at the surface. The gold had not been lost, but it was temporarily invisible. When Christ turned and looked at Peter as the cock crew, Peter remembered the Lord's promise to pray for him and his burden was lifted. The gold – his faith – much more valuable than it had been before, could now begin to gleam again.

3.   Faith is *more precious than gold that perishes.* The reason is that the faith does not perish – the gold ultimately will.

4.   It is interesting to compare this analogy with the one that the Lord used when telling Peter he would deny him: *Satan has asked to sift you as wheat…* (Luke 22:31). Just as the process of purification of gold is designed not to lose any gold but make it more valuable by freeing it from impurity, so the sifting of wheat is designed not to destroy the wheat but to separate the valuable grains from weed and other kinds of "impurity". We might note in passing that Satan's intention was to destroy the purposes of God, but his power is limited and God can and does use him to refine the faith of believers.

5.   Peter's key message, therefore, is the same as that of Paul. Knowing what life and its pressures can and cannot do to us, under the hand of God, can bring us great assurance that our faith will be guarded until we reach home.

Incidentally, it is difficult to see what the point of our Lord's intercession could be, if the faith in question were not Peter's faith but a faith that God had given him as one of his unconditionally elect. The P in TULIP – a thoroughly biblical doctrine, though not for deterministic reasons – is at odds with the U. The reason Peter and you and I can have assurance of enduring faith is not because God's election is unconditional, ensuring the elect will endure by definition; no, it is that we have a high priest who ever lives to pray that our faith should not fail.

John 17 has often been described as the high-priestly prayer of Jesus. It gives our Lord's own explanation of what is involved in his preservation of the faith of his disciples:

> *While I was with them, I kept them in your name, which you have given me. I have guarded them, and not one of them has been lost except the son of destruction, that the Scripture might be fulfilled… I do not ask that you take them out of the world, but that you keep them from the evil one.*
>
> (John 17:12, 15 ESV.)

The only one lost was Judas, but he is not an example of someone who genuinely believed and then lost his salvation. It is true that he was part of the group of disciples that Jesus called, yet even though he was the treasurer and (presumably) went around preaching with the others, our Lord himself makes it clear that he never was a believer in the first place and never became one:

> *For Jesus had known from the beginning which of them did not believe and who would betray him… "Have I not chosen you, the Twelve? Yet one of you is a devil!" (He meant Judas, the son of Simon Iscariot, who, though one of the Twelve, was later to betray him.)*
>
> (John 6:64, 70–71.)

I hope the reader will by now appreciate that Judas was fully responsible for his behaviour and simultaneously fulfilled a role as a "vessel of wrath" within the overall purpose of God.

To sum up so far: Jesus prayed for and kept the apostles, including Peter, twenty centuries ago. He also explicitly prayed for us: *My prayer is not for them alone. I pray also for those who will believe in me through their message…* (John 17:20). Millions of people through the ages have come to faith in Christ through the apostles' message. We can be as sure of Christ's keeping prayer and intercession as they were. Assurance lies in trusting what Jesus promises – relying on his word.

There are, however, people who rely on false sources of assurance – as Jesus himself warned:

> *Not everyone who says to me, "Lord, Lord," will enter the kingdom of heaven, but only he who does the will of my Father who is in heaven. Many will say to me on that day, "Lord, Lord, did we not prophesy in your name, and in your name drive out demons and perform many miracles?" Then I will tell them plainly, "I never knew you. Away from me, you evildoers!"*
>
> (Matthew 7:21–23.)

Human beings will trust anything except God and his word. They will even trust their God-given abilities and gifts rather than trusting in God. There are some people who place their assurance of salvation in their possession of what they call "supernatural gifts" like speaking in tongues, or prophesying, or driving out demons. Here our Lord speaks of such people that claim to have done mighty things in the name of Christ and yet are unbelievers. We note that Christ will reject them, not as people he once knew and now knows no longer, but as people he *never knew*. They also had no root. They never were genuine believers.

This all provides us with further evidence for what we noted earlier, that there are only two groups of people:

1.   genuine believers who prove their genuineness;

2.   people who never were believers.

And as we said before, there is no third group consisting of people who once were genuine believers but have lost their salvation.

Jesus similarly warned his own disciples about the danger of misplaced confidence. On one occasion, described by Luke, our Lord sent seventy-two of his disciples out to teach and preach in the villages:

The seventy-two returned with joy and said, "Lord, even the demons submit to us in your name."

He replied, "I saw Satan fall like lightning from heaven. I have given you authority to trample on snakes and scorpions and to overcome all the power of the enemy; nothing will harm you. However, do not rejoice that the spirits submit to you, but rejoice that your names are written in heaven."

(Luke 10:17–20.)

Their mission had met with apparent success and was accompanied by demonstrations of supernatural power – deliverance from demon possession in Jesus' name. They were delighted with what had happened. Yet Jesus saw that there was an underlying danger of them placing their confidence in the success of their mission. "Don't rejoice in that," he said. That is, don't put your confidence in it. The source of your confidence is knowledge of the fact that your names are written in heaven. And how were they to know that? Simply on the authority of Jesus' word.

Paul had occasion to write the same thing to encourage his fellow workers at Philippi by reminding them that their names were *in the book of life* (Philippians 4:3).

Eternal life involves a relationship. Our Lord himself defined it:

Now this is eternal life: that they may know you, the only true God, and Jesus Christ, whom you have sent.

(John 17:3.)

And all relationships involve trust. Faith in Christ is the key, and that is why God has made such wonderful provision for its maintenance.

CHAPTER 19

Warning in Hebrews

By this stage a question will have been rising in many readers' minds: you have been using the letter to the Hebrews about the role of our Lord as our heavenly high priest, so how is it then that the very same letter contains passages that clearly indicate the possibility of genuine believers losing their salvation?

The main passages in question are these:

> For it is impossible to restore again to repentance those who have once been enlightened, who have tasted the heavenly gift, and have shared in the Holy Spirit, and have tasted the goodness of the word of God and the powers of the age to come, if they then fall away, since they are crucifying once again the Son of God to their own harm and holding him up to contempt. For land that has drunk the rain that often falls on it, and produces a crop useful to those for whose sake it is cultivated, receives a blessing from God. But if it bears thorns and thistles, it is worthless and near to being cursed, and its end is to be burned.
>
> (Hebrews 6:4–8 ESV.)

> For if we go on sinning deliberately after receiving the knowledge of the truth, there no longer remains a sacrifice for sins, but a fearful expectation of judgement, and a fury of fire that will consume the adversaries. Anyone who has set aside the law of Moses dies without mercy on the evidence of two or three witnesses. How much worse punishment, do you think, will be deserved by the one who has spurned the Son of God,

and has profaned the blood of the covenant by which he was sanctified, and has outraged the Spirit of grace? For we know him who said: "Vengeance is mine; I will repay." And again, "The Lord will judge his people." It is a fearful thing to fall into the hands of the living God.

(Hebrews 10:26–31 ESV.)

The first passage seems to many believers to settle the matter – a genuine child of God may be lost. On this basis the passage has been used by some pastors and ministers to keep Christians in order, by warning and sometimes even threatening them with loss of eternal life. Their argument is that, if you teach believers that they can be sure of salvation, this will lead to carelessness of lifestyle.

However, it is very important before we decide on this issue to think carefully about the identity of the people addressed in Hebrews. For, whoever they are, and whatever they have done, the writer says that it is *impossible* to restore them again to repentance. We must allow these words their full force, and then ask whether they can really (as is often thought) describe believers who have lost their way somehow, whose affection for the Lord has dimmed and who have been tripped up by the allurements of what the New Testament describes as "the world".

This cannot be the correct interpretation, for the simple reason that all believers experience rough patches, spiritual low points, worldliness, giving in to temptation, and more; but they have also, as a result of Christ's high-priestly prayer for them, come to a point of repentance and been restored to fellowship with the Lord. They cannot be the people described in Hebrews 6 since, I repeat, whoever these people are, it is *impossible* to renew them to repentance.

Think also of the letters to the seven churches in Revelation 2–3. The Lord rebukes some of the churches for their lack of love, lukewarmness, departure from sound doctrine, and even immorality. He calls on them to repent, an exhortation which would make no sense if it were not possible for them to do so.

If believers who sinned in various ways, let the Lord down, compromised their faith, could not be renewed to repentance, the work of Christ as high priest would cease to have any real meaning or effect. We know that this is simply not true.

So we are back to the key question as to who these people are, whose behaviour is so serious that it is not possible to get them to repent again.

As we pointed out earlier, the addressees of the letter to the Hebrews needed to know about Jesus as high priest because they were people of Jewish background who had come to profess faith in Christ, only to come under enormous pressure to renege on Christ and return to the Jewish fold.

Let us think through the argument. The first thing to notice is that it is impossible to get these people to repent. It does not say that it is impossible for God to forgive them. As we know, God is prepared to forgive anyone who repents, and Jesus taught his disciples to do likewise (see Matthew 18:21–22). Repentance and faith are the prerequisites for salvation, repentance meaning "a change of mind". The problem with these people is that you cannot get them to change their minds. Now, people change their minds over many things, so the question is: what is the issue here?

In order to answer that we need first to see what had happened to them. Four things are said of them:

1.   they had been enlightened;
2.   they had tasted the heavenly gift;
3.   they had shared in the Holy Spirit;
4.   they had tasted the goodness of the word of God and the powers of the age to come.

What do these statements mean?

One well-known response is that of John Calvin and John Owen, who held that these people never had been genuine believers.

Against that Howard Marshall argues that these people had once been genuinely saved and had then fallen from that state.[152] However, there seem to me to be problems with this reading of the text, and I

---

152 See, for instance H. Marshall, *Kept by the Power of God*, London, Epworth Press, 1969.

find myself this time in sympathy with Calvin, although for reasons that are not based on alleged logical consequences of the doctrine of predestination.

First, why does the author of Hebrews not simply save words and explicitly state that these people had been saved? One good reason might be deduced from the author's subsequent subtle shift of language from saying: *For it is impossible to restore again to repentance **those who** have once been enlightened…* (6:4) to *Though we speak in this way, yet in **your case**, beloved, we feel sure of better things – things that belong to salvation* (6:9 ESV). That is, the author is in fact persuaded that the people he is addressing are different from *those who* are in this situation; they are in a better state – they evidence things belonging to salvation. So he is persuaded that they have really been saved. The obvious implication is that the others had not.

But how could that be, in light of how they are described?

Let us take the first term: *enlightened*. Does it amount to salvation? John speaks of the Word as the true light which enlightens everyone (see John 1:9). Nowhere does Scripture teach that everyone will be saved – indeed, the contrary is the case. Hence it turns out that to be enlightened is *not* the same as to be saved. Enlightenment is certainly necessary for salvation, but it is not sufficient. Some people when they are enlightened go on to repent and trust Christ, whereas others sadly are enlightened but then, perfectly aware of what they are doing, decide to close their eyes against the light and reject salvation.

Paul the apostle is an example of the first kind. He describes his pre-conversion days as a time when he was acting *in ignorance and unbelief* (1 Timothy 1:13). He was a well-educated man and thought he knew what he was doing as he passionately opposed the advance of the gospel. However, on the Damascus road he was enlightened as to who Jesus was. Now he knew for the first time what the issues really were, and he decided to repent and trust the Saviour.

Sadly, I have personally known examples of the second kind: people who have studied Scripture with me with increasing interest, until a day came when it suddenly became clear to them who Jesus was. They told me so – but then said they had decided to reject him. Their interest in the gospel evaporated, and soon they had completely drifted away. Christ had knocked at the door of their heart in an unmistakable way. They had recognised it. They had realised who he was, and yet they refused to open the door.

Some weeks after the resurrection Peter spoke in Solomon's Portico in Jerusalem to the crowd that had rejected Jesus as Messiah and had him crucified. He said:

> *Now, brothers, I know that you acted in ignorance, as did your leaders.*
>
> (Acts 3:17.)

Like Paul they claimed to know what they were doing, yet they were still in unenlightened darkness. But now they were enlightened, and they knew who Jesus was. What would happen? To them, as to Paul, God in his great mercy and grace offered forgiveness through the very Christ they had crucified. Peter called on them to repent, telling them that if they did so they would receive the gift of the Holy Spirit (see Acts 2:38). Not only that, but Peter exhorted them to turn from their sins in repentance

> *… so that your sins may be wiped out, that times of refreshing may come from the Lord, and that he may send the Christ, who has been appointed for you – even Jesus. He must remain in heaven until the time comes for God to restore everything, as he promised long ago through his holy prophets.*
>
> (Acts 3:19–21.)

We conclude that enlightenment, though a necessary pre-requisite for salvation, is not sufficient for salvation. This alerts us to examine the remaining terms in the passage in Hebrews 6 equally carefully. The last element in the list can help us with the others. The expression *the powers of the age to come* refers to the Hebrew concept of dividing history into this age and the age to come, the latter referring to the messianic age when Messiah would return and bring restoration and great blessing to Israel – that is, it refers to the *times of refreshing* that Peter refers to in the passage just quoted.

Indeed, Peter had just healed a congenitally lame man at the gate of the temple, giving a foretaste of that glorious age to come, as did the many other miraculous signs that the early apostles did. Thus it was that many people in those days tasted the good word of God and the powers of the age to come. They were physically healed through the power of the Holy Spirit. The question is: does that mean that they all went on to repent, trust Christ for salvation, and receive eternal life? Surely not. The Gospel of Luke tells of a group of ten lepers that received physical healing through Christ himself, yet only one of them came back to thank him. Presumably the others were content to be healed, to take the physical benefit, but were not interested in any further contact with the Lord. (See Luke 17:11–19.)

The sad reality is that seeing evidence for the deity of Christ, being enlightened, and even experiencing the power of God's Holy Spirit in one's own body, is still not the same as salvation.

The letter to the Hebrews has yet more to teach us about these people, as the writer further unpacks the reason why it is impossible to get them to change their minds. Let us look at the flow of the argument in the first passage cited:

> *For it is impossible to restore again to repentance those who have once been enlightened... if they then fall away, since they are crucifying once again the Son of God to their own harm and holding him up to contempt. For land that has drunk the rain that often falls on it, and produces a crop useful to those for whose sake it is cultivated, receives a blessing from God. But if it bears thorns and thistles, it is worthless and near to being cursed, and its end is to be burned.*
>
> (Hebrews 6:4, 6–8 ESV.)

Why *impossible*? Because here is a group of people who have been enlightened as to the fact that Jesus is the Messiah, who have tasted the power of the age to come, and yet who have rejected Jesus – his deity, his atoning sacrifice, his high priesthood – and gone back to the Jewish system of priests and sacrifices that God through Jesus has made obsolete (see Hebrews 7:12; 8:13). They have rejected the better sacrifice, the better covenant, the better priesthood, in favour of a system that can never take away sins (see Hebrews 10:4).

This action means that they are in effect saying that Jesus was not the Son of God, and so he deserved to be crucified: they are crucifying once again the Son of God to their own harm and holding him up to contempt.

So why, we ask again, is it impossible to get such people to change their mind? Well, what could possibly get them to do so? You say, the power of God's Spirit and his message of salvation? But – and this is the central point – they have rejected that. The issue is not whether or not God is prepared to forgive. It is that God does not have an alternative salvation for those who reject Jesus and the power of God's Spirit. There is only one salvation. If that salvation is finally repudiated, there is no other.

The analogy now given in the text explains this.

For land that has drunk the rain that often falls on it, and produces a crop useful to those for whose sake it is cultivated, receives a blessing from God. But if it bears thorns and thistles, it is worthless and near to being cursed, and its end is to be burned.

(Hebrews 6:7–8.)

We notice at once that this illustration closely parallels the parable of the sower, likening people to the land and their response to the gospel to the presence or absence of a good crop. If seed has rooted in a field, then more rain means more crops. If a field only produces thorns and thistles, it is no solution to add more rain – that will only increase the thorns and thistles. No good seed has taken root. The parable is not about believers who have lost their salvation. It is about people who never were true believers.

The second passage in Hebrews that deals with the same issue is this:

For if we go on sinning deliberately after receiving the knowledge of the truth, there no longer remains a sacrifice for sins, but a fearful expectation of judgment, and a fury of fire that will consume the adversaries. Anyone who has set aside the law of Moses dies without mercy on the evidence of two or three witnesses. How much worse punishment, do you think, will be deserved by the one who has spurned the Son of God, and has profaned the blood of the covenant by which he was sanctified, and has outraged the Spirit of grace? For we know him who said: "Vengeance is mine; I will repay." And again, "The Lord will judge his people." It is a fearful thing to fall into the hands of the living God.

(Hebrews 10:26–31 ESV.)

This passage is making exactly the same point as Hebrews 6. Once again the sin in question is not a matter of a believer getting tempted or worldly. It is a very specific sin that concerns a person of Jewish background who has received *the knowledge of the truth*, perhaps made a profession of Christianity, but has then repudiated the deity of Christ with the implication that his blood is common, and his sacrifice and covenant therefore meaningless.[153]

These are very solemn passages that can only be understood if given their full weight. Yet now we need to recall that, although the writer to the Hebrews feels he must issue such a warning about certain people who are not believers, he is actually persuaded that his readers are genuine believers: he is sure of better things – things that belong to salvation (Hebrews 6:9). He makes a sharp distinction between those who and you. He lists the evidence of their genuineness: *For God is not so unjust as to overlook your work and the love that you showed for his sake in serving the saints, as you still do* (6:10 ESV).

The writer is not talking of their works as the ground of their salvation, but as evidence of that salvation. Like the good ground in

---

153 The use of the word *sanctified* here leads some to think, in spite of all that has been said, that genuine believers are in mind. However, unbelievers can in some sense be said to be sanctified – see 1 Corinthians 7:14.

the parable, they persisted in bringing forth good crops. Their faith and love were enduring. They had proved themselves genuine.

Sadly I have personally heard austere preachers tell a congregation that, even if believers serve the Lord faithfully for a lifetime, and then at the end trip up and fall even once, they might well forfeit their salvation. These preachers told me that this was the only way to keep people on their toes – threaten them with loss of salvation. But God is not like that. Hebrews warns of the danger of not being genuine, but it does not threaten genuine believers with loss of salvation. If believers have throughout life been producing evidence of genuine salvation in what they do, and in their love towards other believers, we must not think that God is unrighteous and liable to forget all of that evidence.

In our preceding chapter we referred to Peter's profound analysis of his own experience of tripping up and falling in denying the Lord. He speaks of the trial as a process of refining faith and making it more precious – just like gold. And as he thinks of his readers he writes:

> *Though you do not now see him, you believe in him and rejoice with joy that is inexpressible and filled with glory, obtaining the outcome of your faith, the salvation of your souls.*
>
> (1 Peter 1:8–9 ESV.)

That is, as Peter considers his audience, he sees the evidence of genuineness – they love and trust a Jesus they have never seen, and they rejoice, as Paul would put it, in hope of the glory of God (see Romans 5:2).

And so, in the same spirit as Peter, the writer to the Hebrews encourages believers to push forwards towards the glorious heavenly goal:

> *And we desire each one of you to show the same earnestness to have the full assurance of hope until the end, so that you may not be sluggish, but imitators of those who through faith and patience inherit the promises.*
>
> (Hebrews 6:11–12 ESV.)

CHAPTER 20

Assurance in Hebrews

It would be a mistake to leave Hebrews 6 at this point. The fact that it contains a passage of dark warning means that many people fail to read the whole chapter. That is a great pity, since the second half of the chapter contains one of the most positive messages on assurance in the whole of Scripture. It tells us why we can have *full assurance of hope* (Hebrews 6:11 ESV).

Here are the reasons:

When God made his promise to Abraham, since there was no-one greater for him to swear by, he swore by himself, saying, "I will surely bless you and give you many descendants." And so after waiting patiently, Abraham received what was promised.

Men swear by someone greater than themselves, and the oath confirms what is said and puts an end to all argument. Because God wanted to make the unchanging nature of his purpose very clear to the heirs of what was promised, he confirmed it with an oath. God did this so that, by two unchangeable things in which it is impossible for God to lie, we who have fled to take hold of the hope offered to us may be greatly encouraged. We have this hope as an anchor for the soul, firm and secure. It enters the inner sanctuary behind the curtain, where Jesus, who went before us, has entered on our behalf. He has become a high priest for ever, in the order of Melchizedek.

(Hebrews 6:13–20.)

Abraham is held up for us as a model of what it means to trust God. Like Abraham, we are on a journey towards a future inheritance, and we can learn from his life and experience what it was that helped him push forward, holding on to the promises of God until he saw them fulfilled in his experience. Like ours, Abraham's journey of faith was in stages. We have already briefly considered his inaugural faith in God when he *believed the Lord, and he credited it to him as righteousness* (Genesis 15:6).

In those early days (not surprisingly, if our own experience is anything to go by) Abraham wanted to be assured that God would one day fulfil his promise of giving him the land and a nation to inhabit it. He asked God directly, *O Sovereign Lord, how can I know that I shall gain possession of it?* (Genesis 15:8). God's answer is very instructive: he asked Abraham to take certain animals and cut them in half, making two piles of them separated by sufficient space to walk between. This was an ancient and vivid way of making a binding contract or two-party covenant. The two parties to the contract would walk between the animals, thus expressing their commitment to keeping it – on penalty, as it were, of having done to them what had been done to the animals.

In Abraham's case, though, there was a profound and crucial difference to the way in which the ceremony was carried out. (Note that this occurs before Abram's name is changed to Abraham.)

As the sun was setting, Abram fell into a deep sleep, and a thick and dreadful darkness came over him. Then the Lord said to him, "Know for certain that your descendants will be strangers in a country not their own, and they will be enslaved and ill-treated four hundred years. But I will punish the nation they serve as slaves, and afterwards they will come out with great possessions. You, however, will go to your fathers in peace and be buried at a good old age. In the fourth generation your descendants will come back here, for the sin of the Amorites has not yet reached its full measure."

When the sun had set and darkness had fallen, a smoking brazier with a blazing torch appeared and passed

between the pieces. On that day the Lord made a covenant
with Abram and said, "To your descendants I give this land…"

(Genesis 15:12–18.)

The key point is that this was no covenant between two parties in the usual sense. It was a commitment and a promise of one party to another.

That was an early stage in Abraham's walk with God. The incident referred to in Hebrews 6:13 occurred much later on and is recorded in Genesis 22. It is the occasion when God asked Abraham to offer up his son Isaac, the son and heir that God had earlier promised him.[154] In order to orientate ourselves to understand the point that Hebrews wishes to make in citing it, we should first recall that the preceding verses are concerned with the fact that the Hebrew Christians have given evidence that their faith is genuine. They have done this through their behaviour, their works, and their love for their fellow Christians.

The apostle James cites the same story to make the same point in a passage about the uselessness of faith without works:

Do you want to be shown, you foolish person, that faith apart
from works is useless? Was not Abraham our father justified
by works when he offered up his son Isaac on the altar? You
see that faith was active along with his works, and faith was
completed by his works; and the Scripture was fulfilled that
says, "Abraham believed God, and it was counted to him as
righteousness" – and he was called a friend of God. You see
that a person is justified by works and not by faith alone.

(James 2:20–24 ESV.)

The context, then, is clear. This is the occasion on which Abraham was called upon to justify (to prove the genuineness of) his faith by his works. Now it is sometimes said that justification by works is the

---

154 This account is one of the passages in the Old Testament that raise moral concerns, some of which I have written about in my book *Gunning for God*, Oxford, Lion Hudson, 2011.

opposite of justification by faith; and so it would be if it meant that works were the ground of our salvation. But it doesn't mean that in Scripture. It means evidencing through our works that we are genuinely saved.

It is also sometimes said that we are justified by faith towards God and we are justified by works towards our fellow men and women. And, of course, it is important that those of us who claim to be believers live before our fellow human beings consistently with our faith in Christ. However, that is not the issue at stake, either in Hebrews 6 or in Genesis 22. The Hebrews passage says that *God is not so unjust as to overlook your work* (6:10 ESV). It is *God* here who is interested in seeing the evidence of genuineness in the lives of believers.

That strikes some people as strange – surely God knows whether we are genuine or not, since he can see directly into our innermost beings? That is true, of course, but it does not alter the fact that God requires the visible evidence in our lives. It clearly does matter to God himself what our works are actually like – not, we stress once more, as the ground of our salvation, but as evidence of its genuineness. The need to confirm the genuineness of our faith in Christ by our works and behaviour is a non-negotiable part of basic Christianity. Our good works bring glory to God (see Matthew 5:16).

It will help us understand this better if we think about what actually occurred when Abraham was justified by his works before God: there was no one else there but Isaac.

As we recalled above, Abraham had long since believed in God and it had been credited to him as righteousness. God had accepted him, and nothing would alter that. Yet Abraham's faith, like that of Peter, needed to be refined, as the account in Genesis makes plain. As we saw in Chapter 13 above, with the delay in the fulfilment of God's promise to him of a son, Abraham began (with considerable help from his conniving wife Sarah) to entertain the common idea that faith amounts to "God helping those who help themselves". He therefore attempted to see the promise fulfilled by employing a surrogate mother, Hagar, who bore him Ishmael. It was a hard, bitter, and lengthy lesson for Abraham and Sarah to have to be taught by God that this was not real faith at all. God's promise would be fulfilled, not by their efforts and deeds, but through God's supernatural power. Like salvation through Christ, the new life would be a gift that is *not by works* (Ephesians 2:9).

The arrival of Isaac was a red-letter day in the lives of Abraham and Sarah. God's promise had been fulfilled in a dramatic way by his supernatural intervention in rejuvenating their physical bodies. It is clear from the Genesis account, and perfectly understandable, that Abraham made every conceivable provision for Isaac's security. God's great promise for a nation to come from him was centred in Isaac's survival – so Abraham sent Ishmael and Hagar away, he dug wells, he had armed servants, and he made treaties with nearby tribes. Nothing was going to prevent Isaac growing up and being an ancestor of the nation promised to Abraham.

It was when Abraham had just concluded a security pact with the Philistine leader and his army commander that God spoke to him and made an unexpected and devastating command:

> *Take your son, your only son, Isaac, whom you love, and go to the region of Moriah. Sacrifice him there as a burnt offering on one of the mountains I will tell you about.*
>
> (Genesis 22:2.)

How shall we understand this request, or rather command, in light of the fact that all of God's promises were in Isaac? Hebrews 6 is about to base one of the most powerful statements of Christian security on what God said to Abraham after this most painful testing time, and that gives us the necessary insight to focus on what is central: where does security really lie?

We have already seen that Jesus warned his disciples against the danger of finding their security in the supernatural powers with which he had gifted them, rather than in trusting his word. Surely it is the very same issue with Abraham, but at a deeper level. For Isaac was God's supernatural gift to him. Isaac had become the centre of his world and was in danger of displacing his trust in God. More generously, perhaps, we might say that Abraham was at least in danger of trusting both God and Isaac.

Trusting God plus anything else is dangerous, especially if security is the issue. Abraham needed to learn, as we who trust in God through Christ need to learn, that there is no real security to be had unless our trust is "in Christ alone", as the beautiful hymn of that name says.

The Genesis account of this event is prefaced by the explanation, *Some time later God tested Abraham* (Genesis 22:1), and it was a test that stretched Abraham's faith to the limit. Hebrews sums up what happened:

> *By faith Abraham, when God tested him, offered Isaac as*
> *a sacrifice. He who had received the promises was about to*
> *sacrifice his one and only son, even though God had said to*
> *him, "It is through Isaac that your offspring shall be reckoned."*
> *Abraham reasoned that God could raise the dead, and*
> *figuratively speaking, he did receive Isaac back from death.*
> (Hebrews 11:17–19.)

Abraham reasons the thing through with remarkable logic. God has promised that Isaac will be the progenitor of a nation. He believes that will happen. So if God now takes Isaac away by Abraham's hand, then he will have to raise him from the dead. Abraham has already experienced something like this on a minor scale – the birth of Isaac was a supernatural regeneration of his and Sarah's "dead" bodies. God can do bigger things for Isaac, should they be called for.

So Abraham went together with his son to the mountains, bound his son to the altar, and raised the knife to do the deed... when God dramatically intervened:

> *"Do not lay a hand on the boy," he said. "Do not do anything*
> *to him. Now I know that you fear God, because you have not*
> *withheld from me your son, your only son."*
> *Abraham looked up and there in a thicket he saw a*
> *ram caught by its horns. He went over and took the ram and*
> *sacrificed it as a burnt offering instead of his son. So Abraham*

called that place The Lord Will Provide. And to this day it is
said, "On the mountain of the Lord it will be provided."

(Genesis 22:12–14.)

Now I know, said God. He had seen the evidence, and he now not
only repeated and confirmed his promises but did something entirely
new: he gave his oath to Abraham using a form of confirmation that
Abraham would clearly understand and from which he would derive
the highest level of assurance and security:

I swear by myself, declares the Lord, that because you have
done this and have not withheld your son, your only son, I will
surely bless you…

(Genesis 22:16–17.)

Hebrews 6 points out that, in human disputes, swearing an oath is
often used to bring matters to a conclusion. In courts of law today
this process is still used, with people swearing by someone higher
than themselves (that is, God) "to tell the truth, the whole truth, and
nothing but the truth". But there is no being or power greater than
God. So God swore by himself. That brought immense assurance
to Abraham. It is also geared to bring the same assurance to us, as
Hebrews explicitly says:

Because God wanted to make the unchanging nature of
his purpose very clear to the heirs of what was promised,
he confirmed it with an oath. God did this so that, by two
unchangeable things in which it is impossible for God to lie,
we who have fled *to take hold of the hope offered to us* **may**
be greatly encouraged. *We have this hope as an anchor for*
the soul, firm and secure. It enters the inner sanctuary behind
the curtain, where Jesus, who went before us, has entered on
our behalf. He has become a high priest for ever, in the order of
Melchizedek.

(Hebrews 6:17–20.)

That assurance is guaranteed by two things: God's promise and God's oath. It is impossible for God to lie. The use of the term *impossible* reminds us of when, towards the beginning of Hebrews 6, the writer spoke of it being *impossible* to get certain people to repent. They turned out not to be true believers. But now the writer is speaking of true believers whose security is guaranteed by another impossibility – that of God to lie.

There is yet more – our hope concerns the world to come, and Jesus has already gone there as our forerunner. To make sure that we arrive in turn, he is now a heavenly high priest, there to help his people to face the deepest decisions of life. We have an anchor in the other world – not in ourselves, our circumstances, our feelings, or anything else that is in this temporary world. After all, it is foolish to put an anchor inside any ship.

The application to the recipients of Hebrews is clear. The pressure was on them to turn back to Judaism, to its priesthood and sacrifices. But there was no security there. Security was only to be found in the sacrifice and priesthood of Christ – and in him alone. Not even partly in one and partly in the other. "In Christ alone our hope is found."

God called upon them, as he did on Abraham, to demonstrate the genuineness of their faith by their works, in giving up what Hebrews describes as a system involving a covenant, sacrifices, and priests – a system that was becoming obsolete: *and what is obsolete and ageing will soon disappear* (Hebrews 8:13).

What about us in our day? There is increasing pressure in many cultures, particularly western, to water down or abandon many of the distinctives of Christianity, the uniqueness of Christ as Son of God, the supernatural witness of his deeds and resurrection, the efficacy of his sacrifice for sins once for all, and the morality of that atonement in his role as the only high priest of God. Hebrews 6 challenges us to make sure that we make no compromise with such defection from Christ.

As we look to the future, let us take a final encouragement from the writings of Paul:

... being confident of this, that he who began a good work in you will carry it on to completion until the day of Christ Jesus.

(Philippians 1:6.)

I always thank God for you because of his grace given you in Christ Jesus. For in him you have been enriched in every way – in all your speaking and in all your knowledge – because our testimony about Christ was confirmed in you. Therefore you do not lack any spiritual gift as you eagerly wait for our Lord Jesus Christ to be revealed. He will keep you strong to the end, so that you will be blameless on the day of our Lord Jesus Christ. God, who has called you into fellowship with his Son Jesus Christ our Lord, is faithful.

(1 Corinthians 1:4–9.)

I am determined to believe that.

Epilogue

We have now reached the end of our long journey, but not the end of the discussion of the issues raised in the course of the book. They will be discussed until the Lord comes and tells us what we should really have thought. My objective has been to challenge deterministic arguments that claim to be based on something I do not challenge – the biblical doctrines of the sovereignty of God and human responsibility. I remain as convinced as I was at the beginning of this work that God is the great initiator in salvation who draws men and women to himself. That salvation is in Christ and no other; it cannot be merited; it is by grace and is received by faith in Christ as Saviour and Lord, faith which is not a work or meritorious act but its opposite.

Finally, I have considered the important question of assurance of salvation and the guarantee of eternal security that is at the heart of the glorious doctrine of the high priesthood of Christ.

My hope is that I have at least stimulated thought about some vital issues. In order to do so I have had to quote people with some of whose views I disagree. I trust I have done so fairly. I would once more like to make clear that disagreement with some statements a person has made by no means implies disagreement with everything they say, nor does it signify an *ad hominem* attack, any more than their disagreement with my take on things would imply such an attack on me. This is particularly important in regard to the authors I have quoted, since I have gained from them much that is helpful in many other areas. It is precisely because I respect them that they have caused me much thought regarding the particular issues I have focused on in this book.

I have no doubt that their motivation has been *Soli Deo Gloria*. I trust that mine has been the same.

Questions for Reflection or Discussion

Part 1

1. What in your opinion are the essential characteristics of freedom?

2. What is your view of the relationship between freedom and justice in civil society?

3. What freedoms do you think human beings have, and why? Consider occasions when there is no liberty, liberty of spontaneity, and libertarian freedom.

4. Why do some people think that religion is a threat to freedom? Is there any justification for this reaction?

5. To what extent do you think someone's concept of freedom is dependent on their worldview?

6. What are the similarities and differences between atheistic and theistic determinism?

7. How would you express the moral problem connected with determinism (that is, of course, if you see one)?

8. Are labels helpful or unhelpful; what are the pros and cons?

Part 2

1. What are your initial thoughts about the biblical teaching on divine sovereignty and human responsibility? What for you are the decisive biblical passages relevant to the topic?

2. What in your view is the range of meanings covered by the concepts of foreknowledge, predestination, and election?

3. What is meant by "unconditional election"?

4. Do you think God's foreknowledge eliminates true freedom?

5. Why is it important when we see the term "elect" or "election" to ask the question "for what purpose?"?

Part 3

1. What in your view was the damage done to humanity as a result of the first sin?

2. What do you think "faith" is? Give biblical examples for your view.

3. What does Paul understand by the contrast between faith and works? Is it possible to turn faith into a work, either inadvertently or deliberately?

4. In what sense, if any, may faith in God be construed as a "gift"? Does this make it independent of human response?

5. Do you think that God always takes the initiative in salvation? What does that mean, precisely?

6. In your view does faith precede or follow regeneration? Give your reasons. Does the difference matter?

7. What does it mean to say humans are "dead in trespasses and sins"? How does that affect their capacity to respond to God? Does the example of Adam in Genesis throw any light on the issue for you?

8. Does "drawn by the Father" imply unconditional election? Do you think that God's grace can be resisted?

9. What does the fact that Jesus expected people to follow his moral arguments imply about their responsibility?

Part 4

1. Why in your view did Paul write Romans 9–11? How do these chapters fit into the message of Romans as a whole?

2. In this passage what distinctions, if any, does Paul make between Israel and the church? Give your reasons. In what category does Paul place himself?

3. What reasons does Paul give for Israel's unbelief?

4. What do you conclude from the description of the process of the hardening of Pharaoh's heart?

5. In what sense was Israel responsible for its unbelief?

6. What are vessels of mercy and vessels of wrath?

7. What do you make of the imagery of the olive tree and its branches? Does it indicate a future for Israel as a nation? Give your reasons.

Part 5

1. Thinking of your own journey, what has your experience of assurance been? What considerations have hindered you, or helped you, in gaining whatever assurance you now have?

2. What is it about the nature of salvation that promotes assurance?

3. How does the parable of the sower relate to assurance?

4. Once a believer, always a believer? How important is it to allow Scripture to control experience in thinking about this issue?

5. What does the high-priesthood of Christ mean to you in everyday life?

6. In what way do the warning passages in Hebrews contribute to assurance of salvation?

Index

INDEX

Index of Scripture References